The S.K.A. at Carnarvon

A
TROJAN
AFFAIR

Michael Smorenburg

First published in the United States of America by *CreateSpace* in 2014.
Copyright ©Michael Smorenburg, 2014
All rights of Michal Smorenburg to be identified as the author of this work has been asserted by him in accordance with the Copyright, Designs and Patents Act of 1998.
All rights reserved. No part of this publication may be reproduced, stored in a retrieval system, or transmitted in any form or by any means, electronic, mechanical, photocopying, recording, or otherwise, without the prior permission of both the copyright owner and the above publisher of the book.
Every effort has been made to trace or contact all copyright-holders. The publishers will be pleased to make good any omissions or rectify any mistakes brought to their attention at the earliest opportunity.
Some of the concepts and quotations expressed in this fictional tale first appeared, some in a different form, in various print or electronic expressions by the originators, authors or presenters so named.
3 5 7 9 8 6 4 2
www.ska-at-carnarvon.com
www.MichaelSmorenburg/TrojanAffair
FaceBook.com/MichaelSmorenburg
MichaelSmorenburg.com
MichaelStheWriter@gmail.com

Updated Edition

House of Qunard Publishing

Copyright © 2014 Michael Smorenburg
Copyright © 2016 Michael Smorenburg & Qunard Publishing
All rights reserved.

ISBN Print: 978-0-620-62576-0

ISBN eBook: 978-0-620-62577-7

Cover Photo Credit: Mike Peel (licence details at):
https://commons.wikimedia.org/wiki/File:SKA_site,_South_Africa_2014_60.jpg

DEDICATION

This novel explores the drama humans create for themselves.
It is dedicated to those who have lost their lives and suffered unnecessarily
at the hands of intolerance and irrational fears

*"News is like the wind; it comes over mountains and
valleys and brings with it the fragrance of flowers and
also the stench of other things."*
                                        Bushman Proverb

The Square Kilometer Array Telescope
At Carnarvon

In this work of fiction based as it is on fact: names, characters, places and incidents are products of the author's imagination and are used fictitiously. Any resemblance to actual events or locales or persons, living or dead, is entirely coincidental. The arguments for and against science and theism are originated by minds greater than mine; I borrow them for dramatic effect and send all credit for them to the many inspired authors and books on these topics; shelves of which I devoured in research for this work of fiction.

For your ease and convenience;

A glossary of technical and foreign words and terms appears at the back of this book.

Also by Michael Smorenburg:

- Ragnarok—*Qunard Publishing*—*2016*
- The Praying Nun—*Qunard Publishing*—*2016*
- LifeGames—*Qunard Publishing*—*1995 & 2016*
- Business Buyer's Kit—*Career Press 1997*
- The Everything Sailing Book Part 1—*Adams Media 1998*
- The Everything Sailing Book Part 2—*Adams Media 1999*

ACKNOWLEDGMENTS

My appreciation to the many people from both sides of the divide who, over the past five years of research, helped me come to grips with the arguments, rebuttals and general confusion that abounds when science and faith begin to tussle.

Thank you to darling Kirstin Engelbrecht for your tireless line-by-line edits and putting up with me in all ways.

My thanks to Gordon Clark for his wealth of experience in storytelling and creativity; to Jacqui van Staden and Kate Lill for earlier cover designs; and to the very humble artist who didn't want to be named for the design of this cover... thank you, it is fantastic. Much appreciation goes to Lin Sampson for her hard-hitting critique and to my very special friend Patricia Glyn who always finds the time to hear me out, and give great advice and YouTube interviews.

Thanks to all proofreaders and others, particularly: Butch Coetzee, Craig Campbell, Dino Contario, Leverne Gething, Noel Harman, Charmaine Hoffmann, Mondy Holliday, Glenda & Kitt Lill, Meredith Martin, Christy McCullagh, Denzil Newman, Lynne Newnham, Frank Ortmann, Paul Prinsloo, Chyrisse Torrente, Debbie Wilding, Catherine Winn... and too, too, too many others for my flitting mind to remember—please forgive! You all gave so much input, feedback and encouragement along the way. I am enormously grateful to Peter and Francy Schoeman, and Nestie and JD Smit for their hospitality and huge volume of feedback and experience as residents of the impacted area that the SKA will cover.

Thank you Hans Pietersen for taking an entire working day to do an emergency last minute proof-read to iron out some *gogos* that had crept into this updated version.

I am grateful to my many friends who patiently listened to my unceasing babble about this undertaking over several years; I apologize to my online friends for my unceasing posts, 'keeping you in the loop' as the project drew to a close.

PROLOGUE

The world is shrinking. Everywhere, new ideas bursting in on the blissful isolation of traditional cultures; modern thinking driving wedges between the generations; doubt creeping into long-cherished religious dogmas of small communities.

In the 1990's, an Afrikaner, South Africa's President, FW De Klerk brokered the end of apartheid. On paper and in theory, all citizens and ideologies became equal. But culture is no slave to politics, and hardened stalwarts in forgotten corners continue to march to the beat of an older drum, resisting outsiders and their threatening new ideas.

On 28 May 2012 the decision was made to build Sciences biggest infrastructure in history—the *SKA, Square Kilometer Array* telescope—around Carnarvon, South Africa.

The SKA will find the origin of the Universe.

Thing is… Carnarvon is bible country.

This is one of those stories. It is set in Africa and echoed in small towns all around the world.

Chapter 1

Dara was slight of build.

Indeed, with his diminutive proportions, twinkling eyes and a complexion like a tenderly airbrushed glossy, he risked being pretty—a dangerous liability in his sudden predicament.

Still shaking from the confrontation, his mind was a clutter of competing thoughts.

"What th…" his mouth began of its own accord to speak up, but he cut it short. With his persecutor still in shoving distance, this was not the moment to vent.

"Don't you *beckchat* me boy. Don't you *dare*…." The guttural voice from the unlit corridor behind him barked, "You GET OUT!"

This scrubland he was marooned in; this village, this *dorp*—Carnarvon in South Africa's Northern Cape Province—had never felt more like a prison.

The muted sounds of the school corridor fled as he reached the threshold. Beyond that doorway—outdoors—freshly minted enemies waited.

The teacher's voice from behind demanded that he keep moving. This was the *"final warning"* it threatened.

He ignored it a moment to steal a glimpse heavenward and the sun glared fiercely back. Like a biblical God of old it commanded him to avert his foreign eyes.

The sun here was a different beast to its insipid self back in England. Here it was a cruel master. Dominating every outdoor ambition from horizon to horizon it seemed in no hurry to vacate its daytime throne.

Everything in this place was in no hurry to do much at all. Lethargic and slow paced; everything but the insects and flies that delighted in aggravating with their manic agitations.

Everything was parched too. Years of drought left the powdery residue of fine grit on every surface.

The zinging din from the cicadas was now a wall of sound plaited into the sweltering heat, amplifying his misery.

He squinted out over the arc-lit gravel wasteland where shadows seemed to hide on tiptoe. As he scanned the school grounds, clutches of kids were engaged in small private dramas, distinct groups apart in different places. *Apartheid*, the forced separation of races had not yet relinquished its grip here.

He huffed in resignation and pocketed his trembling hands. *Predators would feed on fear*, he reminded himself.

This was now home. For the next three months this lot would be his lot, so he set his shoulders and stepped out into Hell.

Manufacturing a leisurely attitude that he didn't feel, he aimed his hands-in-pockets amble toward the shade of a flat-topped acacia thorn tree that promised some threadbare relief from the cloudless sky.

As he approached, the clutch of brown boys loitering in the shade there halted their conversations and eyed him with suspicion and a look of dread.

In the distance beyond them, oblivious to the oppressive temperatures, a noisy game with a ball was in full swing. Big boned lads, all white, charged about while a group of girls looked on admiringly. Most had blonde hair but one stood out, hers lustrous and full of body even from this range.

"You're the new one they're talking about?" The boldest of the boys inquired directly.

"Till the end of term," Dara confirmed, relieved that the pitch of his voice was only a breath too high. He offered his hand and the most nonchalant smile he could muster. The boys looked at the trembling offer as if it dripped with disease.

"Best you keep opinions to yourself then," said the wispy lad with a yellow tinge to the brown of his skin and a shrewd oriental set to intelligent eyes.

"I haven't expressed any," Dara pointed out, giving up on his attempt at a handshake.

"*They* say you have…" the accuser motioned toward the big-boned boys, "you challenged the teacher, the domi..."

"Oh hogwash…" Dara retorted, his confidence flooding back at the lie. "That teacher… *he* told me to tell the class why I'm here."

There was an awkward moment of silence, the boy studying Dara's effort to subdue private terrors; in it he saw his own reflection so he extended his hand and a smile of encouragement.

"I'm Dawid… they call me '*Dawie*'," he pronounced the '*w*' as a '*v*' and drew out the '*a*' so it sounded like two '*a's* and a '*v*'—"*Daah-Vee*"—he introduced the others.

Dara greeted each in turn, starting to ride the exhilaration of overcoming terror.

The adrenaline had spiked Dara's mind and he'd taken the whole scene in at a glance.

Dawie had hair echoing the sparse pockets of bush in the desert just beyond the school's fence. It tufted in clumps on his head. That and his startlingly high cheekbones and small ears struck Dara as peculiar.

The eyes of one boy caught Dara's attention; they were green as emeralds and just as crystal clear. With his dusty blond hair and pale skin, he seemed strangely out at odds with this group in this divided place.

Dawie saw the small question in Dara's frown.

"This is Tjaardt," he introduced, and the boy's face lit up. "He's also a foreigner."

Tjaardt corrected him, his mother was from the Baster community in neighbouring Namibia, but his father was local; and he'd been born in the town.

"Ja... but you're not really one of us... and you're not one of *them*..." Dawie's head again motioned toward the ball game, "...so you're a foreigner."

As if arranged by divine intervention to emphasize the point, a wave of tension suddenly dashed through Dara's new friends with a shout from the field beyond them. The game had momentarily halted and there was some consultation between several of its participants, one brute clearly the ringleader. He was glaring toward Dara and the huddle under the tree. Nods of agreement and an unmistakable hand gesture flicked in their direction, emphasized by a rasping curse in the local language that only just carried on the still air.

The boys in the shade pretended not to notice—but darting glances betrayed their fear. Though the game resumed, this newcomer in their midst had them in jeopardy. Dara felt the thing within trying to grip him with its terror again so he spoke carefully in a measured voice to assure himself all would be fine.

"So, they think I've ventured an opinion? And...? What's wrong with my opinions even if I had? It's a free world."

"Free?" Dawie laughed the word out. "In this place if you don't say what *they* want to hear, that is opinion enough. And it's worse for you because you're black...." He emphasized the condemnation with a scrawny finger poked at Dara's forearm.

"I'm Indian," Dara corrected.

"Ja... whatever... you're a *coolie*. Brown, black... you're like me... makes no difference. You don't have an opinion," Dawie assured him.

Dara looked down at the offending dark skin of his forearm; the son of an Indian father whose father in another era *had* indeed been a *coolie* according to the word's definition—an unskilled native laborer from India's south.

He was proud of his Indian heritage but he'd not really noticed its blackness like this before. Here though, under the intense glare of the African sun and the fierce scrutiny of the locals his blackness seemed his standout and perhaps *only* defining feature.

The news got worse and worse, they explained—he was the darkest with a strange accent that didn't fit the expectation the locals had for how he *should* talk; his *larney*—his *posh* British accent, hated so much because it was, well… British and, the British had burned their farms and imprisoned their women a century earlier. To the bitter end… they would never forget it.

"He says," Dawid motioned toward the distant tormentors, "they'll shut your mouth for you if you open it again."

"I'm not scared of them," Dara parried and forced the involuntary swallow he felt coming to leave him—it would negate the dismissive claim he needed to believe.

"Well then you're a fool. They'll fuck you up. Don't you understand?"

Today had been his first full day at the school.

The last class he'd attended before this lunch break had been *Life Orientation*.

The teacher, a Mr. van der Nest, was a tall thin man with a hawkish face and ferocious eyes inherited from generations that scan distant horizons. He was not on staff but an outsider who filled in *pro bono* to teach various guidance subjects both in and out of the curriculum.

Van der Nest in an increasingly ill mood had checked his watch and halted class early.

"*Sit julle Bybels weg,*" he'd instructed the class. He'd wanted all bibles safely stowed before allowing this little black foreigner to speak the heresies that the school authorities had insisted he must.

He'd then fixed Dara with his most intimidating glare and gruffly told the boy to introduce himself; to explain to the class who he was and why he had come to their Carnarvon.

The order for this introduction, he'd explained to the class in Afrikaans in the tone of an apology, had come from a higher authority.

"They say to treat him like an *ambassador* for the project," the Principal, Dr. Deon Louw, had earlier told Gert van der Nest. "I've been instructed by the department that, as the first of the scientists' kids, we need to formally welcome him and allow him to talk on their behalf. Now... I don't like it either Gert... but I'd rather he do it in your class because I know you can get it over with in the *right* context. As long as you let him have his say before the end of class, we've done our duty."

Van der Nest didn't like being told what to do or how to do it; it was one of the advantages of volunteering his time. For years everyone had turned a blind eye as he'd ignored the State's official curriculum in his Life-Orientation subject in favor of his own doctrine.

But the situation had become even worse... He'd only just stomached the unfortunate news that a foreign scientist's son would soon defile his turf when, ahead of the school assembly that morning, he'd realized the boy was a dark skinned Indian with flashing white teeth and the charm of the devil; one who'd quickly drawn several of the white girls into a tittering mob around him.

If many more like him were threatening to come, Gert had determined that he'd set the mood for their welcome with this one; so, with all bibles safely out of sight, he'd rounded on Dara:

"Explain to the class why you're here... and make it quick," he'd made Dara's presence sound like an accusation of some dreadful sacrilege.

Dara understood the tone clearly enough but was clueless as to its murky motivation. For him, the straightforward question without a hidden sleight involved two sets of answers—Dara had elected to come to Carnarvon school to meet friends, avoid boredom and kill the last three months of the year before his final year of schooling, which would see him in a private Cape Town boarding school next year.

But to get to that explanation he'd first needed to explain what had brought him to Carnarvon; and that had required him to explain his mother's career....

Since most of the kids were the offspring of sheep farmers or farm laborers, Dara had imagined that expanding on the details of the most exciting technology ever conceived in science coming to their very doorstep would be riveting and welcomed.

With this in mind he'd enthusiastically waded into the details, trying to inject excitement into his delivery:

"My strange accent...?" he had begun as jovially as he'd planned to, while pinning up posters of huge radio dishes superimposed onto their desert landscape, "...It's from England."

The class had reflected a few mild smiles dotted in a sea of blank or suspicious faces, the smiles mainly from the girls he'd chatted with earlier—and the teacher had given each of them a withering look to extinguish their welcome.

"My mother's an *Astrophysicist*, studying the physics of the universe. She's from Boston, but she graduated from *Caltech*. Now she's on contract from the European Space Consortium and will be here for the next five years. My dad's from India... he graduated from Oxford and studies *Evolutionary Anthropology*, so his work has him travelling a lot. He's in America right now promoting his newest book and doing a lecture tour, but he'll be visiting here soon..."

He'd finished fixing the posters to the board.

All the while the teacher had been pacing the class irritably, deliberately drawing attention away from Dara and to himself.

"...So... mine is a family of scientists; the first of many new residents who'll soon come to this area to work on one of the greatest scientific infrastructure ever; the SKA... I'm sure everyone here knows what it is...?"

From the back of the class had come a response; *"Ja... 'n rooinek duiwel gedoente"*—a foreigner's devil contraption, someone quickly translated for his benefit.

The class had erupted with laughter and out of years of habit van der Nest had scowled, trying to pick out the culprit and decide what to do. Since he'd agreed with the sentiment he'd done nothing but growl "*STILTE!*"—The class went instantly dead quiet.

"I'm sorry—I don't understand...?" Dara had asked.

"It's nothing... *Jus'* get on with it! We know what it is—*that* telescope..." van der Nest had snapped, "...your *SKA*. Hurry this up...!" He'd stalked to the window and looked out at the nothingness beyond the parking lot.

Dara had seen how the class minutely scrutinized the teacher for his smallest reactions, hardly watching the presentation at all.

Van der Nest's demeanor had begun hostile and steadily deteriorated from there; to ensure there'd be no misunderstanding he'd huffed and clucked noisily, making a scene out of advertising his disinterest and irritation.

"Well, sir... Yes... the SKA. It's a radio telescope, not an optical one. Radio's a longer wavelength of light so you don't use lenses like a normal telescope; the SKA uses giant dishes... like satellite TV dishes, but these are as big as houses. South Africa's sharing the project with Australia; eighty percent of it is being built in South Africa and..."

Another disruption; a heckler shouting out again in Afrikaans had led to a short but enthusiastic discussion with derogatory overtones about the raging sport rivalry between South Africa and Australia. Van der Nest had reluctantly *shoo-shed* this more interesting diversion.

"...SKA... *Square Kilometer* Array... it gets its name from the total collecting area of its three and a half thousand dishes spread all over Southern Africa and out as far as Madagascar, Malawi and even Nigeria. Together they make up a square kilometer... that's a million square meters of collecting area. Now, here's what's amazing: It will collect more data per day than the Internet produces in a year... so much data that if it was written to compact disks, the stack would grow by a kilometer a minute. That's sixty kilometers an hour."

By now, Van der Nest had retired to his chair where he'd sat with his knee jumping incessantly on an arched foot, irritated and enduring this offensive boy with only a slender veneer of self-control.

The unpleasantness had got to Dara, his own voice had seemed to him to be coming from outside his body, his vision had bounced to each pound of his heart but he'd pressed on.

The facts of his mother's career and the instrument she was helping to build had stunned him when he'd first learned of them. But though he'd used simple language, the teacher's reaction and blank stares he'd received, had convinced him that a cultural disconnect in his telling of it must be the reason, so he'd tried another tack from his prepared pitch:

"Three hundred years ago when Galileo pointed his telescope to the sky, he increased our resolution of the stars by ten-times—but the SKA will increase our knowledge not *just* by ten but by ten-*thousand* times... As you know, Galileo was nearly burned at the stake by the church for being right… This is going to be a lot bigger and Carnarvon is going to be its very centre."

The silence had crackled with that statement—all eyes had gone to van der Nest, whose face had cragged, his eyes slitting with ever more outrage with each word that Dara had spoken.

Dara had shuffled and stammered not knowing what he'd done to offend and how to turn it around, so he'd pushed deeper into the features of the unit and deeper still into the morass of the teacher's wrath:

"The scientists don't even know how they'll manage all the data, but when it comes on-stream in another decade or so, computer technology will have increased according to Moore's Law so tha…"

But it had been all too much for van der Nest, who had stood to his full height from his chair cutting Dara off mid sentence; "And what will this *donnerse ding*… what will your damned thing do hey? What is it *reeeeally* going to do, this fantastic *masjien* you like so much? What *trrrruble* is it looking for?"

Van der Nest had stammered the question, too blinded by fury to find the English words, his heavy accent rendering it almost incoherent. Dara had stumbled into the literal answer with trepidation.

"We... we're... looking for the origins of the universe—fo... for where everything; the sun and stars, earth and life... where it all came from and how it happened. We're looking for other life in the galaxy or univer..."

"And *where-is-our-God* in all of this?" van der Nest had snarled, his voice low and rumbling with menace.

Dara had seen an angry vein snake its way across the man's forehead and it had unnerved him, "I... I... I don't know sir."

"I'll tell you then you... you little boy," the cautions Principal Louw had only just impressed upon him to avoid racial slurs at all costs with this foreign boy had reined his mouth in, but left it with nothing much else; "...our God is nowhere in there and that... that..." his hands had balled into fists, "... that means..."

He'd not finished his sentence; Face red, eyes bulging; the words had dried in his mouth. His jaw had worked but when all sound abandoned him, he'd slammed his fist into the desk and a classroom full of hearts leapt as high as the pencil tin that clattered to the ground, spewing its contents across the floor. He'd turned and stomped to the door; a moment later it had slammed behind him with an echo and the click of his heels had strode away down the corridor.

"*Jislaaik!*"... a small nervous voice somewhere in the class had said.

The low burble and murmur of children unsure of what to make of a situation had been punctuated by a few nervous giggles. Dara had shuffled his feet and slowly made his way to his desk, careful not to catch anybody's eye, careful to keep his hands closed to fists so they didn't fidget.

A few moments later the bell had rung in the corridor outside and everyone had begun to file out until Dara had been almost alone.

The last to pass him had said, "Meneer van der Nest is die *Dominee*... the town preacher."

Dara had listened till the corridor outside had become quiet and deserted.

He'd collected his belongings into his bag and left the classroom. School rules so recently impressed on him required all students to vacate the building for the duration of breaks but given the sudden crisis, he'd preferred some solitude to think so he'd sought out a quiet corner that nobody would be likely to check.

It hadn't been long before the prowling teacher ferreted him out, identifying him as the newcomer who didn't know any better. He was spared further sanction and unceremoniously ejected onto the playground.

Now outside, the heat was wearing on Dara. His emotions frayed, the effort of keeping up a brave attitude sapped his energy and he felt exhausted.

Just then the school bell rang again, calling an end to lunch break and everyone began traipsing back toward the squat face brick school building.

Tjaardt and the other boys went directly inside but Dara lingered a little talking to Dawie, reluctant to be in the throng, delaying the misery of yet more tension as long as possible.

"Whether *you* think you did or didn't talk against God doesn't matter," Dawie was explaining. "If *Dominee* van der Nest thinks you did, you did... he makes those decisions for us."

Dara couldn't grasp the blind herd mentality of it, "Nobody around here ever thinks for themselves?"

"On this topic? No... I do, but I'll never talk about it."

"Well if none of you talk about it perhaps everyone disagrees with the preacher?" Dara suggested.

"Perhaps some do but I'm not going to find out."

"Kom julle… OPSKUD!" shouted a teacher from the parking lot. He was pointing an accusing finger at them and motioning them to GET A MOVE ON to the building.

Their short delay had the two new friends entering the corridor, briefly within view of the distant adult, then swallowed by a clutch of stragglers from the field who had accelerated to catch up, all speaking Afrikaans

Before he'd realized it, Dara was shouldered apart from his new companion and swallowed by the mob, the ominous laughter peculiar to boys in a horde began pummeling him as they closed ranks around him, a sea of tall uniform walling and screening his view on all sides.

A sense of foreboding gripped Dara, but he committed to ignore it and win his way to the next class through bluff alone.

The press of bodies surged as they funneled through the unlit passage, so cool and dark after the brightness of the African sun.

When it came, he didn't feel the punch—it detonated solidly at the base of his skull with a thunderclap of sound and he collapsed like an imploded smokestack.

Looking up, blinking, his vision reverberated; a sea of faces leering back. An acrid smell from the impact stung him. The ring of faces looking down on him jabbered excitedly, jostling and shoving over him lying prostrate, the din in his ears from the impact of the blow obliterated all hope of comprehending a word or gist.

Through the fog he realized two camps; one half trying to move the other half away from him, the antagonists trying to get past them to land new blows.

There was a timid and testing kick in his ribs and someone stamped on his ankle, but he hardly registered these as pain, he only felt the nausea.

Then something wet, a glob of thick liquid smacked him in the face.

Instinctively he wiped at it with the back of his hand and a roar of laughter went up as it clung to his wrist; the unmistakable opaque muck of spat mucus.

Looking past it through the strobe and swirl of vision he saw the girl with the hair from the playground. She was fighting mightily, wrestling to push someone back, giving it her all to stop the figure reaching Dara.

He felt revolted to see the ferocity she endured for him, ashamed to be lying so helpless while she fought. Then she was gone, flung aside; and through the haze, surging into view where she'd been a moment before appeared the smirking culprit—as ugly as a fortress with close-cropped hair squaring off a head like a block of granite, his nose crooked across his face.

His name was Vermaak, Neels Vermaak—the ringleader from the playground ball game, the *bad-news* Dawie had just moments ago warned him about.

"Mister Prrrrretty boy…" said the piece of granite with a drum-roll to his *'rrr's*, *"Jou klein swart moffie duiwelaanbidder. Kom… staan… ek klap jou weer."*

The throaty challenge to stand up for another smack needed no interpretation; Dara had already picked up enough of the local intonation to know he was being goaded with accusations of homosexuality and devil worship.

The words washed over him in a dream state, all in slow motion as the boy deliberately wiped his own mouth to emphasize who owned the gob.

Then, suddenly, the crowd evaporated and a lone adult was looking down on Dara.

Lying in the sick bay the kindly old secretary in a hideous blue floral dress acted as nurse. She had an icepack to his neck.

"Now you jus' lie still, you hear?"

She was plump and genial and thick of accent; "Poor boy. I'm sorry for you but it's your own fault… this is why you're forbidden to horseplay in the corridors."

Principal Louw, judge, jury and executioner, had quickly convened an impromptu hearing; the girl with the blond hair was among them, the block of granite was absent.

The principal wagged his finger sternly at the girl's bowed face severely admonishing her; *"Wat sal jou Pa se? Staan jy nie op vir jou eie mense nie?"*—His tone said it all; the disappointment her father would feel and questioning why she wouldn't stand up for her own people.

Judgment was swiftly delivered: Dara's clowning had caused the slip and fall that had cracked the back of his skull on the floor. He was firmly reprimanded for putting the school's good name at risk. Conduct like this strictly contravened school regulations—he would be dealt with and learn the consequences once his concussion had been assessed.

Dara was in no position to argue against the gang of witnesses hastily assembled. He didn't care to, as he had no intention of returning to face sanction anyway.

His mother would be relieved with this decision, he thought. Marsha had been against him enrolling in the first place.

Now what he most dreaded was her inevitable, *"I told you so!"*

"I *told* you... I warned you! You know I'll always back you up but why must you confront these people?" Marsha scolded Dara as they arrived at her car but she stopped and hugged him before she opened the door. "This is very upsetting."

They got into the BMW, its sleek air-conditioned interior an oasis of familiarity.

"I *didn't* confront them, Mum."

"The principal just gave me an earful, how very *insulting* you were in class, …no *respect* for your hosts…"

"What?"

"I'm merely repeating…."

"That's *ridiculous,* Mum. I already *told* you what happened."

"They see things differently—this is what I alerted you to…"

She'd been called at work to come and fetch him, and on their way to the car Dara had briefed her about the class incident, the playground tensions and the ambush punch.

They drove in silence through the school gates and she put her hand on his knee and squeezed it.

"I'm not attacking you. I'm just concerned you don't quite understand. They're different to us... different to anyone you've met."

"I didn't try to *change* them, Mum. I didn't even bring it up. The teacher asked me to talk about your work."

She was silent a moment. "How're you feeling now?"

"I'm fine Mum, you're making a big deal over nothing."

...But she knew he wasn't and saw how he kept his hands pressed firmly to his thighs as he replayed events though his mind in the silence, tension in his shoulders.

They stopped at the clinic where, after an hour's negotiation, Dara triumphed and was discharged.

"You're making such a big deal of it," he griped as he opened the car door. "It was nothing, Mum..." he got in and shut the door. "I've had worse playing soccer."

"Enough, Dara," she admonished. "The doctor agreed... an overnight observation is normal."

"But not around here..." Dara repeated what the doctor had conceded after Dara had used every argument to escape a whole night in a hospital bed for observation. "I'll sleep in your bed and you can watch me all night," he assured.

A few blocks later Marsha turned the car off the broad main street into a side road and parked outside a drab pale-blue building, fenced from the street with coiled razor wire topping its perimeter.

Flagpoles stood outside, the flags flaccid against the dazzling blue of the sky. A blue *"South African Police"* sign jutted above the charge-office door.

"Why are we stopping here?" There was alarm in Dara's voice.

"We have to lay a charge"

"No Mum! No way! I'm not a coward."

"We have to do it, Dara," she asserted, knowing that fears of cowardice were his demon.

A hulking man in a straining police uniform filled the doorway, his back to the road. As they stopped he peered at them over his shoulder, a cigarette smouldering between sausage fingers held behind his rump.

Slowly he turned and studied them more closely, lifting the cigarette to his mouth and drawing on it thoughtfully. The smoky exhalation came slowly through his nose and his ice-blue eyes explored the contents of the vehicle, scanning its occupants as a predator picks prey from a herd. He puffed the last of the plume and a hint of an approving smile appeared at the corners of his mouth.

The giant nodded a barely perceptible greeting; it seemed more ominous than welcoming.

"Men don't lay charges," Dara was insisting.

"It's *not* about being a man and it's got *nothing* to do with cowardice, Dara. The ones who ambush from behind are the cowards."

Since Marsha and her husband had begun spending extended periods apart, each involved in careers that forced them to different continents, Dara had assumed a fiercely protective role.

He bridled at what he took as a misguided suggestion from his mother that he was somehow weak; "I'm seventeen! I can handle this."

"That's ridiculous, Dara."

She knew the look he was giving her now, fresh from winning the battle at the clinic his jaw was set and his eyes squinted with determination, ready to assert his rights again. In this mood he would not cooperate and she certainly didn't wish him to dig his heels in among strangers.

By now the policeman in the doorway had half turned and was clearly talking about them to someone inside, alternately glimpsing back at them… nodding agreement to something either said to him or to his own thoughts.

It unsettled Marsha and she re-started the engine.

As she pulled away the man's penetrating stare locked onto Dara, the boulder that was the policeman's head slowly swiveling to track them. His expression betrayed a process of actively filing that face in his police brain for future reference… it made Marsha check and re-check her rearview mirror until they were well away.

They passed through the town centre under the shadow of the forbidding NG Church spire that dominated the landscape.

"You shouldn't have gone anywhere near talking about their God," she advised.

"Oh come on...!" Exasperation in his voice, "... they said that to you, too? It's as if I'm in a parallel universe. Mum, have you even been listening to me? I *didn't*."

"These people..." Marsha gestured toward the spire; "they're not thrilled to have us here. We're not just newcomers, Dara; we're the enemy. That preacher's incensed about the SKA."

"*Now* you tell me..." Dara said sarcastically. She could see him regaining his full confidence and it pleased her.

"I didn't know till now... the secretary just told me," Marsha admitted.

"What's his problem?"

"She said he's angry that we've come here to search for the Universe's origins. He feels it's a direct challenge to the Bible, to Genesis or something."

"That's really pathetic..." Dara huffed, "...Childish."

"Childish it may be but they take it very seriously and that's what I warned you about. I didn't know they're at fever pitch with it right now but I warned you that they're Calvinist, Old Testament obsessed. They've created an angry God who holds each of them responsible for *everyone's* behavior... and they enforce it with fists."

"I know that Mum, but...."

"No, you've *just* learned it, Dara. I'm concerned that you still don't understand. You like a good argument but these are zealots and it's a volatile situation, so I'm emphasizing it. You're out of your depth."

They were silent a while, Dara contemplating her words.

The town slid silently by and gave way to asphalt through scrubland and undulating hills with a smudge of mountains in the far distance. They turned onto the access road to the SKA staff compound, sited on a farm.

Dara explored the lump at the back of his head and it hurt.

For three days he lay indoors, immersed in the satellite TV and fibre optic Internet feed, his pride hurting more than his injury.

Marsha called at regular intervals from work to quiz him, alert to signs of complications from the concussion.

The house staff regularly checked on and fussed over him. From the questions they asked and the way they studied him, they were clearly under instruction to report any hint of symptoms back to his mother.

Outdoors the heat remained relentless; indoors a climate-controlled heaven.

Slowly as his morale strengthened Dara ventured out to the swimming pool but the loneliness he'd aimed to avoid by attending the local school in the first place began to bite.

Marsha was at work all day and often into the night.

Dara was accustomed to sophisticated company; the house staff, friendly as they were, were simple country folk.

The 250cc off-road motorbike the landlord, a farmer, had lent Dara became his saviour. It came with restrictions of course; he was several months shy of eighteen, the age limit on public roads for that engine capacity. Marsha underlined this law with her own ban. With the unpleasantness of the town still so fresh in his mind he had no intention of violating these rules. After all, he had the run of the vast farm, endless tracks leading through the scrub, up into the hills.

Although Dara was naturally gregarious and preferred to have the company of friends of every stripe, he began to bury his feelings of isolation in the exhilaration of chasing around the vastness.

Soon he knew every corner of the extensive farm. The region was arid and devoid of the large wildlife that most people presume proliferate in Africa. In the intricacies of the insects, birds and small animals Dara found increasing fascination.

His father's career as an evolutionary anthropologist had infected him; he knew that the area was dotted with caves containing Bushmen paintings from centuries ago… the legacy of these hunter-gatherer peoples who had been driven by indigenous African and European invaders to the arid interior of Southern Africa.

Dara's world became exploration. He'd always done it through books but now it was hands-on, it was real. He'd been at it now for weeks and was already successful in his quest to find rock paintings, not knowing if he was the first to see them since their creation. Finding a fossil by chance, his horizons broadened. Now he spent hours intensively researching the prehistoric environment of the area.

Over dinner each evening he'd enthusiastically recount the new discoveries of his day and lay out his plans for the morrow. Often they'd spend time with others in the compound, Marsha's colleagues and visitors and Dara would be riveted by the many facets of the development they where here to attend.

The prospect of living in a commune had been a foreign one to Dara but the longer he stayed the more he became captivated by its advantages; so many great minds in one place to tap.

Chapter 2

It was weeks since the classroom incident and, with the initial shock of it over, Dara had derived some amusement from its retelling.

He'd shared his story far and wide across social media but none of his friends could grasp what the fuss could be about.

Confirmation that the corridor attack was a direct reprisal for Dara upsetting the preacher was all around town, returning to him from many angles. Even the house staff ventured an opinion, "*Kleinbaas*"—*Small boss*, they called him—"…you can't go saying things like that."

"Things like what?" he'd asked.

"Things that make the *Dominee* angry… when the *Dominee* is angry we must all be angry," they'd declared.

And the *Dominee* was evidently angry; very-*very* angry. He'd been angry about the SKA development before but now its implementation had a face, the dark face of a devil child who did not know his place, an arrogant strutting peacock of a boy who had come grinning into his class with his very white teeth and his very white eyes cast around on the very white girls. And that devil child had been so smug and proud to announce that the Almighty Bible and Genesis were wrong.

Word also had it that the preacher's sermons in the town were, since the incident, about almost nothing *but* the SKA and the blasphemous stain it would put on his town.

Dawie had verified all of these things to Dara, that he remained the talk of the town.

Since the initial furore had died down, Dawie had become a regular visitor at the compound, walking the hour it took from his own home. Sometimes he'd bring along the other boys Dara had met on the school's playground—Detlief and Tjaardt—Tjaardt with the emerald eyes.

The house staff wasn't finished with their opinions either; "It's a *skandaal kleinbaas*—scandalous—to look at the white girls like you did," they warned.

Dawie upped the ante and the other boys nodded in solemn agreement: "They're still out to get you—Vermaak wants to *donner* you."

"Donner *me?*"

"Ja, man… to beat you up."

Neels Vermaak with the granite head thought the situation more than scandalous—he was treating it like a blasphemy. His girlfriend, Dawie explained—the one with the striking blonde hair, the one who had tried to intervene at the attack—had been so disgusted by Neels' assault that she'd broken off their long relationship.

The only son of a wealthy farming family, Vermaak carried clout in the town. Dawie detailed his pedigree; he was the *Dominee*'s *protégé*, the youth leader in the NGK congregation and a star on the sports, and especially rugby, field. He had backup.

By now Dara had the whole scoop on the parched town—its people suffering from a crushed economy, desperately reeling from a prolonged drought. With the worst El Niño ever recorded amplifying the effects of climate change already in full force, rain hadn't fallen in almost three years and the farms were in crisis. Prayers for rain at the local church had come to naught.

Undeterred and oblivious to these matters, Dawie's people were planning to gather soon to shuffle and dance and beseech the ancestors to save the land from the ravages of man.

Against the backdrop of these tough conditions, small human dramas were playing themselves out.

Detlief was up from Cape Town staying with extended family. The gang violence of his home suburb in the city had boiled over and drug-related killings in the slum streets there were a daily occurrence. His mother had shipped him out when he started moving with the wrong crowd; given the depravations they lived in he could hardly have avoided it.

Tjaardt's pedigree was now also cleared up—he'd detailed it with great pride so that there could be no confusion… These categories were important he'd insisted, as they pegged each person into a hierarchy. The brief history lesson he extolled came with solemn nods of agreement from the other boys and house staff. He pigeonholed himself into his mother's ethnic linage; he was a Baster. Derived from the old Dutch word for *bastard,* an early ethnic mix between the original Dutch settlers and indigenous African population. Tjaardt seemed extremely proud to have the blood of the *Trekboers* in his veins… even if their ancestors in the town and on the playground rejected any hint that he was any part of them.

Tjaart's uncle was the local *Burgemeester* or Mayor. His position was not a welcome one to the white community of the town. His affiliations to the ruling political party of the country, whom they hated, were bruised but still too strong for most to stomach. There was a general sense that he was an undeserving recipient of the position was rife.

When Dara thought small town politics couldn't be any more outrageous, on his latest visit Dawie updated the threat to *Defcon Level-1*.

"Vermaak says he's going to kill you… and me."

"What for *now*?" Dara sighed it, exhausted by the seemingly endless litany of escalating threats and hostility constantly rumbling toward him from the distant town; were it not for Dawie's obvious concern, it would have seemed farcical.

"They know we're friends and they know I come here… but mainly because of your mom."

"Because of my mum? Because of her work?"

"Yes… but also because…" he hesitated, "…because your mother went to the police—and the Constable is an elder in the Church, so it went right back to *Dominee* van der Nest, and then to Neels."

"What? My mother went to the cops?" Dara was outraged, feeling betrayed but he knew that he couldn't do anything until his mother returned home—at work she was not to be disturbed by calls.

"This is absurd...."

His mind was suddenly a tangle of a thousand thoughts.

Fragments of memories and tumbling thoughts came vaulting through his mind, falling into place.

More than once he'd seen a *bakkie*—a pickup truck—someone screened within it watching him intently from the national road as he rode his bike on an adjacent farm track.

The previous week while shopping in the town with his mother a passing car had jeered him.

He'd thought little about these unconnected matters at the time, but with Dawie's input connecting them, his predicament suddenly felt ominous. A trickle of ice seeped into his veins, the adrenaline of fear traced a cold trickle of dread to his every extremity.

Something sinister slid within him, a foreboding.

He pushed it out of his mind.

In a few weeks his mother would take him down to Cape Town for a vacation. He'd enroll there at boarding school there and remain away for months. All this madness would blow over and be long forgotten before he returned.

Suddenly it felt like a race for survival until the date of their departure.

I'll keep a low profile... stay on the farm, I'm fine here, he silently consoled himself.

"They call you *Mister Prrrrretty boy*," Dawie reminded him—and the way he rolled those '*rrrrr*'s struck like a tuning fork, resonating with that agitator's shout-out in the town. The *thing* slid through Dara's gut again and he shoved his hands into his pockets to quell any tremor and manufactured a scoff of laughter.

When his mother arrived home that evening he took her to task and it erupted into an unpleasant shouting match.

He stormed to his room and slammed the door.

Later his mother came knocking. He eventually relented and opened the door.

He knew she was right, though; she had made a statement so that the incident at the school was on record. The African sergeant who had recorded it already knew the details and name of the assailant before she even described him and battled to pronounce his name—*Neels Vermaak.*

It was on the record—that was all she wanted.

Chapter 3

More weeks passed, but still the hoped, prayed and danced-for rains remained stubbornly absent; the experts said the situation would persist.

Dara's perch high above the escarpment should have provided a dazzling vista of bloom for which the *Painted Desert,* as the Namaqualand region was called, was rightly famous. Carnarvon lay at its boundary.

The postcards of what *should* be out there now were mesmerizing but the ancestors in their unfathomable wisdom seemed happy to ignore all pleading and leave the place dusty with a rugged masculine beauty.

Somewhere out there over the horizon; Dara gazed in the general direction, knowing it was far too distant to spot; lay *Verneukpan*, famous for its land speed record attempts. His father was a speed enthusiast and had promised to take him there when an event was next scheduled.

Dara's parents had been forced by career to live apart for some years but the arrangement was purely practical. Contracts had taken them to different parts of the world so that clinging to the ideal for a relationship was more corrosive than allowing one another to be apart in mutual agreement. When they came back together it was like nothing had changed for those all-too-brief periods.

His father was currently in the United States promoting his fourth book popularizing breakthrough science. He was scheduled to visit South Africa later in the year to tour sites of early mankind; the entire region north and east of Carnarvon also bordered the enigmatically named *Cradle of Mankind* where a graveyard containing dozens of *Homo Naledi* bones were found deep inside the impossibly tight and meandering *Rising Star* cave system. The announcement of the find had rocked the world of science, begging deeply searching questions about the point in the *hominid* timeline when the evolving human species had developed a sense of self.

As Dara had begun to appreciate, this part of the world was a veritable treasure trove for learning. It was an irony he thought, that the inhabitants so roundly rejected the evidence of these facts etched into nature so close at hand in favor of Calvinist dogma from so far away and long ago.

His father had told him of the significance of the local peoples—the *Bushmen* as some of them preferred to be called rather than the more popular and politically driven *Khoisan;* the living fossils of humanity's deep prehistoric past.

Those calling themselves Bushmen had explained to Dara that *Khoisan* refers to a specific clan name within the Bushman community. It was Dara realized, not unlike *McGregor* would not do as a collective label for all Scotsmen.

Dara had proudly explained as much to his father.

It had all come to life for Dara—the very earth of the place now held a magnetism, as if the DNA in his fibres recognized its ancestral home. Each day, England drifted ever further away from his yearning.

The drama that had played out over these far and barren lands was reverberating deep inside of him. In the theatre of his mind he visualized the scenes back a hundred thousand years. The roving bands of hunters stalking small game, sheltering in the caves that were now his playground—families and generations under the rash of stars and the Milky Way that had brought his mother; a new kind of explorer.

The rocks reflecting the lanky figures and their speared quarry captured in paint on the living rocks, their footprints found impressed into ancient petrified mud and the middens and bones they left as fossils—these were the things that would soon unite his parents and make them briefly a quasi-family unit, all in that other great quest for knowledge that seemed to surge through the family genes; with doctors and engineers on both sides of his linage.

Cutting down through the deposited rock strata, as Dara had now taken to spending his days, the time-machine ran backward with each layer; from the time that our recent Paleolithic ancestors were making stone tools—past the Jurassic of the great lumbering dino-beasts—to the reptiles that pre-dated them in the tropical swamps that once abounded in this now dry space.

It was the little yellow-tinged people, Dawie's folk, who fascinated Dara.

Many of the house staff and those in the town bore the classic features that came to them down sixty thousand years of genetic linage and a culture distinct from all other peoples of the earth—the small ears, tufting hair and sometimes oversized rumps. *Steatopygia*, his father had called it.

Dara had looked it up: *"an accumulation of large deposits of fat on the buttocks, especially as a normal condition in the Khoikhoi and other peoples of arid parts of southern Africa,"* the encyclopedia confirmed. It was an evolutionary bulwark against the deprivations of endless drought in these barren lands.

The plight of any population crushed by history is always a point of contention and in contemporary politics a potential powder keg for its remnant descendants.

The modern predicament of the Bushmen had its first foundations in equatorial Africa nearly a thousand years earlier and four thousand miles north, as population explosions in the black groups there sent an undulating wave of migration south, the black Nguni tribes—the farmers and herders—marched steadily forward generation after generation, valley and plain after valley and plain.

Ahead of them they enslaved and pushed the escaping hunter-gatherer bands ever further, ever southward toward the coast.

The process was a slow seep of humanity, the subtle differences in appearance but vast differences in cultural organization creating a patchwork of group-to-area designations.

Squinting to pick it out from his vantage point, Dara thought he could *just* make out the thread of asphalt that offered an eight-hour drive southward to Cape Town; *The Mother City*.

Five hundred years on from the first dramatic migrations that he was imagining in this dry interior, the *Heeren XVII* or *Lords Seventeen* of *The Dutch East India Company* had promulgated their orders for the first of the European explorers to join the coming *mélange* of cultures assembling for collision.

Ship after ship, they arrived slowly but steadily, planting their flag at the foot of a comely mountain that embraced a welcoming bay.

Within a century, their numbers bolstered, religious instability in Europe and enmity between its nations sent shockwaves that set them on their way, fanning out to the north—columns of mostly Dutch descendants bringing their guns, language, culture and Bibles.

They in turn had pushed the Bushmen north again. The Bushmen's path blocked by the Nguni in the North and East, were diverted and crushed into this arid West where Carnarvon lay—into the desert badlands of scrub and hardship.

The Europeans brought disease too—smallpox and other plagues—against which the incumbents had no or little resistance. Alcohol, unknown to roving bands, decimated those who survived the other apocalypses. Few bloodlines of Bushmen avoided mixing. Fewer yet maintained the wandering subsistence culture.

Subsistence back then meant following the seasons and masses of game; now, with the great herds decimated by guns, and barbed fences penning the last traces of quarry in and the subsistence hunters out, it meant handouts and stipends from tourists along the national road or near game park entrances, traded for trinkets and small change.

As Dara sat imagining it all, possibly no single human left still held to the *old* ways.

"When the last is gone Dara," his father had said, "we lose the biggest part of ourselves."

"*The biggest part?*"—It sounded rather an exaggeration and Dara challenged his father.

"I mean it literally Dara," his dad had assured. "They are our anchor—our lifeline to finding out who we *are* today in our psychology, in our sociology and anthropology. These are important questions. We live in vastly complex societies full of different cultures and competing political ideologies each with their own basket of economic systems. But we're still only collections of individuals, and for half a million generations… millions of years of hunting and gathering, our individual psychology evolved to cope with a few other individuals—mostly extended family members forced to live highly cooperatively with no concept of possession over things or others. At most we've been in larger communities and dealing with strangers for five hundred generations, and that is not enough time to overcome bred-in psychology that held sway for a thousand times longer. For one, two, three or more million years not much changed from generation to generation until the concept of farming and with it *ownership* arose—and then *everything* changed. And we're watching the last of our species give up that ancient simple lifestyle."

Dara learned how even the benign but necessary act of paying cash for an item at a store involved a prescribed exchange that was unnatural to our deepest selves; how it ran contrary to our wiring for close cooperation with kin; how that exchange introduced a barrier between the parties that reinforced the emotional distance between them—and ultimately drove competition and enmity.

These thoughts mulled in his mind as he looked out over the lands his and every other human's own ancestors had certainly once wandered.

Until recently these concepts had been academic to him— theoretical. But barefooted and dusty with this earth; he was growing small roots into the Africa under his feet; and with his intimate acquaintance with Dawie and other indigenous workers around the compound, the theoretical was fast catalyzing into the emotional. Only a generation or two from humanity's 'wild' condition, Dara could detect the difficulty these Bushmen still grappled with as they tried to slot into the modern world.

Dawie was a spectacular find for Dara—almost royalty in this regard, his grandfather a clan leader of the Bushmen. His grandfather's grandfather in turn recognized as the last of *"the wandering Bushmen"*—living wild off game, indigenous plants and especially wits.

But Dawie had posed a conundrum Dara could not yet get his mind around:

"A Zulu man can wear a suit and take his seat in the National Assembly of our country's parliament, and a Xhosa woman can be an I.T. expert or sit on the Board of a multi-national," Zulu and Xhosa are splinters of the Nguni nation, "and nobody questions if either are a *real* Zulu or a *real* Xhosa. But I'm a bushman boy who loses his cultural identity if I put on shoes or use a mobile phone."

It was true—Dara had already detected that prejudice within himself.

Dawie's family had been driven off the land and forbidden their traditional rights—now, outside of academia, they were not even considered 'Bushmen' or Khoi—but the collective noun 'coloured'; a catchall designation for anyone not white, black or Asian. The coloureds numbered in the majority for the region—nearly ninety percent of the population so designated; but they held little economic or political sway.

It was deep into afternoon; Dara donned socks and shoes and began to make his way home.

The wind had risen and tall thunderheads like the phalanx of foreign invaders in centuries past marched abreast steadily forward. And then salvos of thunder began to reverberate off the surrounding mountains. As Dara passed, a lazy windmill on borrowed time groaned at the labour the rising wind was forcing on its dusty gears.

Just then the first lonely drop of rain splattered out of a darkening sky, a dollop of hot water doled from the heavens.

Dara looked skyward just as *two… three-four* more globules slapped his visor. He opened the throttle a little to beat the deluge and smiled in praise of Dawie's people and their unflinching conviction that the ancestors will always protect the land from the ravages of man.

Chapter 4

Three days later, mid morning, Dara was on the bike, bound for the hills five kilometers to the east where he'd have a good view of the blossoming *veld*. It was a spot where he'd found interesting fossils of tropical ferns some days before. But before he'd gone a kilometer the bike spluttered and coughed and he quickly felt below the tank and flipped the fuel lever to '*reserve*'. This would give him a few extra kilometers but too risky on a deserted dirt track to ignore, so he doubled back. Back in the garage, he found the fuel drum empty.

"Fuckit...!" he bellowed. Though he'd been told not to do so countless times, the gardener was always topping the lawnmower off with Dara's stash of fuel and once again the petty pilfering had run Dara's stockpile dry.

Dara was furious—he stormed off to find the man but couldn't locate him.

He went inside again intending to find something else with which to busy himself; to abandon the outing. But, try as he might, he was already fixated on the far hills and couldn't find a distraction from it. More than that, he heard the old echo of cowardice taunting in the shadows of his mind, questioning why he was *really* so reluctant.

"What's out there that's so important?" he asked of himself, already knowing he was about to break a rule.

He was under a spell that only Africa casts, becoming African, craving it raw and untouched before the imminent departure back to city life.

The clock in his head and fall of the shadows agreed that it was near ten in the morning. School and its dangerous inmates would still be in session for two more weeks, those in their final exams should be hard at their studies, and there'd be next to no traffic to speak of, so he dared himself.

It would be less than a twenty minute round trip—illegal.... *"Yes"*... but the engine capacity, he convinced himself, was only *juuuust* over the limit his age allowed; very quickly he convinced himself it would be the right thing to do—to not let the calls of cowardice within defeat him.

The heat of the day was already up, yet he wore longs and sleeves with gauntlets and his visor was mirrored; normally, protection from a fall; today it thwarted prying eyes.

It proved to be a milk-run into town—he only passed two cars, instinctively he'd dropped his head down into them. He kept his visor down for the duration of the refuel.

There were only two pumps, one of which was out of order. As the pump attendant tried to squeeze the last drops into his tank, a pickup passed and immediately slowed. With a slide of terror within, Dara saw the brake lights come on. It pulled over to the side then completed a U-turn, entering the lot right behind him. Dara's heart thundered in his ears—he dared not to look as he felt the bumper pull close up behind his rear tire, the clatter of its diesel engine a din.

Without looking back he overpaid the attendant and stalled the bike within a pace of pulling away, kicking it frantically back to life. His breath was rasping as he glimpsed two occupants in the rearview mirror on the handlebars, but his darted look was not enough to confirm more than that. He over-revved his pull away and turned onto the road that took him momentarily past the vehicle. It hadn't pulled forward to the pump but the driver was talking to the pump attendant and looked past the man straight at Dara as he went away.

Against his best intentions to appear calm, fear gripped Dara; he hit the gas and dropped onto the tank, winding the screaming engine up through its gears.

By the time he pulled into home the engine popped and pinged in outrage. The terror was gone, replaced by the exhilaration of winning over fear. He never sang, but he belted out a popular tune. Removing his jacket he smelled the sweet reek of adrenaline sweat and his hands still shook, but he didn't care; he'd had a victory… perhaps a victory over no more than his own timidity.

By the time he caught up with the gardener, the excitement of the sortie had planed the edge off his anger, and all he could muster was a tepid rebuke that didn't carry much authority; the gardener adopted a dull look in his eye as if he didn't fully comprehend it, just earnestly repeating *"Ja kleinbaas"*.

An hour later Dara was in the hills, the drama forgotten.

Chapter 5

A delegation was in town, come to inspect the SKA site and progress.

On Friday they'd done their fieldwork.

Today was Saturday; a banquet had been laid on in tents pitched out on the local school grounds. Dignitaries and prominent citizens were present for various speeches and presentations.

On Sunday the same tents would be used to drum up enthusiasm for the less prominent citizens of the area, laborers and farm workers. The agenda for that upcoming event would be to detail the promised benefits that the SKA investments would bring to the area.

Marsha had been speaking at some length with one of the visiting politicians who had presented a keynote address. Guests milled, joined them and broke off to chat with others. The topics Marsha and the Minister had talked about ranged widely until the drift of conversation allowed Marsha to bring up the incident.

"My son ran into some trouble at the school, quite unpleasant really…" she went on to describe the details.

"I think it's an isolated incident," he assured her. "We *were* originally presented with a petition but our PR people took care of it—the town council is fully behind us now."

"Oh I don't doubt the council," Marsha agreed, "but it does seem that the religious groups are… how shall I say…? *Underwhelmed* by the implementation."

"Yes," the Minister declared, "it's a small group who are unhappy about the loss of farms and other conveniences," he made light of it.

"Of course there are legitimate gripes—I'm talking about something much more unsettling. It seems that we're treading on religious toes...."

"Oh, the zealots," the roll of his eyes suggested he knew about them. "I think you've uncovered the *Israel-Visie* a lunatic splinter of the church. There are just a few of them that we've identified, mostly old men past their prime who have to hide their affiliations or they'll push the enlightened younger generation away from the church. Regardless..." he went on before she could challenge him, "...the infrastructures we're bringing in are going to continue isolate them as the youngsters adopt new thinking. The new IT infrastructure at the school... new tar roads... upgraded airport... fastest fiber optic internet connection on the continent..."

Though the politicians weren't bringing anything tangible in, they unashamedly took full credit with an inclusive '*we*' to the very people who were bequeathing these things; but Marsha let the petty point go;

"Sure... But how much do the farmers value these things going on in the town when we've cut all wireless connections to their farms...? They're feeling isolated. There's a lot of discontent. Maybe it's one of your old men, but at least one of the teachers at the school is putting real negatives into the kids' minds. He's the local pastor, so..."

"I wouldn't worry about that. If you look at church influence it is plummeting," said the Minister confidently. "Thirty years ago they had nearly a thousand members out here—it's a third of that now. He has no real influence anymore. I know this because it was an early concern and my office looked into it. We got it resolved."

"I hear your assurances," Marsha conceded, "but with all respect I don't sense it is resolved. The church's influence may be down in numbers, but the world over their attitudes are sharpening. My husband's an evolutionary anthropologist and author. His work has hit a lot of headwind, especially in America."

"Well, that's America for you," the Minister smiled with a practiced sincerity that was anything but. "We're not in America." He aimed his reminder at the flock of eavesdroppers, voters, that Marsha was an outsider with an American accent.

"I must disagree," she persisted. "I think there is cause to worry… These people seem very passionate, and..."

"I have no doubt in my mind that this significant project will serve as a catalyst to improve learner performance in the area of mathematics and science and to prepare learners to take advantage of the opportunities that will emanate from the developments associated with the Karoo Array Telescope, the MeerKAT and the SKA."

The minister had just repeated *verbatim* an extract from the speech he had just delivered from the podium. This wasn't a conversation, Marsha realized, it was just more political cheerleading for the small audience listening in.

Chapter 6

Constable Andre Kruger had not been invited to the banquet; as a rank and file policeman he'd long ago accepted that the closest he would ever come to such an event would be to attend the parking of dignitaries.

No, he argued; what rankled him was the insult to his standing as *Diaken;* a Deacon was second only to the *Dominee*. The position *demanded* respect. But these godless outsiders had snubbed it.

Like his father before him, rising through the police ranks had been his childhood ambition until this 'communist', as he called them, black government had come to power decades ago. And since then his rank and prospects had been stillborn and pegged. He'd long since abandoned all hope of that changing—the passion was dead, and the grind of it had become a job-for-a-wage.

So his passion and energy to pursue meaning in life had diverted into Faith. After the *Dominee* he was now the most respected man in the town, even if the outsiders shunned his position.

"It's not worth troubling yourself, that's why I turned down my invitation, Andre" the *Dominee* Gert van der Nest assured the constable.

It was a Saturday night; the time families traditionally gathered at one or another's home for the men to watch their beloved sport on television and heap meat onto the coals, while the women flocked to prepare salads and sharpen gossip.

"You won't hear any truth spoken there—just these *rooinek* foreign scientists telling their lies to politicians and politicians making their empty promises back to them," Gert assured.

The last glow of dusk had evaporated and the Milky Way was a pale rash overhead. Crickets had taken over the night chorus from the retired cicadas of the dayshift. With the meat cooked and consumed, the women had retired to the kitchen to clean. The younger children were in bed and the older allowed an extra treat of television.

Kakpraathout was crackling on the hearth; the wood colloquially named for its noxious fumes that taint meat if used as coals in the cooking process. *Kakpraathout*—wood that made men with tumblers full of fiery liquor in their hands talk shit.

The two men—preacher and policeman—stood contemplating, eyes cast skyward as they'd done countless times since they were lads and friends. The twinkle and milky rash overhead tonight was particularly crisp and clear.

Sonja, Andre's daughter came outside and silently threw her arms around her father's ample bulk, snuggling her temples against his chest. She was a tall girl and took him to the armpits.

He held her fast and sniffed her head. An elastic band held a single ponytail and he pulled it out, releasing her thick blonde mane.

"*Pa-aaaaa!*" she complained, singing her protest.

"Go help your mother" he told her. "This is men's talk."

She snuggled deeper and held tighter.

He nuzzled her scalp with his nose.

"She's a good girl," the *Dominee* said.

"My special girl," her doting father assured. "Getting her a car next year when she goes to Cape Town," he added proudly.

"Seventeen already?" Gert asked with some amazement, he hadn't noticed the years.

"Almost eighteen," she smiled at him coyly then buried her face in her dad's chest.

"And you still want to follow a course *on* mathematics?"

"Ja *Dominee*," she responded in muffled tones. She'd known him all her life; he had christened her into the Faith.

"She'll teach them a thing or two," her father assured and beamed.

"And your boy?" asked the *Dominee*, "still so difficult?"

The *Dominee* had not uttered Andre's son's name in nearly a decade since he'd married the foreign woman and become like them; he was determined to never relent.

"...So much going for him, what a loss... But, you see, Sonja... when you mix in with the wrong people..." he let the warning hang as an accusation.

JJ—Johannes Jakob—was Sonja's older brother by almost two decades. Not yet forty, he had already accumulated wealth that his father could barely comprehend. When he visited it was in his own airplane or by expensive sports car that needed to be nursed over the rough country roads. His end-goal focus had him spending more on speeding tickets than on fuel.

Andre was ambivalent toward his son. Secretly proud of JJ's achievements, he was also as deeply disappointed as the *Dominee* for the man's soul. Since going to the city to study law, the prodigal had strayed from the culture, married an American and resisted all efforts to win him back. He no longer attended church and was frustratingly argumentative.

"JJ is a good boy at heart," Andre said, placatingly. He knew JJ's apostasy hurt the *Dominee* the way any son's rebellion hurts his spiritual father. "I'm proud of him... he must just spend more time with his people."

They stood silently a few minutes longer in contemplation of the heavens.

"They want us to believe it's getting bigger... expanding," Andre said, jutting his chin at the sky. "Sonja comes home with these kind of stories; *neh* Sonja?"

Sonja said nothing and the *Dominee* huffed; "Our Lord's place is big enough Sonja," he assured with conviction. "There's no end to the nonsense they tell these poor children." After a few moments contemplation, he went on; "There's a science center at the school now; a new teacher with it. They're even wasting money on this high-speed *interweb*."

Andre's huff was weighty with despair, the burden of these sudden invasions into his quiet corner of the desert almost too much to contemplate.

"You and I, Andre, they know our faith is strong... *unbreakable*... they'll *never* shift us. No... they want our children...." He too shook his head with disgust at the cunning.

"Gert..." Andre rarely used *Dominee* van der Nest's first name, "I don't know..." he sighed. "I don't know what this world is coming to."

They stood a few more moments longer and Andre went on. "That black devil from your school has been riding his bike out on the national roads. I did some checking and he's not yet eighteen—he can't have a license. If I find him..." He let the threat go unspoken.

"Better you find him than our Neels does hey."

They both chuckled in prideful agreement.

Sonja's body went instantly slack and she released her grip, turned and walked indoors, shoulders rounded, irritation in her attitude.

Andre eyed her suspiciously, instinctively filing her reaction, as any good policeman should.

"Strange..." Gert pondered aloud.

"Strange?"

"Strange her reaction Andre, the way she just walked away."

"It's the trouble with her and Neels," Andre speculated hopefully, wanting to shift the course of the obvious observation. "She hasn't wanted him at the house for weeks."

"Hmmm..." Gert weighed news. "They've been so close a long time."

"Committed," Andre confirmed. "I think she wants to break it off. Going their different ways next year... with her off to study."

"No... Her attitude changed when you talked about that boy Andre. She looked very irritated."

"Never!" Andre said emphatically, a lance of ice thrusting within; he'd felt it convulse in her the instant the Indian boy had been mentioned, Sonja's body going rigid, betraying her anger; but he would never allow anyone to speculate such a disgusting thing that she'd side with a *rooinek* over her own kind, certainly not with a dark *rooinek*.

"Well..." Gert let the contradiction of his old friend's words whither on the air to spare him the further shame of truth.

"I'm sorry about this with Neels though… To have a son-in-law like that… but girls these days…" Andre paused to mull what might have been.

"Ja. A special man that boy will become," Gert agreed. "He thinks of you as a father, idolizes you my friend. I know you know it but I don't think you realize quite how intensively he admires you"

Andre knew it was true. It filled him with vast pride to have the prince of the town's youth so enamored of him—of *him*, with such a lowly rank in his police career. And, Andre thought, how miraculously and ironically his Lord worked, that his lowly rank in the police could bestow so much more untold weight to the boy's admiration. Had he attained his ambition to follow his own father's passion for policing to the rank of Captain and beyond… had these corrupt and undeserving black bastards not stolen that dream from him; the admiration that Neels and others with a backbone like Neels' might have favored him with would not have carried the weight it now did.

Andre shook his head in wonder thinking about it.

No, that it was and could only be his unshakeable Belief that drew Neels to him made him burst with pride and give all honors to God for imbuing him the gift of boundless Faith.

"The father of the boy is Indian," the *Dominee* changed the tack back to Dara, *"No need to rub Andre's nose further in his children's scandalous behavior",* he thought. "Another troublemaker Andre. He's in America now, my friends there tell me. And he's coming here soon. I have some eyes on him, selling his ungodly books there… what when he gets here?" He was insinuating a challenge. "This family Andre… *duiwel besete."*

"What do these people want with us Gert? There's going to be trouble… they're looking for it, they just won't stop. This is our land and our town. Every street in this town the name of our *Dominees—Alheit, Sterrenberg and Stremme…"* Kruger listed them. "This wouldn't be a town and there would be nothing but bush if it wasn't for the mission and the church. We didn't just proclaim the gospel, our forefathers built this place."

"But they *think* it's theirs Andre. Just listen to the name, 'Carnarvon'—that's a *bliksemse Engels naam*—they must always change to bloody English names," Gert pointed out. "Yes, we named the streets but they stole the whole town and called it theirs... now they bring these *verdomde* people."

And it was true—the village's original name, Harmsfontein, was changed to Carnarvon to honor the British colonial secretary Lord Carnarvon. Henry Howard Molyneux Herbert, the fourth Earl of Carnarvon, studied for his BA degree at the University of Oxford and became under secretary of Colonies in 1858 and State Secretary in 1866.

They looked heavenward again in askance.

"They say they're here for the quiet of our little piece of heaven on earth—because there is no radio pollution to interfere with their listening to the sky. What a joke; these scientists must come and disrupt our simple world to escape the radio *'pollution'* as they call it, pollution they themselves have made. I'm telling you, it's ridiculous is what it is." Andre's voice was strained with frustration.

"This is the devil at work," the *Dominee* solemnly assured, "...and it's God allowing us to be tested. A test so we can show our mettle. We will overcome."

Both men huffed in unison. They were of one mind in how they'd meet the test.

Chapter 7

"We're in the headlines," said Dr. Deon Louw, School Principle and NG Church elder, "but for all the wrong reasons."

It was Monday mid-morning, the second last week of school for the year.

"*Luister hier,*" and he began to read off a printed sheet stapled at its corner:

"Dust swirls as reed-thin children file into a marquee erected on the sports field of Carnarvon School to attend a community *Imbizo*—a gathering to discuss the SKA radio telescope that is being built on a remote site 80 km from their town."

"*Waar kry jy dit?*" Van der Nest asked of its origins with a scowl.

"One of the parents brought it in—their boy found it on the computer; it says here "*b-d-live*-its an interweb newspaper—Business Day newspaper, the heading is 'Carnarvon's poor place their hopes in the SKA project'."

"I will tell the children to look out for this sort of thing and report it to me," *Dominee* Gert assured.

Deon read on, "…Whether their presence is motivated by genuine curiosity for the project or the prospect of a free meal, is hard to tell.

While the SKA project is intended to provide astronomers with the world's most powerful radio telescope, not fix a broken town, scientists and engineers responsible for implementing it have also to manage community expectations. It is a delicate task, one they are trying to manage head-on."

"*Wat 'n klomp twak!*" Gert spat out his rebuke against the article; Deon kept reading.

"The telescope will span Africa and Australia, with its core in the remote reaches of South Africa's Karoo. The world's most powerful radio telescope will help scientists to answer questions about how the first stars and galaxies formed and probe the nature of dark matter…' And on and on it goes…" Deon pushed his glasses back up his nose; his glasses always slid down when he was irritable; he read on, "…'Inside the tent, hopes run high that the telescope will provide an escape from a life of grinding poverty—people complain freely to the gathered dignitaries'…"

The secretary came into the room to clear the teacups.

"Dankie Trudy."

"Plesier…" she said.

Deon ran his finger down the printout, his lips murmuring, seeking something provocative to recount; "…'It's barely noon yet plenty of the locals gathered in the marquee have clearly had more than a few drinks. Many children carry the mark of fetal alcohol syndrome…"

"That's how these people are… but somehow *we* are to blame, *neh*?"

"Ja…" Deon held his finger on the page, keeping the place he'd stopped reading; "…'Outside the school grounds lies a town with a single general practitioner and a barely functioning hospital that does not even have hot water, never mind a doctor.'"

"What? A single practitioner!" Gert frowned, looking deeply offended. "How old is this report?"

"Now… from this weekend," Deon re-checked the date on it.

"Well… there you are…" he announced with a dismissive wave. "Our new clinic just opened, so what *kak* are they saying *'a single general practitioner'."*

"Ja… exactly. Like the rest of it—rubbish… and you know it's Andre's boy who put the money up? For the clinic…" Deon asserted.

"Really?" Gert was genuinely surprised.

"Ja."

"He never said anything to me."

"I'm sure… He's quite embarrassed by it. Says that if his boy could put this kind of money in, why only do it when the foreigners are here? Why donate it through them? Why did he wait all this time?"

"I agree with him. That boy, Deon… I know it has cut Andre deeply… the disappointment."

"I feel for him… And Sonja? She's under their influence too. With that incident I had to remind her of her priorities; I don't want Andre to find out what she claimed…" the principal harked back to the inquest into Dara's head injury in the corridor when Sonja had admitted that Neels had sucker punched him; her evidence ignored and her priorities called into question. "You know that we just hired that new science teacher… That Fiske…? Well… here's what they report; 'The schools cannot recruit science teachers into such a backwater…' So you tell me… dishonest with every word they print."

Chapter 8

Across town Marsha was reading the same report from the *'bdlive'* web page out aloud to a visiting friend, Chris Weber.

"…'While the SKA project cannot uplift an entire town, it is sensitive to the effect that such a big construction project has on the lives of locals, and is investing in human capital development programs that may provide a step up for some of them.

It has already provided hundreds of bursaries and scholarships to university students in mathematics, science and engineering.

Earlier this week it launched a quarter-million dollar e-schools initiative with industry partners who will provide three hundred and fifty laptops and Internet access to five schools in the area. Those laptops are preloaded with mathematics and science learning resources'."

She stopped reading and frowned in contemplation; "They're actually very nice people, Chris"

"The workers…? The poor in the article's heading?" Chris asked.

"No… Well yes. The workers are very nice, very charming. But the farmers, I mean, the local Afrikaners… really lovely people. Some of the old guard is particularly edgy right now. But this whole development, it is having an impact… a lot of farms are being bought up to accommodate the project and not all of them are keen sellers. They've got a lot of generations invested into the land and they're feeling aggrieved and robbed of heritage."

"Sure… like any big civil engineering project that displaces people. I'd be angry too if I were them," Chris suggested.

Chris Weber was a Quantum Physicist working at CERN's Hadron Collider. He and Marsha had been friends for decades and, since he was in Cape Town on vacation, she'd invited him to spend some time in the hinterland.

"This impact's bigger than most projects though," Marsha pointed out. "If you're building a dam, you flood a valley and displace a few families who get compensation… But here its millions of hectares that we need to push a century back in time. You can't live on a modern farm under the conditions we need, they lose all the conveniences of modern life… no mobile phone coverage, no engines, no planes… They can't use those things once we're operational. The problem's that radio is such a slippery medium and our sensitivity to it is off the charts. We can't even allow windmills to turn because the friction in their mechanisms interferes with us. Just that alone sets in motion an environmental impact on the game and sheep that rely on the scarce water."

"Granted, but it's a desert… what are we talking? A few dozen families… maybe a few hundred?"

"More than that… because they have staff and the towns are totally reliant on the farming economy. The towns die if the farms stop working."

"But you'll pick up the slack… provide employment?"

"During construction, sure, some. But tens of thousands of jobs…? That's a stretch."

"Why'd they take it on here then? Australia was also bidding."

"Rumours around town are that the original numbers were fudged. I can't confirm it because I wasn't on the bid committee. The farmers reckon that the bid understated the economic activity of this region."

"Why don't these folks complain then," he frowned with skepticism.

"Depends who you talk to… they *are* complaining, complaining bitterly, but they say they're not being heard. I can *kinda* see their point, you and I peer in as outsiders. We see a bunch of mainly-white farmers howling about losing their mobile phone signals and satellite TV, or maybe being forced to sell their farms and we think. '…It's in the name of progress for the betterment of all humans…' or '…your apartheid past doesn't give you the best platform to complain now about mistreatment…'. Who outside of this impacted community is going to listen to their gripe…? We see them as the products of institutionalized bigotry, so who cares about their hardships now?"

"Okay… wow… and I thought it was all going swimmingly."

"The project's steaming ahead beautifully, just these tensions are weighing on me."

"Why take it on…? It's not your problem."

"The thing with Dara…" she looked at Dara sitting quietly listening, "…it highlighted for me that there is a problem. It was suggested to me that he reaped the whirlwind I'm part of causing."

"You can't feel guilty about the whole situation, you're not paid enough to worry like this. Just do your job and let the decision makers do theirs."

"I'm a fool, all liberals are… we think too much. The boy who hit Dara was just acting out on what he hears from the adults."

"Don't excuse it," Chris admonished.

"That's not what I mean, and Dara knows it… I mean that the younger folks… the kids and even their parents. The ones born after apartheid began crumbling; they're more open to negotiate this out. It's the older generation that are implacable."

"A big generation gap?"

"Like anywhere going through rapid modernization, sure."

"Well… it's going ahead, so you have to choose and then live with it." There was a long silence until Chris piped up with a cheerful ring to his voice, "It's a hell of a project wherever it goes," he tried to lift the mood of gloom. "Exciting time in all the sciences."

Chris had been on the team that in 2012 had announced the confirmation of a Higgs Boson—a sub-atomic particle so elusive that the media had dubbed it *"The God Particle"*—derived from the frustration scientists expressed in looking for *"that Goddamned particle."*

The relevance of uncovering the Higgs would keep echoing down through all of the sciences and cosmology well into the future, Chris went on, connecting for Dara how the very small of his quantum mechanics were the foundation of the cosmology that his mother, Marsha, was a part of studying through the SKA project.

Still silently soaking it all in, Dara was a sponge in this type of company, and occasionally he'd deliver a question or observation that could derail even the smartest among these hyper-thinkers.

The Higgs, Chris explained, is that impossibly small component—possibly just a dancing filament of pure energy—deep within and intrinsically part of the nucleus of every atom. It is the Higgs that causes the atom to interact via its own *Higgs Field* with other atoms—attracting them. Collectively, this attraction we experience as gravity.

It is gravity that gives mass to matter, he explained, it is therefore the Higgs that makes 'things' *weigh* something. Gravity was the cornerstone of the entire cosmos—on the biggest scales, causing gas clouds in space to collapse in on themselves to become suns, in the process of nuclear fusion, cooking simpler atoms of hydrogen and helium into the progressively more complex atoms—Carbon, Oxygen, Calcium, Sodium… Chlorine and all other elements, and radiating heat and light in the process.

The language of Chris' professional world was not English or any other human language—it was the language of the cosmos, mathematics. The concepts of quantum mechanics, expressed in English or any language other than mathematics made next to no sense. Quantum, he explained, is not a philosophical or even a logical deduction, it is purely a mathematical reality that is borne out by observation.

"But what good is it?" Dara asked.

"Thirty five percent of the United States' GDP relies on a thorough knowledge for the application of Quantum mechanics," Chris immediately responded. "Without our understanding of quantum theory, electronics simply don't work. And, forget the thirty five percent of GDP—without electronics we go back to the stone-age."

It was sobering.

It reminded Dara of his mother telling him that the Wi-Fi he took for granted had its invention in her own field—"An Australian Astrophysicist in the nineteen fifties was looking for Black Holes in deep space and invented a type of mathematics to tease the signals he sought from the background radio noise—

and it is that development that Wi-Fi uses to allow multiple electronic components to all communicate seamlessly in the same space."

Blue-Sky investments they were called—these mega-scientific investments; Hadron Colliders and SKAs. They set out to looked for one thing and quite often found many others by accident.

"They're *Moon-Shots*, Dara," she'd said when she'd told him that she was going to accept this new position at Carnarvon, and she would have to move them down from a cushy lifestyle to Africa.

Dara had a commercially orientated mind, so she'd sold the move to him in those terms; "They're called *'moon-shots'*... like NASA's Apollo Mission of the sixties, they're vast in scope, have a defined objective but generally return investment by non-anticipated discoveries. Apollo is said to have returned a dollar and sixty two for every dollar invested via unexpected spin-off commercial products. Teflon is just one."

Now, Chris and Marsha were heading into realms of discussion to which Dara, for all his stockpile of knowledge, could not yet follow them:

"The most powerful shortcut for completing the supergravity calculations emerged some time ago from the discovery at our CERN Laboratory," Chris explained. "We found that gravitons behave like two copies of gluons, the carriers of the strong nuclear force, which "glues" quarks together inside atomic nuclei," Chris had pointed out. "This 'double copy' relationship between gravitons and gluons has shown up in every variant of supergravity our researchers have studied, and they expect it to hold in the correct theory of quantum gravity, too, *regardless* of whether super-symmetry exists in nature."

Dara's mind boggled. He had no idea what they were on about, but he was impressed that they did.

Marsha smiled. Evidently she knew what it meant, "So in practice, the discovery means that once a gluon's scattering amplitude has been computed in a particular form to a given level of precision, extracting the gravity amplitude is child's play?"

"Indeed, yes. The double-copy property is more than a calculation tool. This is very concrete. It makes it absolutely clear that gravitons and gluons really do belong together. They really should be part of a unified theory."

The details were getting further away from Dara with each sentence they spoke, but he kept listening; satisfied that if two intelligent people understood, he eventually could too.

And, he noted, it was not a superficial pretense at understanding or a philosophical one—it was one vested deeply in observable and repeatable disciplines. The words of Richard Feynman, another of the great contemporary thinkers and acquaintance of his mother came to Dara's mind. Richard had once said, "Stick to the facts, ignore opinions. Nature doesn't lie."

"We are subjecting *N-equals-eight supergravity* to an unprecedented test," Chris went on. "We intend to calculate what happens when gravitons collide to a level of precision known as *"five loops"* in a fictional world with four point eight space-time dimensions."

"Of course, fractional dimensions can't really exist," Marsha added for Dara's sake in case he misunderstood.

Chris nodded agreement

"Of course," Dara replied—more than a little out of his depth, but he was fascinated and didn't want to divert the conversation; he made a mental note to quiz his mom later and she'd explain it then.

"We've seen that the five-loop calculation for four point eight dimensions roughly corresponds to a much more difficult seven-loop calculation in the dimensions of the real world. The harmonious interplay between the particles in *N-equals-eight supergravity* would go beyond what we currently understand."

The discussion of high-science had gone on a while until it returned to the more mundane but pressing issues of economics with the context of the deprived community into which this relative opulence of academia had inserted itself.

"If the SKA had gone to Australia," Marsha was saying, "I think we'd have seen a whole lot fewer problems... Or more accurately, *different* problems. The reality is that this community has some money, but it is very concentrated. There is a huge contingent of have-nots who are looking to us as a fairy godmother. That fact is that if we force farming to stop, the towns die and countless livelihoods are lost. We're constantly bogged down with these sort of social responsibilities that go along with local politics."

"I hear you," Chris agreed. "You only need to look around. When we dropped in at the event yesterday—the one report you just read from—I could feel for these poor and desperate people. So much hope in their eyes, so much enthusiasm in their singing and dancing; but there's not a lot the average person around here can hope to get besides handouts. What you're telling me is that the social problems may increase, not decrease?"

"It's something I'm not qualified to answer," Marsha admitted. "I'm just seeing the tensions and feeling for all parties... Some of these people have been on the land for half a dozen generations and more. You watch a grown man cry..." she swallowed, her own eyes misty as the memory of witnessing it washed over her for a moment. "...Cry for the loss of land he's worked a lifetime to hand to his kids. You see the hatred in his eyes for what we're doing to him. It's not easy," she shrugged, "...but, like you say, I have a job to do."

"I've met some very clever kids," Dara volunteered, feeling uncomfortable for his mother's anguish.

"Dawie and Tjaardt," Marsha agreed, taking the escape door that Dara had opened for her to close the topic. "Especially Dawie... Why don't you get Dawie over, Dara—I'd like Chris to meet him."

Dara went to make the call.

Chris remarked. "How many more years left for Dara?"

"This coming one will be his last at school," she replied.

"Are you worried about the project...? The opposition to it. Second thoughts?" He looked concerned for her stress.

"I hate politics and I hate that we're causing stress to the locals and maybe ecology."

"Things like this can go pear shaped if the locals don't feel invested," he observed just as Dara came back.

"The government Minister I spoke to about the religious backlash... The *Israel-Visie*, they're called. I looked them up, and they're crazy. I mean, genuinely barking mad."

"Yeah... seems that crazies are everywhere these days."

"I think this level would be hard to beat."

"Dawie's busy with chores, mum. He'll let me know later if he can make it."

"I'm here for a few more days," Chris assured. "Plenty of time."

"One of the problems, Chris, is world-view," Marsha had re-gathered herself. "When you're born in a place like this, so isolated, I guess you don't grasp the scale of things. The only thing the local population, and I mainly mean the labourers here who are in the majority... all they know is what their employers, the farmers, are doing, or what the church is doing. There's really not very much other economic activity to speak of. There's certainly no industry. The only other player in big infrastructural projects is the government," Marsha shrugged, "The SKA is at a scale that a small town and people with such limited vision really find hard to grasp. They can't seem to make a distinction between their own government and outside investment. I think it may be rooted in tribalism or clan-hood, but the rigid mechanisms of control that are cemented in their minds just won't detach our presence here from their notion that we are a delegation of the political parties—perhaps come to exchange some upliftment for their support. I think this is how it's going to be till we can get it through to them... if we ever can get through to them. Seems we're bound to remain at loggerheads."

"Sort of a cargo-cult mentality?" Chris remarked, his observation harking to a well-known social anthropological reaction by indigenous cultures that experience colonization. The name derived from the apparent belief that ritualistic acts lead to a bestowing of material wealth. "The way they all broke into song, yesterday. Chanting, shuffling in unison, almost a trance-dance... choreographed, as if they've been practicing. To get a bunch of Europeans to do that sort of singsong you'd spend a lifetime of practice. It was quite spectacular to watch."

"Watch their local TV news here and you'll see it at every political rally, and not just down in the masses; up on the stage the leaders are completely in tune with it." Marsha pointed out. "So, I don't know... There's a vast disconnect here between getting the infrastructure designed and built so that we can get on with this exciting work. Its very frustrating to keep having to stop and deal with a myriad of social issues that I'm not vaguely qualified to deal with. Don't get me wrong—I understand and wish I could help—but it's not the best use of my time and I don't really have the aptitude."

"We hit the same headwind with anti-investment at CERN."

"The same...?" Marsha cocked a brow.

"Well... Fair enough—not the same; not the same league, impact or intensity, I grant you." Chris recanted. "But it's the same kind of disconnection—goofy ideas the public get that aren't logically connected to the issue at hand; 'You could buy millions of baby incubators,' the vegetarians will tell us, '...rather than waste it on studying atoms'."

"The vegetarians?" Marsha inclined her head.

"Yeah-yeah... the lentil-eaters... tree-hugging pinko-liberal *commy*-socialists... present company excepted. You know me, Marsha; Vegetarians is a good catch-all name that summarizes the reactionaries; I haven't changed."

She liked it in Chris—he was a realist and full of humor and quips; he didn't' take himself or anything but his work too seriously.

"It's our era," Marsha sighed. "We have to keep reminding ourselves that we're very young at this science-thing. A few hundred years into systematic thinking is all that we as a species have under our belts. A few decades of major science infrastructures built... This is just a start. It's not like we're far enough down that path to have brought all humanity with us yet. It's not enough time for those not intimately involved to have wrapped their heads around the outcomes we'll achieve in the long-term. And the situation's hugely amplified around here with so many living at the subsistence level, just focused on the *now*."

"Yep."

"I've got to prepare a keynote address and, with the resistance rising, it's a political tightrope. As I said earlier, a sect of the farmers and white townsfolk here aren't much better," Marsha lamented. "The old guard... they've got this old-school fire-n-brimstone thing going. They take their Bible very seriously—very literally, and they try to influence the moderates with it."

"Oh… it's going to be fun then when Al arrives then!" Chris was referring to Marsha's husband, Dara's Indian father, *Alok*, and his fame for writing and teaching evolutionary studies.

Alok had a long running spat with American creationists who regularly disrupted his debates and book launches. The internet was full of epic debates he'd held with leading theologians—the topics of which ran a full gamut of sub-topics within the wider standoff between science on the one hand, and religious fundamentalism on the other.

Marsha rolled her eyes, "As if Dara and I haven't stirred up enough trouble to prepare the way. What a family, hey?"

They laughed. Dara was immensely proud of his father and his special capacity to communicate sometimes-complex ideas in easy terms.

"I'm getting hints that this lot here are connected to the Evangelists in the States."

"Not impossible." Chris agreed.

"They know about dad and that he's coming," Dara confirmed. "Dawie says the grapevine's abuzz with it."

"Yep… but Al's a big boy," Marsha assured. "He can look after himself, even here."

Dara had been pondering the public's opposition to investment into the sciences that Chris had mentioned a few minutes earlier.

"I don't understand the concept of 'wasting money' on science," Dara reverted back to that segment of conversation. "With a science investment, billions of dollars are brought into the country and spent on salaries and equipment; and the salary earners spend that money on food, and cars, and petrol, and other things. How can that be a waste? It's just money going round and round. The local people can get their hands on it if it's brought here and spent here. If this investment isn't made, the money never comes."

"From the mouths of babes," Marsha proudly smiled.

"I'm hardly a babe, mum," Dara complained, and Marsha playfully ruffled his hair because he hated it.

"You'll always be my babe," she hugged him to her cheek and he kissed her on it.

"You've got it." Chris agreed. "I can't put it any better... I'm wondering what it's like with two famous scientists for parents?" he quizzed Dara.

"It's... *normal*," Dara suggested.

"I'd hardly think so... You don't seem normal... I mean, in maturity—you're far ahead of your years."

"Thank you," Dara knew how to take a compliment.

"Question is, how normal are you going to *be*? No little rebellion coming on? Maybe some weed or chase bad girls... Or, maybe you'll go to the other side and join a cult?"

"I doubt it," Dara considered the musing quite seriously, "I guess I like predictability too much."

"Predictability?" Chris tested.

"Well... with two scientists for parents, I've learned that science is predictive, religion isn't. It makes religion is unstable... why would I follow an unstable system?"

"Unstable? That's an odd word," Chris kept pressing.

"How many versions of just Christianity are there? It's unstable because it constantly splinters... the interpretations of holy books are too wide open to interpretation; I don't like that." It seemed like he'd finished, but before Chris could respond, Dara summarized it, "...that's why the modern world is made by scientists, not by theologians."

"Did *you* teach him that," Chris was impressed. "It's pretty tight reasoning."

Marsha was impressed and a little taken aback, though not shocked, by the impromptu speech her son had just given, "Not in as many words," she admitted, "But we all only know what we've learned, so I'd like to think I put some of those thoughts in this baby," still in her arms since she'd hugged him, she kissed his head, "...but they're his words. I was always careful to teach him *how* to think, not *what* to think," Marsha added.

Chapter 9

Oom Karel had the skin of a parched lakebed.

Oom was an adoptive word from the white Afrikaans culture—it meant 'uncle', but was widely used in the generic sense to address or mean any older male.

The *Oom* was a small man with the darting eyes of a marmoset. But those eyes were becoming glassy now, opaque with years.

The more gaunt his features grew with age, the more prominent his high cheekbones stood, making him look ever more Oriental with each passing season. It was another of the hallmarks of his Bushman heritage.

He loved to be asked his age; "I am as young as the most beautiful wish in my heart," he'd declare, "…and as old as all the unfulfilled longings in my life."

Empty bags of skin hung in gathered folds all about his withered body that in his advanced years had become scarcely more than a sack of bones; yet he put in a full day's work five and a half days a week. People often remarked that if he ever grew into all those wrinkles he'd be a giant, and it never failed to send him into paroxysms of laughter that always ended in a hacking cough. He'd eventually choke on it, bring up something colourful and spit it into the dirt.

Always into the dirt—he was never *not* in the dirt with his bare feet. He lay or squatted in the dirt under the sun or a tree, even if there was a level of cast cement and comfortable chair alternative. He declared that the contact with the soil was his roots and nourishment, "You never find plants growing on rock bed in a cave," was his mantra.

It was the wild tobacco and whatever else it was he packed into his ancient yellow ivory pipe that kept him hacking and spitting. The putrid smoke that engulfed his head much of the day fortified him against the cold of the winter and fierceness of the summer's heat. Against the pangs of hunger and agonies of teeth now rotted away.

Most of all it killed the pain of loss, the loss of dignity and freedom, the loss of his culture and kin, nearly all gone now.

"My boy," he told Dawie, "it is soon my time to go."

"Your time is a long time off," Dawie assured him. The old man had looked the same and said that same thing for as long as Dawie could remember.

"It is different now Dawie. I know I have said it many times, but I didn't really mean it. I have loved my life. It has been hard and I have seen many things. But my family are now all gone." *Oom*'s brother had died two months before and it had cut him deeply.

"We are your family," Dawie reminded and assured the old man.

"You are, my boy, all of you are. I am proud of you all and happy to have lived my last days with you. But my *real* world has passed—has passed long ago. When I was a boy I had great grandparents and brothers and sisters. And there were cousins, and later came the children of these, all of my family, yes. But they have gone now, all gone. They were the people who knew me as I *was*, when I was a man. Strong! I could run all day. I could track an animal on the run for three days without sleeping or eating. They knew *that* me. Now I am alone in remembering that man; I am the only one still alive who knew the real me."

Dawie was about to protest, but *Oom* stopped him.

"No my boy. I am not sad—I am happy. I am not complaining—this is as it should be, that the old leave a new world for the young. The world is changing and you are like a green branch that can bend with it. Look at me…" he held out a withered old arm that looked like it belonged to a mummy. "I can no longer bend. I can't adapt to the changes. `I must go while I have dignity and my memories."

He went on, in the bushman tradition of word of mouth history, reminding Dawie of the clan's remote past, it's folklore; of how they outsmarted the newcomers for so long, until the newcomers had taken their livelihood—their game—shot it out, penned it in behind fences.

He disappeared into the dreamstate, his eyes glazing, travelling far back through time; marveling at the springbok that he saw as he went—the native antelope of the territory, moving in herds that spanned from horizon to horizon, millions in number; now all gone. All hunted to near extinction in his lifetime.

Now their sustenance and staple were owned, he sighed. Everything reduced to being a commodity with a profitable value.

And his mind was gone again; dredging the painful memories of times when they too were hunted; his people hunted, a bounty on each head, out in the deep bush. Their crime; no traceable linage recounted in *The Big Book*—the Bible—the only law the *Trek Boer* frontiers men carried or cared about. It consigned *The First People*, as they had subsequently come to be known in our more enlightened era, to be numbered among the animals back then.

Now they too were owned, he admitted; also just a commodity with a profitable value in menial labour… and perhaps more than that.

Back then, before the game were gone, even the authorities—the British and German colonial masters—had sold licenses to hunt and shoot the ancestors too; whole families, men, women and their children on the run from hunters with guns; a practice only abandoned in the 1920's.

Dawie had heard it all countless times before, but culture dictated that he should drink it all in as if it was the first time of hearing, and so he did, sitting with his grandfather under the shade of a thorn tree deep into the late afternoon.

"There are big ears coming to our land soon," he told Dawie, "steel ears with roots into the ground, listening to the sky; the *Dominee* came to tell me this."

It snapped Dawie out of his stupor of listening to oft-repeated recounts of their place in history. *Oom* Karel hated the *Dominee*—

he had never capitulated to the angry Christian God that they had tried to threaten and bribe him and the clan into.

"The *Dominee* says?" Dawie's shock was unmaskable.

"Yes, my boy. He and the *Baas* and some others came to see me. I have been thinking about what they said. They told me of what you also told me—about the big ears to listen to the sky."

Dawie always fed a constant stream of news from the village and school back to the farm where his grandfather and family still toiled. The SKA and its giant dish antennas, 'ears', was a hot topic of course for him—the younger members of the family imagining that they would somehow see their lot improve immeasurably—what, with the new tar roads, construction, airstrip and countless other exciting-sounding developments coming to town.

That not one of them and nobody they knew had personally ever been in an airplane, driven a car or done more than shop for the basics seemed to elude them; if these things were coming, surely, they reasoned with their timeless optimism, they would participate in it?

Now Dawie wondered, what was up with the *Dominee* bringing this news to the old man? What did he want? This was unprecedented. The masters never came to the servants to engage them or seek their opinion. Yes—sometimes they came to get support; maybe to win election votes; but that was dished out as an instruction leaving no doubt that an *"or-else"* consequence stood behind it.

The way the old man was talking now though, it seemed that the *Dominee* wanted something—wasn't demanding something, but was seeking help; almost like an equal.

It was most suspicious.

"The *Dominee* said they are going to listen to the sky with the big ears," *Oom* Karel was repeating. "And the *Dominee* said that his God has already put His voice in *The Big Book* so these troublemakers can now only hear what the *Devil* wants them to think."

"And you believe this, *Oupa—Grandpa*?" Dawie quizzed carefully.

"Hell no...." the withered old man chuckled. "That *Dominee* is *mal*—he's crazy! He always thinks there's a devil behind every bush and shadow, but I've never heard him say the devil is also in the sky! That is where his God lives... that's what he usually says... So, who knows? Maybe the Devil is visiting his God up there?"

He broke off into peels of laughter that ended in hacking and spitting, "I believe they are listening for what you told me they are listening for; a different kind of light—light we can't see, like sound we can't hear... even though the sound is there."

The culture worked both ways—the old also listening intently to the children and parsing what they heard through the filter of possibility to see if it could defeat any dogma they held; it was the only way to survive nature.

"What does he want then *Oupa*? Why did he come to you, to us?"

"He says that the ears are going onto *our* land and that we must fight it and stop them."

"*Our* land?" Dawie was stunned and disbelieving. "The *Dominee* said it is *our* land? Ours...? What does he mean?"

"Yes my boy. It is *our* land now. His people's farms are now on *our* land because it was our ancestor's lands... lands he says they are protecting for us with their laws... or we would otherwise destroy it because we are backward. He says he can show us how to protect our heritage with their laws—with the new Black man's laws, he says. That is the claim he makes; but we all know it is only their interests they want us to protect." He laughed again. He laughed a lot. There were very few things he didn't laugh at.

Dawie instantly gauged and understood what was afoot. The country was rife with land-claims under the new *South African Constitution*—groups of mainly Nguni tribes and clans laying claim to pockets of land that their ancestors had farmed before the white man had arrived. Successful claims on land by Bushmen were pitifully rare; unless it was settled, the courts were disinterested in entrenching the rights of those that wander; it was a farmer's law, not a huntsman's.

"So are they handing the land back, then?" Dawie asked shrewdly.

"You are a clever boy. That was my first question," the old clan leader said.

"You asked the *Dominee* that?"

"Of course not!" The old man's eyes twinkled, "That was the question I asked myself… When you find your Eland, do you race unchecked over open ground to kill him immediately?"

The Eland is Africa's largest antelope—large and rare—they occupied a deeply mythical realm in Bushman lore. A Bushman, certainly not by an elder of *Oom* Karel's standing, did not lightly choose an analogy to an Eland.

"When we hunt, we don't let our quarry know that we are a threat."

"Did the *Dominee* also go to the Xhosa for their help?" Dawie asked.

The first community of farmers to permanently settle in the area was a Xhosa faction under leadership of Gert Kaffer. By all accounts, the Cape government of his era had cordial relationships with the Xhosa and wished to use them as a buffer between the colonists and the troublesome Bushmen.

In 1839 the Cape Governor, Sir George Napier, officially granted 98,000 morgen of land to the Xhosa people. Before the end of that year 110 Xhosa families had settled in this area.

"The *boere* are too cunning to take it to the Xhosa," the *Oom* predicted, "The Xhosa run the government and they will make it their own idea and cut the white man out completely. The *Dominee* thinks he is safer with us yellow men; he thinks he still controls us."

He started to laugh again until he choked and spat.

Chapter 10

"Karel is on board" Gert, the *Dominee*, assured them all.

A group of half a dozen men of the older generation were over at Andre's house, sitting about the kitchen table while their women folk sat apart in the lounge. Sonja was in the scullery washing dishes from dinner. She'd volunteered for the chore even though the house staff would normally handle it the next morning. She took her time, carefully avoiding any noise so that the men forgot she was present.

This was not an arbitrary group of friends; it had a purpose; a self-styled militia, though now only loosely formulated. But once, not long ago, it had had a formidable reputation for influence.

They were a *brotherhood*—a shadow and husk of The Afrikaner *Broederbond*, the once secret exclusively male Calvinist Afrikaner organization dedicated to the advancement of Afrikaner interests in South Africa and its influence abroad.

The *Broederbond* was founded in 1918 and was known as *Jong Zuid Afrika*—Young South Africa. Two years later it adopted what became a chilling name for any who opposed them—*Broederbond*.

For most of the 20th Century the organization had enjoyed a vice-grip over the South African political system and its leaders. In this, it may reasonably be compared to *Freemasonry*, or at least the legend of what *Masons* are according to conspiracy theorists.

But the *Broederbond* was no illusion; it was all too real. They achieved their greatest heights during apartheid, the divisive racial system that was a *Broederbond* brainchild in the first place.

Officially, the organization no longer existed.

Though these men had lost the power that their fathers had wielded, they had not lost the attitude or self-assurance.

They maintained an iron-cast conviction that the Afrikaner *volk*, its people, had been planted in the country directly by the *Hand of God*; destined to survive as a separate volk, apart from all other influences with its own calling directly from the gospels. It was a *meme* that gripped and held them in its grasp, a meme they were determined would live on in their children and grandchildren; they worked hard at cementing it there.

"Could that old Bushman even grasp what you wanted?" Jan de Villiers, a *Kommandant* under the former government's army infantry asked.

"It would be a mistake to think that one is stupid, Jan," Willem Bauer, owner of the farm on which Karel lived and worked cautioned, "…he's as crafty as a bag full of monkeys."

"You are right," the *Dominee* agreed. "Karel is like a clever *bobbejaan*. The first he'll go to with this news is to his nephew… that *donner*… Bennie Pieterson."

Tjaardt's uncle, Bennie Pieterson, the town's *Burgemeester* or Mayor.

A coloured of mixed race and distantly related to *Oom* Karel, Bennie had been a prominent member of the ruling government until he'd been forced out of favor and to the backwaters under a cloud of rumour and intrigue. And even as the town's coffers strained under the weight of the drought, Pieterson flaunted newfound wealth that seemed to be steadily growing.

Much as Bennie claimed to be a scapegoat, that he had taken the fall for illegal shenanigans that went up to Presidential level, the group gathered here this evening and the white community at large, would hear nothing of it. Ordinarily they would love to see the President brought down by small fry like Pieterson, but it suited their local agenda to rather perpetuate the distrust in Pieterson in spite of these claims of Presidential collusion.

In short, they wanted Pieterson out, at any costs. He wielded too much local power and influence for their liking.

"I didn't fall off the turnip truck yesterday," said the *Dominee*, adopting a cunning expression. "We've out-thought him already… I chatted to Willem earlier. He'll see to it that this can't happen…"

Willem Bauer was *Oom* Karel's employer; he nodded, endorsing Gert's words.

"The Coloured who outwits me has not yet been born… and we have an ace up our sleeve," Gert smiled.

"The *Discover Group*…?" Andre blurted, then checked himself. Developments with the American-based *Discover Group* had been on his mind since Gert had discussed it with him in private the previous week.

The *Dominee* shot him a glare.

"*Discover Group?*" Jan asked cautiously.

"We may need cash to do this," Gert pointed out. "Enough said."

"Understood." Jan nodded, "it's need to know.…"

"It's not that you don't need to know, Jan. It's just best to keep our powder dry as the *rooinek* says. I'm working on something."

"So long as the *Boesman* is with us, I think that's all the powder we'll need."

"Old Karel says he must meet with his '*advisors*'." They all laughed at the notion, "But I'll buckle the old fool, yes. Willem can put some pressure there too," the *Dominee* assured.

"It's not like it used to be in the old days, *manne*. But I still have some influence" Willem suggested with a smirk, and the way he'd said it made the men laugh again. "But my concern is when the Xhosas get wind of it? You know the way they're going everywhere else—next thing you know they will think this is a clever idea… an idea just perfect for them."

"We have the claim over them all—we have the documentation, they only have stories," Gert, the *Dominee*, assured them. "And I'm reading this from the official history of this area."

He opened a giant old dusty book he had already marked for the meeting.

"The first documentation of the pre-history of Schietfontein—of Carnarvon—comes in the form of the official granting of grazing rights by the Cape Government to Pieter Hugo on 26 September 1758. For this privilege an annual rent of 20 '*rijksdaalders*' had to be paid'… and-so-on, and-so-on."

He stopped reading, "Now, that's a hundred years before anyone recognized the Xhosa in the area—so they are out of the claim when it comes to land ownership. It is only the Bushman's right to protect the land from development we're motivating... only the usage of the land and their claim to a spiritual priority. We *must* stay far away from any notions of an actual land claim and ownership. They just deserve heritage status so their spiritual wellbeing is not damaged."

"Ja... But I'm still worried about the Xhosa... those filthy *rooinek* lawyers will smell money and jump on the cause. They are very tricky, especially the Jewish ones... you know how they got into bed with the Xhosa long ago... with Mandela, and even before that." Jan warned. "The first thing they're going to claim is that some ragtag bunch of their ancestors roamed the area hundreds of years ago before our people and used these hills for initiation rites, or something."

"I still don't understand why we are following this one issue..." Willem Bauer interjected. "The main problem for me, *Dominee*... and I say this with all respect... goes beyond the insult to our beliefs, real as it is. I am keeping my farm..."

"For now..." Andre reminded him.

"Yes... for now," Willem agreed to the implied threat that still kept him awake at night that some day the dreaded call may come as it had for so many that he was now in the path of the next phase and would have to sell, "...and I'm sorry for the families who are losing theirs, but even keeping my farm I can hardly cope. I have no mobile signal, they're making me take down the satellite dish I use to link to the Internet... I can't do banking, I can't make phone calls. My windmills are all coming down, so I can't water the sheep... I can't even kick start a motorbike and this *fokken* SKA machine gets disturbed by the spark. I must live and do business like a *voortrekker*... They've pushed us back a hundred years and call it progress. Without even the security of a phone, how do I protect my family if they get attacked and murdered in a country where life means nothing?"

"Because," Gert assured him, "when we tried to deliver that argument at the meetings nobody here cared. Nobody came to the meetings... how many out of hundreds of farmers? Less than ten. Nobody would put money up for a legal challenge. Our people won't stand together, it's our fault… But when you challenge our beliefs…" he said with conviction.

"It is true," Andre backed up his *Dominee* as a Diaken should. "Our beliefs are our culture."

"I have a plan," Gert assured him. "Don't you worry yourself, we can get outside money for this fight… I have very big guns lined up."

Chapter 11

When not out on the range, Dara had taken to experimenting with debate. In the tiny peer group he'd established since arriving in Carnarvon there was nobody who had his worldly experience and his level of sophistication. He liked to share with his friends, but he was hungry to learn too, so he took his curiosity online, adopting a pen name—*'Memes'*.

The name portrayed what he intended to learn and hoped to share. It encompassed the *meme*, a concept his father had taught him.

"Memes, pronounced *'meem'*," his father had taught Dara, "are cultural analogues to *genes*; infectious ideas that self-replicate, mutate and respond to selective social pressures."

The concept of memes was first conceived by Professor Dawkins, a world-renowned *evolutionary anthropologist* whom Dara's father aspired to.

The word had gone on to gain momentum, almost a life of its own; it had become a cultural phenomenon of study in its own right. Memes, it turned out, explained so much of psychology and social anthropology—through racism to religiosity, fashion to conspiracy theory.

"A meme is *'an idea, behavior or style that spreads from person to person'*," his dad had refined the definition for Dara. "It is the unit that carries cultural ideas, symbols or practices, transmitted from mind to mind through writing, speech, gestures, or rituals."

Assuming the pseudonym *"Memes"*, Dara went to work. *Memes* became a buffer that allowed Dara to begin testing and researching the minds of strangers of every ilk. *Memes* commented in various medias, established a blog and quickly gained new likeminded friends on social media. He gathered enemies too.

From a memetic perspective, Detlief's story had become particularly fascinating to Dara.

Detlief, of course, was up from the city; from Cape Town; sent to Carnarvon to keep him from peers and mischief in the drug infested and dilapidated slum his family had fallen to. Worse yet, many of Detlief's closest family members had been drawn into the drug trade and were constantly revolving through the prison turnstiles. They had rank at different levels of the various ferocious "numbers" gang culture that raged and killed indiscriminately in the streets every night; it was a warzone.

Beyond the squabbles for turf among the gangs, an equally vast and potentially lethal opposing group had grown up too. It was religiously based in Islamic heritage; imported as Islam had been to the Cape by the Dutch who favored Malaysian slaves and laborers over African ones in the 17th and 18th Centuries.

The Cape Malay, as they were once known, practiced a benign form of Islam that was not radicalized to the degree emerging elsewhere across the globe. These *Moslems* as they were otherwise known, stuck to themselves; they possessed a violent hatred and grudge toward the gangs.

They quite literally met fire with high caliber fire.

There were contracts out on heads and, in the unlikely event that Detlief somehow managed to avoid direct involvement in the methamphetamine drug known locally as *'Tik'*, his head was all too often in close proximity with others that might attract a blizzard of flying lead.

Detlief was characteristically rough and ready. He had a gentle spirit but his unceasing brushes with violence and brutality from birth had scarred him... his memes were negative. In Carnarvon, until his recent troubles, he had been on the straight and narrow, but his wheels were buckled. Staying on the straight was an unlikely probability; life had programmed him to veer without warning.

Dara had picked Detlief's plight as inspiration to express his very first essay on an Internet blog:

"The cells of our DNA do not belong to us—they belong to the collective—we borrow them for a short life and then hand them on to our issue, who, in their turn, pass them forward to a later generation.

A billion generations of ancestors; a river of raw data; stands at each of our backs, a deluge of genes flowing down the eons from the primordial soup and through ancient seas, creeping among dinosaurs and dragging its knuckles across Africa's plains.

But before this journey erupted from Africa an epoch ago, the broth that is the hominid-gene had birthed a strange new thing, a new form of data that took its hold as master of our destiny: The accumulated information of chemical gene created 'meme'— infectious awareness; small ideas that weave webs in thinking, meshes that trap and milk us of our industry; some building our empires, others returning no more than blind conviction as their reward.

The meme has spun its cultures, fashions and religions too; through those faculties it evolves, it hacks the R-Complex—the brooding reptilian brain that lurks in each of our heads; the seat of our aggression and territoriality; and there it draws its battle plans for self-preservation.

It sings its challenge from the minaret, its rival clangs a response from the church bell close across town."

That first piece drew some praise from those who thrilled to the cultural perspective from a poetic stance. It of course left many unmoved. It also reared a few who threw derision at Dara for imagining that *memes* were in fact any kind of study at all. This latter group was hostile to the idea, Dara came to understand, not because they could show it to be inaccurate or nonsense, as they claimed it was—but because its initiator was Dawkins, a man of science whom they hated.

Dawkins had, long before Dara's father had added his voice to the debate, written landmark books on the topic of human evolutionary origins through natural selection.

These books had drawn the unrelenting ire of conservative Christian creationists, particularly those known as YECs who believed in a *'Young Earth'*. YECs took a literal view of biblical interpretation, insisting that the earth and universe are less than ten-thousand years old.

"They're a relatively small group, Dara," his father had told him, "but they're very vocal."

Creationists considered that any proofs that contradicted biblical notions were anti-God and therefore inherently evil.

In quick succession Dara, through his pseudonym alias, *Memes,* had followed his initial blog essay with dozens of others. He'd publish a new one every few days, just as soon as the dust of argument had settled from the previous one.

The reading audience polarized into two sharply opposed groups, friends and foes. Many, like *'Memes'*, used pseudonyms that provided the person behind them a shield from scorn and praise alike.

Marsha was in the habit of reading online news during morning coffee breaks and she had been watching this new personality, *Memes*, as he or she had gathered both a fan club and enemies. She had no idea that the mind behind it was her boy until one day, by chance, she saw a half-way finished essay on his computer that, a day later, she saw published.

She had brimmed with pride but kept her discovery to herself, responding to Dara by creating her own pseudonym arbitrarily selected to have no connection, *'Kimberly-A'*, through which she could engage *Memes* to tease and test his knowledge.

Among those who aligned with and had befriended Dara in social media was a pseudonym, *"VoorVel"*—*Foreskin* in Afrikaans.

The name was intentionally provocative, intended to irritate the conservative Afrikaans opponents that he enjoyed riling in conversation. He derived it during an argument over the religiously inspired practice of circumcision blindly followed.

During the ensuing weeks the two pseudonyms, *Memes* and *VoorVel*, had befriended one another on social media, had messaged one another and joined the same discussion groups where theists and non-theists thrashed out their differences.

Dara had found the experience of the blogs and these groups a catharsis; a place he could speak his mind openly and hear a range of opinion—some inspiring and mind-expanding, some outright insane.

VoorVel, Dara discovered, had been born in Carnarvon. He had grown up and attended the local school many years earlier. Many of the teachers from that era were still at the school, so they had some areas of intersection to discuss.

Dara was extremely excited by the prospects that lay ahead; *VoorVel* was coming to visit in a week.

Neither Dara nor his new friend wanted their identity or association known around the town so they arranged to meet the following Wednesday at a coffee shop in *Loxton*. Loxton was a neighbouring village on the Cape Town side of Carnarvon, sixty kilometers to the south.

"I'll be there by 3pm. Let's meet at *Blou Schuur Kafee*," VoorVel suggested.

"How will I recognize you?" Memes typed.

"I'll be up in my car… you can't miss it." VoorVel had replied.

Farmers usually drive big pickup trucks—on that description, Dara imagined it would be a monster.

Quite how he would get to the meeting—half an hour's drive south—would be another story. "Perhaps," he dared himself, "I'll take the bike."

It certainly would be an exciting prospect to consider.

Chapter 12

The firewood had been uncharacteristically green and moist so that the whole affair had got off to a slow start; the result, an impressive hillock of discarded alcohol cans and bottles had begun to mount.

There was a mix of music the whole evening and Sonja had danced her way through most of the boys, laughing from the belly at slapstick pranks and teenage jokes round the fire where the spit-trussed lamb was dripping hisses into the coals, its aroma tempting the predatory passions of the inebriated to swell.

Wherever she went, Sonja towed behind her a small pack of darting eyed admirers. Like hyenas near a lion kill, none were bold enough to stake a claim, instead they were satisfied to snatch a morsel where they could; a dance or flirtatious word when Neels, the pack alpha, was distracted by the celebration rituals that his 18th birthday demanded.

For Neels, it had been a spectacular day. It had started with the new truck from his father. She was a beauty; fat tires, 5 seats, turbocharged diesel grunt and spotlights for night hunting on a bar above the cab. His right to earn a full license and legally drive was now a reality, and he could retire the lesser farm diesel he'd sometimes used.

Well before sunset the Vermaak farm, one of the wealthiest in the region, had become a hive of activity—every kid from the district had come to pay homage. A vast marquee housed a bar, dinner seating and a dance floor—with the cooking fires outside.

Neels was already well oiled long before the sun approached the horizon, his vision swimming and his voice roaring, almost hoarse.

His dad watched his lad with pride—it took some constitution to have swallowed what Neels had managed and still be accelerating well after dark.

Neels, so preoccupied all day with the stuff of men had hardly given Sonja a second thought; suddenly, though, something in the fog of his most primitive self tugged him in a new direction and off he went in search of her, the truth that she'd split with him weeks before anaesthetized by the grog.

She saw him coming and tried to give him the slip, ducking surreptitiously into the thick of the crowd's throng. Her gaggle of admirers also saw him beginning to prowl and they too abandoned their hopeful attempts and evaporated out of contention.

She checked her watch and saw with relief that it was almost 10pm, the time her father was scheduled to collect her.

Tonight, Andre was on duty and so would be in the van and in uniform.

She ran her eye over the pockets of adults at the periphery of the revelers, but no sign of him yet. Andre's booming voice dishing out greetings would precede him in the event she'd missed his arriving car.

"Why so early?" Andre had asked when she'd requested the pickup time.

"Entrance exams, *Pa*. I have to be up early tomorrow to study."

It was of course nonsense, she could easily stay till midnight without harm to her university ambitions but she'd anticipated something like this from Neels. Indeed, she'd preferred not to have come at all, but that would have made it worse with him and triggered a scandal across the community. Over the past weeks the more she'd withdrawn from Neels the more insistent his advances had become.

Cat and mouse; Sonja had played with Neels for long minutes under the marquee, flitting from group to group, keeping anything or anyone tall enough to obscure her from his searching eyes, breaking off conversation when she estimated his next drift might bring him in her direction.

Neels knew Sonja was here, somewhere in this crowd.

Earlier when she'd arrived he'd embraced her roughly to the jubilant cheers of his minions.

After that he'd seen her several times, out on the dance floor… each time he'd scrutinized the level of threat posed, but judged that her intimacy with *that* partner did not require him to intervene and end it.

And, no matter where he looked, she seemed to have evaporated.

There was no doubt in Neels' mind that she would have left the party early. If she'd dared to do such a thing without a goodbye, news of it would have quickly found him through his network of eyes.

Lately, he admitted to himself as he puzzled her invisibility, she'd been immensely frustrating; ever since that incident with that *Prrrretty* boy at school, he pondered for the thousandth time, she'd been disdainful and disobedient to his calls for more of her time—breaking off dates he'd made with her.

The correlation between the Dara incident and her unacceptable behavior as 'his girl' was unavoidable, and it infuriated him, raising the stakes now.

Even on this momentous evening of his coming of age, he contemplated, that he'd managed only the briefest of words with her before she'd somehow each time spirited herself away rather than hang close at hand as she normally would and properly should.

The longer his intensive search went on, the more exaggerated his craze became. It was *his* birthday, he reminded himself, and about time that the queen of this town submitted to its king. His passions were charging, alcohol fueled as they now were, he could feel them becoming volatile.

Knowing him as she did, Sonja could see he was hunting her, his urgency in the search beginning to escalate; she needed an escape. Her moment came as he was distracted by a small throng who insisted he drop yet another measure of the powerful local farm-made liquor down his gullet. She slipped out through the back of the enclosure, unnoticed.

The tension of escape had taxed her and she needed the relief of a few minutes away from people, so she drifted into the dark and surveyed the parked cars for the police van as her eyes adjusted to the dark.

The sounds emitting from the tent retreated, becoming a mélange of voices garnished with an occasional whoop or pepper of laughter, the music an underscore.

Neel's farm fortunately had not yet seen its mobile phone coverage severed, and earlier she'd sent text messages to her *Pa*, urging him to hurry, and now, away from the noise, she called him—the phone began ringing.

"En hier loop my bokkie," Neels crooned from the darkness, close behind her—unashamedly calling her a plaything... "Making a call to someone?" he asked with sarcasm ringing in his voice.

Reports that she'd slipped out back had found his ears and in the dark the light of her phone homed him in on her position like a missile.

Sonja froze, ice surging through her veins; it was the worst possible place for him to find her. At that instant her father's phone went to voice mail and she let it record, hoping if he got it, it would raise his urgency:

"Aggghh, Neels," she tried to make light of it, "I'm just not feeling well. My father will be here in a moment."

The urgency of that unexpected news, news of her imminent departure, raised the stakes for Neels, so he closed in.

"Put the phone off. Let's dance," he instructed.

His right-handed snatch was so fast that she didn't feel her phone go, it was in his hands and he cut the call in one deft movement. His left arm was around her, his hand at the small of her back, controlling her center of gravity, pulling her pelvis urgently towards him.

As her crotch impacted with his, she felt it; unpleasant and unyielding as it was at this ugly moment—the thing urging him on, the madness that made no sense. She tried to retract but he was too strong, oblivious to her poorly concealed and rapidly growing revulsion.

"Please Neels, I really don't feel well."

"I can make you feel better," he assured; his breathing ragged, the acrid smell of alcohol on it.

He'd pocketed her phone, allowing his now-free right hand to move swiftly over her body, sizing her breasts and then quickly round her back, at her waist searching for a gap between the layers of shirt and skirt.

"No Neels.... My father is *reeeally* coming now, I don't want him to see us...."

"He won't see us," his voice was urgent the pitch rising sharply with his lust. "Let's go to the hedge."

His fingers had found the breach and in one smooth movement his rough calloused hand surged down inside the skirt, under the elastic of her G-string and over the mound of coccyx in between the melons of her buttocks.

She wriggled as strongly as she could but his left hand held her expertly so that no matter which way she squirmed, he kept control over her.

"Don't mess my clothes—*Pa* is a policeman, he sees everything."

"I know your *Pa* is a policeman," Neels reminded her, ignoring her implied threat, "...I leave no evidence."

"Please Neels... I'm really not well."

He just laughed at her. The cushions of her buttocks either side of his searching fingers were turgid, solid with taught muscle, soft with luxurious skin, padded by femininity in the flush of youth.

Like a diviner finding the well, he sensed the humid blush of womanhood before he touched it. It drove him forward, madly and insistently.

She knew she dared not cry out for help, there was too much risk of social fallout if she did. All she dared do was make muted protestations, her voice thin and strained by efforts to squirm away, to defend herself as best she could in a brutal grip.

But Neels heard none of it. In his mind her moans were passionate, passion that he confirmed by the slip and slide he found in her.

In the months of their relationship, they'd had many *liaisons*. At various functions on different farms she'd been accommodating to his advances; she'd let his hands explore her womanhood.

He'd come to expect the indulgence.

She always felt hairless and smooth under his fingers and this excited him to a mild insanity; he'd never seen her in the light, but her fine silky body hair offered no suggestion of shaven stubble. This curiosity obsessed him. The other girls he'd been with always presented a gritty abrasion of hairs rolling under his fingers as he explored their curious folds to eliminate the false entrances. But Sonja presented an enigma he could not get enough of.

In the past encounters Sonja always seemed encouraging, opening up willingly; or that's how he remembered it; but now she forced him to proceed with increasing effort that felt like a game.

Then, slowly, through the fog of booze and lust, the reality dawned on him that she was clenched as tightly as she could, that what he presumed to be her uncontrolled breathing and staccato pants were the clutches for air that come with fear and tears.

She was crying.

"What the hell's wrong with you?" He retracted his hand and shoved her away.

"I told you, I'm not well."

"Rubbish," he said. "You're talking shit. It's something else *'ne?* It's that black bastard... that *Prrrrretty boy*! You've be been pulling away since I gave him a little *klap*."

His voice rang with outrage and Sonja feared for an instant that he'd open-handedly hit her, she cringed and he glared. He'd done it before, slapped; not her but other girls.

She was sniveling and hating herself for it. She wanted to agree with Neels—say it out aloud, *"Yes… It's Dara and what you did to him. He is intelligent, decent… cultured. You are disgusting! You are a coward to hit from behind and then throw me aside; bruise my arms that I had to hide from my family."*

She wanted to tell Neels the truth of *who* and *what* he was; a pig and a bigot—not even a man, just a cowardly brute.

But too much rode on her blurting that; there was just too much community intricacy.

Instead, to keep the things of her heart secret, she forced herself to protest as best she could—weakly. And the feeling of doing so soiled and degraded her within.

She knew all too well that Neels had an irrational grudge against the newcomer, a vendetta that was backed by the *Dominee* and others—that any defense of Dara, even admitting that she knew and remembered his strange name, would turn even her father against her and too many others with him.

That Neels was hunting Dara, stalking him like prey, was common knowledge by most of the town. They thought it quite entertaining to watch the hunt unfold.

That this foreign boy had touched her affections was not known by anyone.

That Neels had latched onto the truth, accusing her directly in this rage, was deeply unsettling.

These facts were a baying crowd of madness, crowding Sonja as she tried to back gingerly away from the brute.

To protect the newcomer from the outrage that would explode if she admitted any hint of it, she denied and denied, and she denied again the accusations that came streaming at her from Neels with a tempo and ferocity that made her legs buckle. As he drove himself into a rage over it, he walked steadily toward her, she backed away; his hostility increasingly laced with a barrage of curses.

"You want to fuck that little black bastard, *'ne?'*" Neels' voice was high in pitch and rising in volume.

"No Neels. Stop, please stop—look, there are people coming this way."

The ruckus he'd caused had been heard from far and a small group of fathers were coming to investigate.

"Wat gaan nou aan?" Neels' father called.

"Niks nie Pa, niks… niks," he assured his father with a bluff.

He embraced Sonja for the approaching men to see, and called an explanation to them; *"Sonjatjie's jaloers oor die meisies, ek gee net versekering."*

His blatant lie, claiming her jealousy of the other girls made Sonja want to retch. She wanted to shout her protest that she needed no reassurances or anything from this vile pig, but ancient cultural sanctions welded her mouth tight.

Neels' father laughed, they were so close she heard one of the men scoff—*"Women!"*

With that the group of recently concerned fathers chortled their disdain for the silliness of this little girl, *"Toe maar, Sonjatjie— niks te bekommer oor Neels nie, hy's 'n* gentleman*"*

A *'gentleman'* they called him—*'nothing to worry about with him'*— she wanted to shriek with hysteria, with laughter and tears at the insult, but she swallowed; *"Ja, Oom, ek weet… Ek is sommer net belaglik,"* Sonja agreed, twisting internally with disgust and frustration at hearing her own voice, the echo of it assuring the men that she was being ridiculous.

Neels let her go and walked away a few steps in the tracks of the retreating men then turned and said, *"Vang!"* as he threw her phone to her.

She fumbled the catch in the dark and the handset clattered to the stony ground. Just then the police van's headlights peaked over the rise approaching the farm.

She picked the phone up and it illuminated in her hands. The device had cost her months of chores and it represented a thread of sanity, a pivot for ambitions that lay in the wide world beyond the village—the lit screen was cracked and she started to cry softly out of humiliation and frustration.

Taking a few moments to gather herself, Sonja straightened her skirt in the dark, wiped her eyes and walked slowly after the retreating silhouettes, heading in the direction of the parking lot where her father would shortly arrive.

She didn't want her father to know about this—Neels was too cunning; even in his inebriated condition she dared not challenge him among men. He'd swing it on her, the fathers and his friends would back him and she'd be exposed for the legitimate liaisons she'd had with him in the past. Her father would be disgusted and blame her for tonight; he'd accuse her of leading Neels on.

Besides, she felt ashamed and just wanted to leave this place without further delay; to shower and be in her own safe space.

More than that, her brother would be here soon. With one word of this from her to him, he had the physical capacity, the financial insulation, and the legal means to wade in and put Neels in his place or somewhere worse—but it would rip everything she knew and loved apart—her family and her community.

She had to simply absorb the insult of it all and contrive to avoid Neels for another few weeks—then she'd leave Carnarvon to study in Cape Town and never have to face this unpleasantness again.

Within a few minutes Andre was out of the parked van and his voice barked its greetings to the group of friends who were approaching him out of the dark. They all shook hands and slapped backs. The cavernous drone and throaty rumble of her father's voice so unmistakable.

Neels had caught up with the men and Andre greeted him warmly and extended hearty congratulations on his birthday and new wheels. They'd laughed together, like a father and son might.

Then Andre saw Sonja approaching slowly, reluctantly; her shoulders rounded. Andre immediately broke and went urgently to her. He embraced her quickly and, for the first time ever, she felt instant revulsion; the feeling of those powerful arms around her so soon after her encounter with Neels making her want to retch.

Andre instantly felt her reaction; Neels saw it too.

"What's wrong my darling girl?" Andre asked urgently.

Neels cut in on her behalf, "She's been feeling sick *Oom* ... and also a bit upset, you know... so many girls here."

"Ag my baby-girl. You're so silly," Andre kissed her forehead and she recoiled within.

Chapter 13

A delegation of politicians and global press was in town and the keynote speech Marsha had mentioned to Chris was upon her.

"There are so many aspects to this, so much I could potentially talk on," she'd told the organizers. "I'm hard pressed to pick between topics. I could stick to my own narrow focus of hard-nosed science; the promised outcomes from this project are tantalizing and on paper, for all humanity into the future, they outweigh the impact on this community many times over. But lives aren't measured on paper. It's a dilemma for me."

"Don't become so emotionally involved," they told her. "It's an ideal platform to direct the international spotlight onto the positive outcomes for local issues. Can you work something like that into it?" they suggested, and there was a clear instruction in that suggestion.

That evening she chatted around the communal table.

"I want to expand this beyond covering the local impoverishments, which I've been briefed to pursue. If I dig too much into that, I'll feel obliged to also detail the stresses felt by the community, and that's not what I'm paid to do," she admitted. "This is about science, so talking about the details behind what we're up to is unavoidable. It's gonna be filmed for a global audience who know little about the underlying implications. I really want to make people who don't care or think about science, to care grasp the *relevance* of this project within the global cultural drift. I want the audience to realize that this is just one peak on a very much larger groundswell of cultural change."

She turned in early and fell asleep thinking about it. When she awoke, her plan was ready.

As she took to the podium her heart fluttered; she hated the limelight but what she had to say was now more than merely going through the motions of duty to the job, it had become an imperative in her mind;

"There is a prejudice…" she began, "a prejudice that in Africa, the world need only focus on seeing that the bare basics get delivered… *elementary* education, some food staples, maybe clean water and some low-grade energy to keep the natives from becoming restless.

I think that, in large measure, this stems *directly* from the charity drives of our recent past. What they did was reduce Africa in the minds of the world to a basket case; ripping up the Hollywood image of Tarzan and jungles and replacing it with dusty, fly-ridden malnourishment. The entire focus became fostering a continent-wide subsistence.

When one stops to consider it from this perspective, it's hard to imagine a more outdated colonial view. We, liberal and socially sensitive as we think of ourselves, recoil in horror from this reflection of ourselves."

She paused a moment to assess the audience's mood—she had their full attention.

"This project, the SKA, is the big break for Africa. At the very least it is a chance to become a world leader in data storage and management… imagine, if you can, Africa and South Africa as the leader in the storage and management of data. Because, no matter what, with the inevitable needs of the SKA to manage and store vast data in ways we cannot even understand at this moment, the onus falls to us to find a solution—a solution that will be commercially used in countless other industries… I'm painting for us a picture of Africa… Africa! Of Africa leading the world in data technologies, with all of the commercial opportunity and upliftment that this implies… teaching the proverbial man to fish.

This project is not going to hand out food stamps—instead, we will give something so much more valuable, we are simply going to force Africa to rise to a challenge that some may think impossible."

Marsha had delivered the message that was expected of her, and she saw the inclines of heads and squints that betrayed skepticism creeping in. She had anticipated this and had the antidote ready for delivery.

"Half a century ago there was nothing to choose between the two Koreas. They were both impoverished peasant societies living, yes… like the image of Africa… *subsistence* lives. The tragedy that became North Korea is too well known to depress you with, but it is the miracle of South Korea who took the high road and grasped the challenge of educating its people… *that* must be our beacon. In practical terms, what transpired for Korean is that, today, half of us are driving Korean cars and using Korean electronics.

The overwhelming message from Korea is that they didn't do all of this by waiting for something from outside to be *given* to them… they didn't do it by clinging to an ideology. They did it through *education* and through *investment* into technology."

Marsha looked about—the body language of the skeptics was changing, she was winning them over so she pursued that tack for a few more minutes, urging the politicians and luminaries in the audience to get behind the project, to see the *blue-sky* potential of it; the unknown opportunities that developing new technologies inevitably deliver, opportunities that can't be planned, opportunities that just arise when breakthrough science unfolds.

She then swung the direction of her speech and expanded on the need to come to grips with the broader and more global social and societal elements of change.

"None of us alive today will see the distant future, yet we care about the survival of our species even though the atoms of our own mortal remains will return via microbes or incineration to the earth.

When we stop and think about it that way, it is curious that we care about the future... Why *should* we care if we are mortal, just a bag of chemicals that returns to the earth to become other things; to become nitrogen in the grass for cattle, carbon for new bodies, and water in new rainfalls?

Yet we, alive today and every generation that went before us, have been universally concerned about how things will turn out long after our consciousness is no more.

Of course, we will leave behind the legacy of our decisions and attitudes... we will leave our DNA in our children—but that is not 'us'... we will be gone. This sort of dry scientific objectivism is often attacked by mystics who hope to claim a point in favor of a deity and an afterlife... Well, I protest; let me categorically say that we care just as much... maybe more... because we *understand the fundamentals and improbability of life and sentience*—and that understanding sharpens our appreciation of it.

I would argue further; that science-based thinkers are even more intrigued by the future and want the best for our species and biosphere because we grasp how impossibly rare our earth and the life on it is, in vast frigidity of space.

Of course, biologists will point out an additional factor that is not obvious to the layperson; that we are concerned because survival of that which makes us, our DNA, *compels* us to care—in the same way it is our DNA that ultimately compels us to breathe, to eat and to seek pleasure... and reproduce.

In a very real and tangible way then, survival of our species is written through natural selection into the very fabric of every living thing. Afterall, those lineages that failed to impart to their protégée this peculiar objective of caring about the future, simply did not see their DNA prosper as ours has.

Put more plainly; the genes that didn't care about the future got out-competed by those with the genes that do care—and each one of us here present, healthy, sane and not entirely psychotic carry them in abundance. The non-carers went extinct—we are not them. The few psychopaths who don't care… who slip through… are simply noise in the statistical probability."

There was a mild disturbance in the audience as a mobile phone rang and the owner squirmed to retrieve it from a pocket without standing up; he extinguished the embarrassment.

"So… we care about the future, *that* is inherent in our genes.

For better or worse, because we're moving rapidly into a highly technological age, humanity's future is now deeply tied with understanding the nature of the very-very small; the quantum world and the very-very large; the cosmic one… We in our mundane every-day lives sit at the boundary between these two extremes.

The nature of the universe is change—yet our infrastructures and commerce is built on the presumption of stability—of no change occurring; Our food supply, our access to the resources of water, energy and raw materials… they're fixed and growing in appetite; we somehow expect to have more of these, but the reality of the matter is that we have less and less.

So… we have developed global systems and infrastructures that are at odds with reality.

The challenge is to manage and protect this world and our future in the long run; and to do that, we need to look out into space to fundamentally understand where it all evolved from; trace it back through time and through an intricate and well understood evolution of particle physics I won't burden you with today."

She paused for a sip of water.

"The SKA is just one important leg of that discovery path. The data that it teases from the universe, together with a host of other major complementary investments into CERN and the Hadron Collider and other mega-science initiatives, will tell us a lot about the accuracy of our scientific theories and models, which in turn will help us to plan and manage the distant future.

Your children and their children will benefit and thank us for what we're doing right here, today.

Deeply passionate as I am about this topic, I must begin to ease toward a close with an important thrust; a message about the environment that science must survive in... and that is the gist of my intention today—to bring science alive in your mind:

In the 1960's, Soviet astronomer Nikolai Kardashev devised a scale to rate the kind of theoretical civilization that we might develop into and of course the kind of alien civilizations that the SKA might reveal to exist elsewhere in the universe.

In broad terms, according to Kardashev, out there in the cosmos there may be intelligent life capable of making contact with us... it will be at one or another level of development. He classified these civilizations as Type-One, Type-Two and Type-Three Civilizations.

For a benchmark, humanity at this moment is... yep, Type-Zero-point-five; we don't rate, we're barely on the scale. This comes as a real blow to our collective ego, especially if we think the whole universe was made only for us."

There were a few stirs in the audience and her teleprompt indicated that she had three minutes to wind up the speech, so she summarized; "For those interested in the details, please do research *'Kardashev Scale'* in your own time."

"As I say—we hardly rate on this scale, yet, we think of ourselves as supremely intelligent and sophisticated. The reality-check is that we're barely three centuries into being a scientifically based species, into being students of the universe; we've barely had three *decades* with technologies that are more than pretty crude mechanical machines.

We need to look at the scale in order to understand the type of global civilization that we can *strive* to be; even at the cost of cherished lifestyles or cultures.

It is urgent to do so *now*, because this epoch, this moment in time is one of *grave* danger, and I cannot overemphasize this... We have the capacity in so many ways to derail our own progress and drive ourselves right back to virtually a Stone Age existence... this is no exaggeration.

The history of our species tells us that *divisions* between peoples hamper their ability to face challenges. Over the past ten thousand years we've gone from lots of small groups to a few large groups... It's the trend I want you to focus on; bands of hunter-gatherers became clans, city-states became nation states and now we see confederations of States.

Europe as a single entity might have teething problems, but at least its no longer wasting resources on borders and armies and internal friction; it's the trend line towards unity, from lots of competing groups to few cooperating groups: Our future as a species lies in unity and for those of you who feel repulsed by that, give me a moment and I'll explain to you why you feel it.

There are milestones on the road to unity—let me list a few:

We all routinely use the Internet; that is the first step toward information sharing at a global level.

I am addressing you in English, the language most likely to assimilate and supersede all other cultures and languages, if only because it is the language of entertainment, commerce and diplomacy.

Global perspectives are rocking cultures and the religions they harbor; in fact... the very word *globalism* has been tainted by the fear-mongers with negative connotations.

I'll bet it really bothers you when I say it... *globalism*. There's an Orwellian tinge to it; I feel it myself.

This is where it is critical to cast off the emotions of propaganda and look at the trajectory of truth."

The convener caught her eye; he was tapping his wrist. She nodded at him.

"The world I inhabit today is less draconian than the one my parents inhabited. And they inhabited a less restricted world than the one *their* parents inhabited; Yes... we all cherish fantasies about the past, but by all practical measures the balance sheet of progress and conveniences our epoch has brought us... our easy access to travel, safe food, painless medicines... longevity; it has all occurred not just against a backdrop of globalism, but directly because of it.

If we follow that progressive line of hard won freedoms we now enjoy back through time, to… oh, maybe our fiftieth ancestor who lived a thousand years ago, only a fool would suggest that our convenient pain-free lives now, are less attractive than the lives of almost anyone who lived in our past.

So, I ask all reasonable people here present today to look to those who shout out against our common humanity… The ones who want us to re-divide along outdated tribal and other lines and consider, understand and realize, that *they* are the enemies of reason and prosperity. They are the foes of progress and education.

They don't want your freedom, they seek to restrict you."

The convener was now pulling his index finger across his throat mouthing, "*Cut!*"

She was out of time right at the climax of the message she needed to deliver and nothing was going to stop her from speaking it. Her audience were locked in on her every word, so she ignored the gesture and pushed on.

"Now I must address our esteemed political leaders in this delegation.

Democracy is a system that *counts* votes, it does not *weigh* them.

In this regard it is an imperfect system. But democracy is the best we have, so I won't talk against it.

We must however remain mindful that when we only *count* votes, wherever in the world that may be, we are counting the votes cast by the *least* informed and comparing them on an equal basis with the most informed.

This potentially results in bowing to the lowest level of understanding, and that in turn leads to retarded political and military infrastructures that cater to and appease the most superstitious fear-ridden minds that are still so anchored in our deep past.

For this reason I *beg* you to be vigilant and guard against the fear, suspicion and superstition by which your electorate will seek to harness and saddle you.

The greatest tragedy of our epoch might prove to be that we are dragged back into our own past by our primitive roots and fears; that ignorance and arrogance will take the steering wheel; and that we commit species suicide through an Armageddon so close to winning the war against irrationality and oppression.

So, as you flick through the news tomorrow morning, when you see the ugly face of terrorism, when you are frustrated by opposing religious fundamentalism and other movements that scream against unity and progress, I ask you to think of my words here today.

Please... Choose bravely.

Chapter 14

Loxton, Dara was pleased to note, proved a much smaller but prettier town than Carnarvon—leafy and green and not the drab utility so common for the region.

The quaint and only coffee shop in the unimaginatively named Carnarvon Street was deserted. It was dappled in shade by a mix of well-established pine and poplar. The tranquil town almost didn't fit with the arid escarpment into which it was set.

Dara had arrived early and parked his bike around the corner.

The road past the shop terminated in a circle with an attractively architected church built on it. The church itself was a smaller clone of the Carnarvon church, though its gardens were greener and seemed better maintained. Like its Carnarvon lookalike, the steeple had a clock set into it that indicated he'd arrived a full twenty-five minutes early. Excited, he'd ridden faster than intended.

Venturing this far from home with nobody knowing his whereabouts had been exhilarating. His heart was still fluttering—so many stimuli, concerns and issues nagging him; but they were all ridiculous, childish paranoias; or so he'd convinced himself.

He calmed himself and selected a seat in the shade. The young coloured waitress came out and wordlessly passed him a menu, then went back inside. Through the glass he saw her consult with an older white woman who studied him as the waitress spoke. The older lady nodded and came outside, directly to him.

"*Hello seun, is jy alleen?*" It was a badly disguised ruse to engage in conversation—clearly she wanted to know what a dark skinned youth—perhaps the first ever—was doing at her table.

"I'm sorry Ma'am, I don't understand," he said.

The cultured Oxford accent startled the proprietress.

"Ooooh, 'n Engelsman!" She bleated in response. "I *is* sorry my boy," she continued in halting and heavily accented English. "I did not know. *Is* you going to be alone, so I can clear?" She indicated the cutlery settings for four.

"I have a meeting with someone," Dara told her, feeling important, and she cleared two settings.

"I get you something while waiting?"

"Water will be fine."

The water was a little brackish, municipal tap water with a tang of chemicals, but it was palatable and Dara's constitution was now accustomed to the local flora as he had a few months earlier.

It was a tranquil and windless day, the cicadas barely perceptible in the distance. Dove and rock pigeon choruses were the lead vocal, strumming out their signature staccato call. No vehicles or pedestrians were about.

A few minutes later, creeping silently, a pickup with a cage at the back rolled by—it had the blue and yellow markings of the *South African Police* and was topped with a blue light over the cab. It had two occupants; a white driver and black passenger, both in police uniform—they studied Dara as they cruised. Their approach and their focus made it clear that they had been called to take a look.

They reached the circle with the church on it fifty meters away and passed out of sight around and behind the shrubbery and building.

Dara's heart was suddenly pounding, his breathing ragged.

"Relax!" he told himself. This was a pickle; a dark-skinned boy in whitest Africa—sixty kilometers from home on a motorbike he was not licensed to ride! The flimsy menu he was pretending to study fluttered so he put it down.

She was watching him through the window—the owner of the shop, talking on her phone.

The van was gone and didn't appear again as it should have if it had kept the same pace; "Surely they would…" Dara assured himself, "if they were coming back…?"

He was gripped with paranoia, trying desperately to relax.

A few minutes passed and the waitress came out again to inquire if he needed anything else. It felt more like she'd been sent to gauge something, but the moment she saw the police van rolling silently back from behind the church she scuttled straight inside again.

Dara quickly fished in his pocket and pretended to make a call on his mobile, hoping it would give him cover and make him appear unconcerned. He orientated himself to watch the road in the reflection of the window, just then the vehicle slid quietly into view. It stopped adjacent to his position and the idling engine cut.

The moments passed at a glacial pace, his mind cramming with thoughts of what might happen next.

He heard the door unlatch and saw the reflection as the driver got out on the far side of the vehicle, donned his police hat and started making his way around the front of the car—now definitely heading in Dara's direction.

Dara was transfixed, watching with horror as the reflection in the glass locked onto him. He did his best to appear unconcerned.

The shop owner was watching too. In the silence he could hear the first crunch of the approaching boot on the pathway.

Just then the policeman in the passenger seat on the 2-way radio called to his walking companion. The man turned aside and went to the passenger window.

Dara felt the urge to bolt.

At that moment the silence was broken by a high-pitched whine and a throaty cough of thunder approaching from the distance, out of sight, beyond the circle and the church.

The engine coughed and coughed again—three more times; blasting suddenly into the howl of a jet engine as the low-slung glistening red car burst from behind the church under throttle—it looked like a predator, crouching low and wide, clinging to the tarmac as a lobster grabs a towel.

The car coughed a final time as the driver flipped the gears down to a halt, snug behind the police van.

There it burbled like a wasp's nest full of smoke; the engine cut.

The policeman had straightened from the driver's window, studying the red sports car pulled contemptuously close behind him on a deserted street.

The door of the Ferrari opened and its sharply dressed driver unfolded his lofty frame from its innards. The policeman suddenly seemed to recognize the man and made haste toward him, but as he came in range the man faked a punch to the policeman's gut. As the cop doubled to the lightly landed blow, the man snatched the police hat off his head and crowned himself with it, displaying a deftness and speed that belied his proportions. It was a friendly gesture, but one only a true friend could get away with.

There was unbridled laughter and a slapping of backs, a bone-crunching handshake and smile-lines creasing both men's faces.

Only then did Dara realize he'd halted his charade on the phone and was watching the scene unfold, mouth agape with bewilderment.

The hat was restored to its rightful head and the two men spoke a moment longer, then the well-dressed young man looked in Dara's direction and gestured toward him. The policeman followed his gaze and the pair said something to one another; the tall man patted the cop on his shoulder said, *"Dankie boet, groete aan almal."*—intimate greetings of old friends.

"Al's reg," the policeman replied his affirmations and returned to his van as the young man with the wide smile and electric blue eyes approached in Dara's direction.

Dara could see both policemen still studying him intensively as they cruised slowly away in the background. The white driver now had the radio microphone up to his mouth and he wasn't smiling.

"Memes?" The stranger asked.

"I'll be in my car... you can't miss it..." Dara remembered those words and now he understood them. The traumatic startles of the past half hour had nearly wiped his memory clean; he'd almost forgotten why he was even here, chancing his freedom.

"VoorVel?" Dara asked tentatively, stumbling over the pronunciation, which required an "F" sound for the "V"s; phonetically, *"FoorFel."*

"Uhmmm, well… yes—but don't say it out aloud!" The man suggested, "It's not something you say out loud… That *tannie* in there will hear you and won't be pleased."

As *Oom* literally means *uncle* but is generically used for any older man, so too *tannie* means *aunt* and has the same purpose as a generic label for all older women.

"My name is JJ… JJ Kruger," the man said.

Kruger was a common enough surname in the area, but it stood out for Dara. It was a significant name, but in this instant of tangled emotions he just couldn't place it.

"How did you know I'm Memes?" he asked as they shook hands; JJ's hand like a brick, thick and solid.

JJ looked around theatrically, "Is there anyone else here who looks like a dirty heathen?" He asked with a laugh.

Apart from the *tannie* and the waitress, the village seemed entirely deserted.

"But I didn't expect you to be so young—you don't give that away when you write."

"Thank you," said Dara, a bit taken aback by it all and at a loss for words.

"The pieces are falling into place …" JJ pondered aloud, studying him. "I heard from my *Pa* that there was some trouble up here with an Indian boy…. Your mother is a scientist?"

Dara was speechless as his predicament far from home came crashing in on him—he'd seen the electric blue eyes before, the colossal proportions—he'd heard the surname—*Kruger*—Constable Kruger, he realized, the hulking man with the predacious eyes filling the doorway of the police station.

He felt the blood drain from his face and he went faint, his mouth dry and tunnel vision threatening.

"Your dad's the policeman in Carnarvon?" He stumbled, trepidation in his voice.

"Don't worry," JJ reached across and enveloped his shoulder in that vast paw. He'd seen Dara's look of terror; the reasons for it were obvious. "We're friends, remember? Same side; I'm not one of *them*."

The old lady in the store was on the phone again, watching them through the window and reporting this outrageous gossip to *somebody*... possibly to everybody.

"So your mother is a scientist?" JJ asked, "Impressive! Rumour has it that she's beautiful too. Smart and stunning."

"Yes," Dara agreed—he was very proud of her.

"It's an exciting project we've got here. I was so excited when it was announced," he sighed. "But my people... they've got gripes, some are legitimate and others are ancient fears and suspicions they're battling to overcome."

JJ did most of the talking, Dara listened; he was a good listener and enjoyed the man's insights, enthusiasm and grasp of many subjects; from the sciences to economics, social issues to personal sensitivity of the prevailing race biases.

"You do know that it comes from fear, Dara?" JJ pointed out. "They think they're strong; they'll trumpet how strong they are in their '*Lord*', and that their *Lord* gives them *this* or *that* authority. It all sounds very convincing, even to them; they even convince themselves that it's true. And in many cases it is true, their conviction of a higher authority to authenticate and authorize their actions does make them overcome what perhaps those without that faith might achieve. But it's all self-hypnosis. I know, I was one of them, a youth leader for half my young life... Until I went to the city."

He'd ordered a beer and offered one to Dara, but Dara refused. JJ sipped and smacked his lips, savoring it, "Delicious on a hot day," he said raising it to Dara.

"Yes... My Mum often allows me a beer, but I'm on the bike," just saying that out aloud made Dara feel quite grown-up—though he cringed within for having preceded it with; '*My Mum allows*'.

JJ saw the boy cringe and felt for him, so he pretended he didn't hear it; "I'm driving too, so I'll just have the one."

The waitress brought some snacks, and when she'd gone, JJ returned to their conversation;

"I'd grown up here and had blinkers on, but at university I had my eyes opened... 'The Bible says *this*' and 'the Bible says *that*'... that was my reference... Don't get me wrong, I wasn't stupid... just misinformed. I wasn't *uneducated*, just *under-*

educated. It was a mess, really... just a tangle of self-assured bigotries put in my head that I kept repeating till they were true. You must remember that where I come from I was taught blacks and coloureds... anyone not European, were automatically stupid, lazy, untrustworthy... atheists too! Atheists were the worst; in my view they were devils and demonic. You couldn't trust them, they had no moral fiber—because in my world, morals only came from the Bible. And then I met these people, these atheists, brown and black people on equal terms. In Cape Town I couldn't dominate them and I couldn't avoid them. I couldn't ostracize them, they were everywhere and they had the same rights as me. If I tried to ostracize them, I'd be the one ostracized by just about everyone else. I had to adapt or die."

His phone pinged with a message and his eyebrows rose as he looked at the screen; "This is what drives me nuts... those cops or the *tannie* are broadcasting... the family knows I'm in Loxton... they want to know what's keeping me." His thumbs were a blur as he typed a response, his brow furrowed with irritation.

Dara made to collect his keys to leave.

"No... relax... they can wait. I just need to also tell the wife I'm safe... she worries... hates this car..." his expression softened to a smile as he sent the second message, "...but, you know... it's the reward I promised myself in the years of sacrifice."

He put the mobile aside; "...I was telling you; when I came home in the early years there was strife. Trouble in my home with my father mostly and trouble in the *dorp* with my old friends and the *Dominee*. My wife's American and not very welcome. I went to church to appease the family but it irritated me, a waste of my time... my mind had moved on. Predictable nonsense—you only see it as an outsider... I didn't go back and the pressure came on... endless guilt trips, threats of damnation, shunning. Jeez, enough to have intimidated me if I wasn't so independent. Eventually the nonsense stopped when they realized it wasn't working."

The *tannie* came outside to ask if they wanted anything more and JJ was very friendly with her. He made small talk in Afrikaans and ensured she didn't hear anything of the heresies they'd been speaking of to feed back into the town's gossip mill.

When she'd gone he went on;

"That was a decade ago, we get on fine now—nobody bothers me about it anymore. I don't come home often, not much for me here. My business is in the city, my friends and life are there. I mainly live in the suburbs but also have a beach house for weekends and holidays."

"What business?" Dara asked—he felt like he was being bad company, just listening with not much to add till this gap.

"I buy hospitals," he said. "…bit of a long story…"

"Gee, that is amazing. Are you a doctor?"

"Oh… no… businessman. I qualified in law and practiced for two years in South Africa, but I didn't enjoy it, so I did a gap year in the States and made a bit of cash as a head hunter with an Executive Search firm… helping place Vice-President and above at HMO, Managed Healthcare facilities all over the States. It gave me a great sense of the medical industry as a commercial venture. When I got back to South Africa hospital privatization was just taking off… Right place, right time; a friend of mine was a doctor at a hospital and I heard it was in trouble. My wife's connected to big money, so we found backers and got our first buy out. It was very lucrative. We now have…" He squinted in thought; things lately had been moving so quickly that he needed some calculations. "Sheeew… it's pretty close to a billion in cap value and it's still a private concern—I'm resisting us floating it. Sorry—you understand what 'floating' means? What cap value is?"

"Sure—floating on the stock exchange—the cap values what your assets are worth," Dara said.

"I forget—you're still at school; but you're so advanced. What were you thinking, going to Carnarvon School? It's a village school, they've never seen anything like you before, of course there was going to be *kak, shees* man!" JJ laughed at him in a jovial way, it was a warm laugh, the laugh of an equal.

"I thought I should get to know the locals, even though I won't really live here"

"And how'd that work out for you?" The question was a politeness, JJ knew all about the incident—and more.

"I made one good friend; his grandfather's a bushman clan leader around here."

"Ahh that'll be *Oom* Karel—nice old man. You met him?" JJ asked.

"No, I only know his grandson, Dawie—Dawid. But he speaks a lot about his grandfather and his people."

"Ja… his people," JJ said it contemplatively, pausing. "…Good kind people, ambushed by history. We've done so much wrong to them… I doubt we can ever make it right."

"Charity?" Dara ventured.

"Alas… Money doesn't seem to help. A big issue is that their culture never developed alcohol—it's lethal to them. What they don't drink away they get scammed out of—they're pretty innocent people. Sitting ducks for every con artist or dirty politician."

"What if they had their own land?"

"I might be wrong, but I think that party's over. Their traditional ways are down the toilet, the game they traditionally subsisted on is gone; poachers will see to it that it stays gone. They realistically can't hunt for a living, and most don't want to anymore. Subsistence doesn't work in the modern world…" He shook his head.

"My dad says the same thing… insoluble," Dara agreed.

"You know…" JJ nodded, "You really must meet my sister—she's seventeen. You're… what, eighteen?"

"No, Seventeen also," Dara said.

"You said you came by bike?"

He looked quizzical and Dara stammered the reply; "Yes… a… a small one."

"Long way for a one two five?"

"It's… uhmm… a two fifty," Dara conceded.

"Hmmm… so… seventeen… no license then…?" JJ smiled knowingly. "Glad you didn't accept the beer or I'd be complicit. Don't let our friends in blue get you," he winked, referring to the police uniforms. He sipped and pondered thoughtfully, "You must *definitely* meet my sis… She's a beautiful lady… beautiful person… Your dad?"

"My dad's an author… a speaker… *evolutionary anthropologist,* so he travels a lot," Dara volunteered. "All over the world with lectures and book launches."

"Interesting… what's his name?" JJ inquired and Dara told him. "Wow—I know his work well, I'm a fan."
"He's visiting soon."
"Hell, I'd love to meet him."
"I can organize it," Dara assured.
JJ indicated to the waitress for the bill.

JJ paid and they bid farewell with a loose plan to meet again during the week.

The car door thunked closed and the predator barked into life. JJ u-turned and the engine boomed a blizzard of sound. By the time the car reached the roundabout with the church built on it, he'd geared up three times and back down a gear to round it; the engine whistled out of sight and the car was gone.

The oblivion of silence settled once more over the town, it left Dara feeling strangely vulnerable and foreign all over again.

He walked quietly round to his bike, donned his helmet and kicked the machine into life. He retraced his path back to the highway, following JJ's path toward Carnarvon.

At the junction he turned right and headed north. There was no traffic through the semi-desert and the sky was its usual aching blue, the temperature as hot as always. A light crosswind toyed gently with the bike.

Dara settled into the ride; he was already past the half way mark and approaching a highway sign that read '*25 kilometers*' to Carnarvon; it meant there was less than twenty to his turnoff; home in ten minutes; and he began to relax.

The road inclined and passed through a cutting into the apex of a hillock. As he crested and began the descent into the next dip there was a small gravel lot obscured by a flanking rock formation. He passed it and in horror glimpsed the parked police patrol van from earlier facing the road. His heart leapt and his eyes flew to the handlebar mirror but the knobby tires made it judder so that the image danced too much for detail.

The engine was screaming and he realized that he had the throttle cranked wide open—he dared a darted look back over his shoulder and could see the van still parked. A moment later he looked again and the van was moving from the slip road to the highway. He was crazed now, the bike shaking and near its limited extent for speed—another stolen look over his shoulder and the van turned onto the highway, it's blunt back facing him; retreating to Loxton.

With a flush of relief he returned attention ahead with only a split second to react; the road was curving away and he was on a collision path with the crash barrier. Time jammed to slow motion again. He fought the bike to match the curve but the barrier was bending faster toward him than he could manage, closer and closer it came. He knew the rule—look where you want to go, not where you're afraid to hit, so he forced his eyes down the road.

It was only a glancing blow; his adrenaline surge anaesthetizing the impact, the barrier slamming into the bike's steel crash-bars, but it gashed his pants open at the knee. The bike swerved, he corrected and over-corrected, it swerved in the opposite direction—the barrier was coming up again. He pumped the back brake and the bike slid, the rubber bit and he corrected again.

The road opened in front of him and he was traveling normally in a straight line as if nothing had occurred. He shut the throttle right down, back down under the speed limit.

His tongue felt like a chunk of shoe leather in his mouth and every finger seemed to be capped by a golf ball. He felt the trickle of icy sweat down his flanks and then the numbness of his knee began to fade, giving birth to sickening pain. He stole a look—it was ugly; blood and gore, open flesh gaping through the rip in his blood-soaked pants.

"Oh... *God*!" He growled through the numbness and pain. It would need a stitch or ten and that would take some explaining.

Another few kilometers passed and his knee was starting to stiffen; the whole leg racked with pain. The bike felt a little different too—felt like it was floating and crabbing, not reacting properly; or perhaps it was just the nausea from the bump he'd taken?

He passed the *Fraserburg* turnoff—home was quite close now, his mind was a clutter; outthinking the questions that would be asked about his knee and the bike—where it had happened and how it had happened.

He needed a story that fitted the evidence; he hadn't fallen, there was no evidence for that. He also needed a story that wasn't too improbable; his mother was incisive in her questioning and she could link the most unlikely things.

To keep the bike, he also needed a story that meant the accident was not his negligence, was not caused by excessive speed—and he couldn't see how he could make that one fly given the probable scrape to the steel of the crashbar.

There weren't too many possible answers he could come up with on a dirt road alibi that fitted what he needed his mother to believe.

All of those problems suddenly evaporated as he rounded a bend, and, directly ahead, the road was blocked. Instinctively, he shut the throttle and stood on the brakes—a police van blocked the road, a single arms-folded blue uniform in front of it.

His options were to run—to double back. On an open tar road his machine could barely break the speed limit and the van would be on him in seconds. He had no option, he had to play it cool—so he rode steadily onward, slowing as any law-abiding citizen would in such an eventuality.

Then another realization detonated in Dara's mind—the man in front of the van was huge, he had ice-blue eyes that bore ruthlessly across the closing distance between them.

Dara's heart felt like a boulder crammed in his chest, it was Kruger—JJ's father, JJ had sold him out.

Just a putting green of distance between them now…

His mind was racing for how to react. He slowed to a halt and the hulk walked slowly forward, nodding curtly with recognition.

"You a *veeeery* long way from home," the cavernous drone and throaty rumble of his heavily accented voice was unmistakable.

"A…. a bit", Dara stammered. It was a weak statement but he was surprised any sound left his mouth at all. His mirrored visor was still firmly down; he knew that he should tip it up but he was desperate to keep any last pretense at anonymity as long as he could—realistically his accent had already identified him; it was a pointless and silly hope.

The policeman walked slowly around behind him, seeming to take forever to reappear. Dara had both feet on the ground and was watching him intently in the rear-view mirrors; the engine pinging from heat and smelling of oil from the strain of the ride and the bump it had taken.

"You ran out of talent," Kruger observed dryly, looking at the gash in Dara's knee. "…Going to need some needle work."

"Oh, it's nothing," Dara tried to sound nonchalant, but with his leg now extended, his foot on the floor, the freshly wind-dried scab had cracked and he could feel the trickle of new blood running down his calf, tickling into his boot. His nausea doubled.

"You'd better get it seen to," the cop's words sounded empathetic, his tone didn't. "There's an accident up ahead though so you'll have to cut through the farm lands," Constable Kruger indicated the dirt road that intersected where the van was parked. "That'll bring you out on the R63—it'll get you into town and you can backtrack to your compound."

Dara was lightheaded with shock, stunned that he was being released.

He thanked Kruger enthusiastically and pulled away, missing then clashing his gear change. The dirt road was loose and rutted, punishing his knee.

He rode on carefully, resisting the urge to run again. He felt exhausted from an afternoon full of so many sudden and unexpected surprises. There was exhilaration too; the recent surge of adrenaline with the policeman had dulled the developing ache in his knee and cleared his head.

"Just nurse the bike home," he spoke out aloud inside the helmet and reminded himself of his dad's watchwords when you're under pressure "Slow is smooth, smooth is fast."

He was very keen to be home fast.

His mind was now filled with concern for what the news of an accident—one sufficient to shut down the highway—might mean.

His mother jumped first to mind. He pushed that fear aside; she worked in a different direction and only returned toward sunset, but the demons of worry that it could be her crept back and he subdued the thought again, checking himself when the urgency of that worry had opened the throttle a bit.

And what about JJ… Kruger's son? *Had* JJ betrayed him? It seemed unlikely and pointless if Kruger had just let him go…

Had JJ crashed, he wandered—JJ had taken off like he had a coal on his seat. But the father would hardly be out on the highway directing traffic if his son was in the accident.

Perhaps then Kruger hadn't realized or been told it was his son? That wasn't possible either; JJ's car was hardly inconspicuous.

Dara's mind was a maze full of escaped monkeys, thoughts bolting in every direction when a new one ran through the frame and began to gnaw at him—his own accent. The cop *definitely* knew who he was and therefore knew his age and no license… and… and… and so many angles, too many surprises for one day—his mind was running amuck.

The road inclined ahead and bore to the right—as he crested over the undulation he looked back and could see the distant intersection with the tar road he'd just left—oddly, the road was empty and clear; no police van stood where he'd just been diverted.

He looked again… and again to make sure he was seeing it properly and the geometry of the roads was right; he wasn't wrong—the intersection was vacant and open.

It was more than strange and the urge to run hard again seized him; the policeman might have thought better of it and could be giving chase. Blind fear gripped him for an instant; but there was no sign of any dust trail.

Regardless of the reason for the open road, there was no way he was going to double back.

Had he dreamed all of this? He seriously considered it. Was he dreaming now? Was he delirious from the collision with the barrier, he asked himself? With the pain he was feeling, he thought he may well be hallucinating.

It was all crazy. Surreal. But he spied landmarks on the distant mountains he now knew so well. In his quest to find caves to explore, he'd intensively studied the area maps and online satellite images. The landmarks triangulated in his head, and they gave him a good fix for where he was; he was between the two tar roads that converged on Carnarvon. To buoy his own spirits he forced himself to laugh at the predicament he found himself in; at least if he was delirious, he thought, his humor and navigation skills were crisp.

He brought his mind back to important matters, contemplating what to do when he'd exit the dirt back onto the tar in the distance, he'd have to take that other highway into Carnarvon and then double back toward the accident to get home.

As he thought this over, he came through another drift, a dip through a dry riverbed and the road veered around a gentle corner. He was traveling mercifully slowly, not much faster than a runner's sprint when something slammed him viciously across the chest, stopping him dead in his tracks as the bike went out from under him. The impact and sound like a gunshot.

There was a loud 'TWANG' as he fell, smashing into the ground, driving the air from his lungs. The motorbike continued riding on its own momentum until it left the road, hit a boulder and flopped over, its back wheel chugging round and round where it lay.

The padded jacket he wore had taken the brunt of the wire strung across the dirt road.

"Look," a familiar voice said, screened by a large bush, "it's our *Prrrrretty Boy*."

Dara instinctively tried to roll toward the direction of the voice, but the voice snapped at him in an accent so thick he could barely understand the words—the tone was enough—"Don't you look at me, boy! Put your face in the dirt."

Clutching for air, ribs smashed from the blow in the front and crushed from the fall at the back, Dara obeyed. He heard the metallic snickers and zings of bailing wire hastily retrieved, coiled and clattering into the back of a pickup—a pickup he hadn't seen from his approach, screened as it had been behind the thick wall of thorn bush the voice had hidden behind.

Self-preservation took over and Dara tried to roll to his knees, but swift footfalls through the dirt closed in on him in an instant and an explosion of sound, light and pain burst in the same instant within his mind. His neck snapped dangerously as the running boot met his helmet; the impact of it rolling him over-and-over in the dirt. He exaggerated the rolls, trying to make distance, but the assailant followed and delivered a steel toecap into the small of his back; he arched to the pain of it.

Rolling again, over and over with grit and grime obscuring the helmet visor, he saw only the outline of the pursuing figure. *"I have to identify him,"* the idea of it urging within his mind seemed ludicrous—he was certain he'd be dead, but he knew he must try.

Rolling away hadn't worked, so he rolled into a tight ball and blows came raining in from every angle; a tornado of fury that made him grateful for the helmet. Then, miraculously, the pain flooded away—Dara only heard the thuds of blows reporting themselves to his numb mind. Everything crystalized; he must play dead, fifteen, twenty blows and kicks arrived in an avalanche as he entered an ethereal dream world where the crocodiles of traumatic hallucination began to play trumpets, its lizards dancing jigs.

With his body protectively curled into a ball, his eyes began swimming in tears; at last the attacker began to tire, the blows arrived less regularly, the assailant's breathing rasping from the effort. And then they stopped.

One last almighty kick arrived, aimed at Dara's crotch—a tester to see if he was truly out cold. It didn't land squarely and the burst of pain he expected was dulled. Dara rode it, completing the illusion that he was unconscious, for he very nearly was.

"Not such a *Prrrrretty* boy now, hey?" The rolled *'rrr's* were muffled by Dara's helmet, but they were unmistakable, and he saw a gob splatter onto the visor, where it hung for a moment then trickled slowly through the settled dust, clearing a runnel of visibility.

Boot crunches retreated, the door of a vehicle opened and closed, and a diesel engine clattered into life. The ordeal left Dara facing down the road and away from the truck; he dared not sneak a look to identify what he could, he felt too numb and weary to bother. The wheels began to crunch slowly over the stony ground, approaching, louder and louder. Through the fog of pain, alarm bells rang through Dare's mind; an urgent dilemma to roll aside and risk betraying pretended coma, perhaps goading the driver to more violence, or lay still and risk being crushed.

The crunch of wheels was close now, and closer still; *"Surely nobody would…"* his mind begged against the evidence of his ears, but a moment later the pressure of a wheel pushed into his helmet, trying to mount it. The hard shell ground against the rough earth, stuttering forward until it seated in a rut and wedged.

The wheel found traction and rode up but fell immediately back with insufficient engine revs; the engine gunned louder and the wheels juddered again, bit and popped up-and-over, the tread imprinting its track onto the clear Perspex, smearing the dust and gob, the rear wheels only slapping him with a glancing blow.

Dara lay in stunned disbelief. He heard the pickup shifting through its gears into the distance and in the silence of its wake the motorbike still burbled as it idled on its side in the drainage trench.

Dara rolled to his back and groaned. He needed the helmet off—the protective shell of it now a prison to his senses. His mind was clearing and the tight-fitting enclosure clamped on his head became claustrophobic, obscuring his vision and hearing in those moments of desperation when he urgently needed his senses on the highest alert to protect his body from further assault and tires.

He must get off the road, he knew it. If he was wrong and the police were still diverting traffic, little traffic as the local highway attracted, a detoured commuter might be in a hurry to buy back time.

He tried to lift his left arm, needing both hands to un-cleat and lift the helmet away, but with horror found it paralyzed, lying next to him at an awkward angle.

With his right hand he reached over and lifted it by the sleeve. It was weighty and dead; it felt detached—severed. The shock of it horrified him—he lifted it high enough to look at, and the angle it described left no doubt that it was broken. With some small joy, he realized it still felt meatily attached; it would only go so far. He placed it across his sternum and it immediately slid from his chest, hitting the ground alongside him with a slap.

He tried to roll but his leg was dead too. Adrenaline coursing his body had extinguished his neural response; everything dull, heavy and paralyzed—cadaverous.

As the shock subsided, the pain came on like a breaking wave, every violated part of his body screaming private agonies, a cacophony to an overloaded brain.

He was weeping, and realized he had been doing so all along—but now it was tears of pain. The sobbing collapsing his rib cage, crushed as it was from every angle.

Dara got a grip on himself, he held his breathe and willed the sobs away, "They won't help you…" he admonished himself. "Focus—move—crawl!"

He tried, but couldn't crawl, so he managed to roll to his good side and inch himself with his good arm across the ground until the stony dirt in his field of view through the visor gave way to the close-up detail of threadbare grasses, the sticks and stones at the margin of the roadway.

The effort of it exhausted him and the movement brought fresh focus to *this* injury or *that* fracture in every extremity, "I'll rest a moment," he reassured himself aloud.

The last thing he saw was the zigzag tire pattern on the outside of the visor.

He could hear that the little bike was still chugging and it pleased him that at least it was not too badly damaged.

Chapter 15

When Dara wasn't home by dark, Marsha called the police but the operator's accent was too thick for her stressed mind to grasp. She had the house staff talk and interpret for her.

The farmer on whose land the SKA compound was built, arrived to assist; he proved invaluable, immediately dispatching anyone who could drive or ride a farm bike to fan out into the mountains where Dara was known to normally wander. Calls came in and false leads were followed, the entire hunt dogged by limited radio communications imposed on the area.

The ordeal became immensely frustrating, with most of the communications in Afrikaans, laboriously translated into English.

Finally, near midnight, the news of a bike accident from an unexpected quadrant came in. A farmer on his way home saw the motorbike and broken body lying to the side of the rarely used road.

He reported the find as soon as he reached mobile coverage near the national road. Since ambulances in the area were a rare luxury, he loaded the kid into the back of his pickup and sped for Carnarvon.

By the time Marsha arrived at the small clinic to identify him they'd cleaned Dara up and were conducting emergency procedures. He was delirious but breathing on his own.

"He's in bad shape but very lucky," the doctor told her gravely. "Three broken ribs. It looks like a crushed thoracic vertebra and a hairline in a cervical one—we'll have to confirm that with MRI. Two weeks ago we'd have been in a world of trouble… this facility didn't even exist then."

Marsha was relieved. The new clinic and its doctor had only just arrived, part of the social expenditure by the SKA investment group and other donors.

"He's our first serious case," the doctor told her. Their respective accents making it clear that both were newcomers to the area.

"Thank you," she said. She was shaking uncontrollably, "What happened?"

"Seems like he lost control... He's pretty beaten up, must have been going like the devil was after him... there are lesser problems; his elbow's dislocated, knee's ripped wide open... arm broken. I'm sincerely hoping we don't have internal injuries. He's certainly concussed—good thing he had a quality helmet."

Marsha was suddenly furious. *'What the hell was he doing off the farm and acting like a maniac?'* she thought, "It's so unlike him," she said, "He's a cautious boy."

"He's what? Sixteen? Seventeen..." the Doctor tried to soften it. "They're all like this; think they're bullet proof. It's a wonder boys ever make it to twenty."

"But it's so unlike *him*..." She kept saying.

"Mothers always think that," the doctor shrugged at the thought, *"their kids never make bad calls."* He gave her a moment, "His father here too? Or are you guardian?"

"Dad's abroad, I'm sole guardian... I've called his dad, he's getting an emergency flight."

"All right. I'm sorry. But it was on a public roadway and the police are buzzing me for details, they want to open a case."

Chapter 16

They kept Dara heavily sedated for the first four days, and Marsha held vigil by his bedside round the clock.

The doctors understood and let her remain, moving a bed in beside him. Her employer footed the bill for additional medical staff to be flown in.

Moving Dara to another hospital was considered, but the decision to avoid an arduous road or air trip proved to be the right option.

The police had an open docket and wanted answers; Dara was an unlicensed motorist on a public road, albeit a secondary un-tarred one. In a farming district the police generally turned a blind eye to a farm boy commuting between farms who stuck to the dirt, but Dara was not a farm boy and his only access to the dirt road on which he'd been found was by a significant distance down a national highway. According to Constable Andre Kruger who delivered the charge, his boss, the Station Commander, was taking a very dim view of the whole affair.

Considering the extent of Dara's injuries, "He must have been going *on* a hell of a lick," the hulking Constable told Marsha in broken English, "and I'm sorry Madam, but the Captain *will* make an example of your boy. So much is changing around here," he added bitterly, "we can't have every newcomer thinking it's a wild-west show with no laws."

The case was by all accounts cut and dried in the mind of the Constable. But Marsha couldn't understand why the recovered motorbike had virtually no scratch on it. The farmer who had found Dara, reported he'd found it laying only a very short stretch from the boy. The bike only evidenced a scratch or two and a minor bend to its crash bar against its rider's pummeling; the whole affair made no sense.

Marsha was no forensic expert, but she went toe-to-toe with the big policeman, insisting that any *reasonable* person would see the glaring disparity in damage between the rider and the machine; one virtually unscathed, the other severely trashed.

The constable grunted and said he couldn't comment. He did offer her friendly advice; that she shouldn't take it up with the Captain for fear of inflaming the situation.

Once he'd stabilized, Marsha left Dara's bedside long enough to visit the scene of the crash to take photographs and some quick measurements of her own. It was clear that although the police were treating the run-up to the accident as serious, they were disinterested in the details of what they'd already judged to be pure recklessness.

At the crash site, there was not much evidence for her untrained eye to see. No skid or slide marks in the gravel, no pieces of the bike; though she hadn't expected any of these since the bike itself and protective wear Dara was wearing showed none of these things. All of her hopes for some obvious visual clues had drawn a blank, but she kept the camera clicking at every angle and minute detail that she'd imagined an actual investigator might record.

Jakob, the farmer who was effectively her landlord, had arranged for Frik, the farmer who had found Dara, to meet up at the site.

The two farmers offered invaluable insight:

Frik showed where and how he'd found Dara, even laying down for her in the scrub to photograph his position and posture. Jakob crouched where the bike had been found lying— the impression of it still pressed visibly into the scrubby weeds days later.

Frik fancied himself as something of a game tracker and he pointed out a place where a vehicle had recently been parked off the road, hard up against a thick thorn bush adjacent to the incident.

He pointed out the discernible tire marks in the dust. There was also a crush of grasses and foliage where the vehicle had stood. "It's within the last few days," he assured. "Since the rains for sure. I don't know what it means or if it can help, but a car has backed in here."

They'd decided that Dara was stable enough to reduce his medication and bring him out of an induced coma.

He groaned, and much as Marsha wanted to scream with joy that the candle of his life was beginning to re-ignite, his labored wincing at every breath and muted whimpers ripped at her heart.

She smoothed the jet-black hair at his temples, shooshing and cooing soft motherly sounds close to his ear.

Then the moment she'd begged fate to grant; his lids parted tentatively, testing the light, his eyeballs tracking slowly and worriedly—bloodshot and fearful.

"It's okay baby, you've had an accident but you're safe…. You're safe." Marsha found herself crying, teardrops falling onto his pillow and she wiped them away, she didn't want the first thing Dara would see to be her fear.

An hour later, Dara was fully awake, clutching for breath through shattered ribs, every movement an agony in another body quadrant.

"What possessed you," Marsha gently lamented. She'd gone through an internal whirlwind of emotions in the past few minutes—gratitude that the doctors said he'd recover fully, anger that he'd done this to himself, urgency to get the answers out of him—and she'd kept a lid on them all, but now she was cautiously testing how far she could push him in this delicate state.

"I'm sorry mum," he winced, his words stilted and slow in coming. "I should have told you. I'm sorry… It was stupid of me, I just wanted to do something on my own… I just wanted to meet with a man I knew from the Internet. We thought it best we meet out of town."

"A man from the internet...!" Marsha's mind went into overdrive—his hadn't been an aimless joy ride—*"A man from the internet!"* Alarm bells were ringing in her head, but she held back and calmed herself.

"What are you talking about, Dara? What man? Why were you on that road? Is he a farmer? You're making no sense." In spite of herself, her rapid-fire thoughts barraged him.

"I was coming back… back from Loxton."

"From Loxton? The town Loxton? Sixty kilometers away?!"

"Yes, sorry mum." He adjusted his position and almost cried out, his arm in plaster, his leg in traction.

"The doctor says you're to lay still. I'm sorry baby, I… I'm just… I really don't understand what you're saying. You went to Loxton and you met someone?"

"Yes Mum—a guy from here, from Carnarvon, but he lives in Cape Town now. That's why Loxton, it's on his way here."

"But why not meet in Carnarvon? Why didn't he just come to the house?"

"It's stupid; now I realize he should have come to the house. I jus…. I didn't want him to know I'm a kid. He was a stranger, I didn't know how it would turn out."

The alarm bells were still going off in Marsha's—her mind still racing to all and any manner of shocking conclusion, *"A man off the internet, meeting my son and he doesn't want the man to know his age…!"* her internal dialogue was a babbling crowd of insistent panic.

"He just said he's too well known in Carnarvon, and our business… the things we wanted to discuss, we didn't want anyone here knowing. It's complicated."

"What business, Dara?" She was agitated and let it show, he was making no sense, *"Perhaps he's still delirious?"* she told herself and decided to back off and just let him talk even if he was sounding deranged. "I'm sorry sweetie. Sorry."

"No mum, I'm sorry. I know what you're thinking and I can't blame you. It's nothing like that, he's married. It's just the stuff I like to write about on blogs and in social media. I've developed cyber friends and he's one of them."

Marsha relaxed; *"Of course!"* she wanted to say out aloud, but kept the anonymity of her own pseudonym observations of him with her silence. But she did want to know who this man was; his pen name. "Does he have a name Dara? I'm not prying but... under the circumstances, though...."

"He also a pseudonym—it's an Afrikaans one, spelled V-o-o-r-v-e-l... It's hard to pronounce."

Marsha had seen that character making comments under the name, a name whose silly provocative meaning was lost on her. She'd enjoyed his dry wit and incisive thoughts but kept this to herself for now.

She nodded, "Okay."

"He was at school here years ago. He lives in Cape Town. He's like, forty or something... buys hospitals, his dad's that big policeman; Kruger; the one from the day we stopped at the station."

The connection slapped her like a wet eel in the face. In her limited interactions with him, Constable Andre Kruger had creeped her out. She willed herself to remain deadpan, but it betrayed in her expression;

"He's a very nice guy mum... my friend. He's very different from his dad and the others round here. We just chatted, it was innocent. I'd have been home and nobody'd have known. I was heading home when I nearly had an accident..."

"You did have an accident Dara" his mother corrected him.

"No mum. I got spooked out on the tar road about twenty kilometers before the dirt, and I hit the barrier; that's how I hacked my knee. But I had to turn off onto the dirt road because the police had closed the last stretch... because of the bad accident. And then a few kilometers on the dirt road I was... something happened... I was attacked... ambushed."

"Ambushed? What...?!" Marsha's mind was doing somersaults again. "Dara. I... what is... just hang on a second." She stood up and paced, telling herself to get a grip. "Dara, you got ambushed? Hang on... What accident closed the road that caused you to get ambushed?"

"The accident on the road coming into town. The police stopped me—JJ's dad, Kruger; he diverted me onto the gravel road that links across to the R63—that's why I was on that road," he said with conviction.

It took a lot of sorting out as Marsha cross-questioned him and Dara tried to explain the sequence of events as they had unfolded. Eventually they had the story straightened out; he got to the point when he'd ridden into the trip-wire that had plucked him from the bike.

She opened the sheets and stared with fresh horror at the livid bruising across his chest. His story fitted, the straight angle spanning his breadth from bicep to bicep had made little sense to the doctors when they'd speculated the cause. The medical staff had assumed he'd hit the handlebars with his chest, but now his claim was that he'd been clothes-hangared by a trip wire perfectly fitted the arrangement of, and the proximity between, where Dara and his bike were found.

"Do you know what you're saying?" She confirmed. "Attempted murder... If that was a wire pulled across a road, it could have taken your head off!"

"I'm certain of what I'm saying, mum. I'm saying what happened."

"This is very serious... and I'm bewildered... I... I'm surprised. Nobody's mentioned any accidents or road closures. In a small place like this, *that* would be big news."

She paused a moment, her mind racing, her emotions wanting to explode but she kept them firmly suppressed in favor of lucidity; this was not the time to react like a mother as her emotional irrationality begged her to do;

"You said it was the Constable that diverted you to the gravel, that he'd said there was an accident?"

"Yes."

"Because I gave a statement to him, to Kruger and he said *absolutely* nothing to me about either a road closure or having seen you. Did you actually talk to him when he redirected you?"

"Yes mum."

"So he knew it was you?"

"I was covered up and kept the visor down—but you'd think he'd know my accent..." Dara cocked his head, "And he immediately spoke to me in English... They always first speak in Afrikaans. He knew it was me..."

Marsha caught herself scowling, horror in her eyes and turmoil in her mind. She sat down again and felt her hands shaking uncontrollably. She needed to arrest them, to not let Dara see the depths of her distress, so she quickly cupped his hand with hers and held it tight. "There is something going on here Dara and I dread to admit to myself what it is."

He adjusted his position in the bed and it caused him to cough. With broken ribs and so much abused flesh, it was an agonized and protracted process.

Marsha cringed but tried to maintain the poker face. Her eye teared for her son and she wiped it so he wouldn't see.

"Dara?" Marsha startled and whirled to face the voice from the doorway. There was a big man with a beautiful girl at his side filling the doorway, just inside the room.

Dara looked their way and smiled a lopsided and pained greeting, "JJ!"… He heaved as he battled to prop himself up to properly greet the man and girl at the threshold, "This is my mother, Marsha."

Dara instantly recognized the girl, she was the one with the hair from the school.

"It's a pleasure, Ma'am. JJ… JJ Kruger," he offered a hand the size of a paddle.

He was very good looking, Marsha saw it at once. His grip was firm, dry and gentle, his eyes his father's; but his body taught and his jaw chiseled. The girl had lustrous hair and an angel's face— the two bore a strong resemblance to one another.

"This is my sister, Sonja"

"It's my pleasure," said Marsha. She was still shaking slightly, so she clasped her hands together in her lap.

Dara's face etched over with growing shock; the coincidences mounting at an uncomfortable pace, friend and foe too closely related to make sense of it all.

His mind raced to the possible agendas; Sonja could be here on behalf of Vermaak to confirm Dara's condition… JJ might be doing his father's bidding to see what story Dara was telling.

It could be very sinister he realized; he hoped his mother understood this too.

Marsha was guarded as she gave an account of Dara's condition, and they reacted with genuine care.

"You did a real number on yourself," JJ summarized it. "You look strong though, you'll be better soon. I just brought Sonja along because she says she remembers you from school, when you had that, uhmm... *incident*."

"I'm sorry, I couldn't say it then because of the Principal at the hearing..." Sonja spoke for the first time, looking directly at Dara. "He warned me that my father would expect me to stand by my people and the community. I feel terrible that they forced me to lie. Neels..."

She was beginning to win Dara's trust.

"...Neels has got so many friends... especially with the teachers. I asked them to check the cameras... the CCTV, but..." She huffed and paused, "...He's the *Dominee*'s special..." she didn't finish her sentence.

"I'm afraid it's all a bit sick... small town politics," JJ said apologetically. "Sonja told me about it and didn't know what to do. Our parents and the Vermaaks are old friends... complicated."

"I'm certain," Marsha agreed, warming slightly to their earnest appearance and genuine expressions of concern, "...it takes courage to speak up."

"I understand you're on Jakob van Breda's farm?" JJ asked.

"Indeed," Marsha agreed. "Why do you ask?"

"I heard Dara had his accident on the dirt road over to the R63." He was about to mention that it made no sense for him to be on that road if he was returning from Loxton, but thought better of it if the mother didn't know about their meeting, so the statement hung in the air.

"I had to divert because of the accident on the main route into town..." Dara volunteered.

JJ looked at Dara quizzically, his head slightly cocked.

"...when your dad said there'd been an accident and diverted me, I was worried it might be you."

"I don't know about an accident or diversion?" JJ frowned.

"That's what I said too," Marsha added.

"Well—I was diverted. Your dad had the police van parked across the road. He said the main road into Carnarvon was closed."

"That's very strange..." JJ said, but he omitted to confirm something that this new piece of information suggested, a detail within his own mind falling into place:

On his way toward Carnarvon that day, JJ had passed his father coming the other way at great speed in the police van.

When he'd recognized his dad he'd flicked his headlights but his father was on the radio and had an intent expression—he'd just lifted a finger on the wheel in greeting and flashed headlong past.

At the time, JJ had imagined that there was some kind of an emergency out of town and he'd thought nothing more of it… until now.

But now, this new piece of information pushed that occurrence into a much more sinister direction.

Sonja read JJ's expression, "*Ernstig..?*" She asked in a single word that the foreigners wouldn't understand.

JJ nodded just perceptibly, *"Yes, it's serious,"* his nod confirmed.

"I've been too busy to chat much around town," JJ told them, "...but nobody's mentioned any recent accidents that would close the highway, and I'm sure they would… I'll look into it."

He needed time to think and find out more before committing his thoughts.

Marsha had seen the exchange between the siblings but the Afrikaans word had been too quick and obscure to betray anything more than the girl's surprise and worry.

"Is there something we need to know?" Marsha made it clear that she knew something was up.

"No, it's just we only stopped in for a quick visit and we must go. I have to drop Sonja out of town but I wanted to see how my friend here is doing. I also thought Sonja and Dara should meet."

Marsha could also play poker, JJ's ruse and cover hadn't fooled her.

"I do intend to find out what's going on," she was deadly focused in her delivery.

"I really do intend to find out too," JJ looked her directly in the eye and she saw that he grasped the full scope of her meaning, and meant what he said too.

"We'd better get a move on—I'll stop by again... You get better my friend," he said to Dara.

Chapter 17

The men were due to arrive for a meeting at the Kruger house within the hour. Prime on the agenda was pushing forward on the next step in their bid to oppose or forestall the SKA development.

Right now, father and son were in heated confrontation and the women of the house had evaporated out of the way. The men's voices were raised, arguing aggressively in Afrikaans.

"You arrive, and the *kak* begins," Andre was furious.

He'd got wind of JJ's impossible-to-miss car parked outside the clinic and he'd confronted his son the moment JJ'd come through the door. There was only one inpatient, so that the significance of the visit was obvious.

JJ had already told his father why he'd gone to the hospital, "I'm interested in this whole project," he'd told Andre. "I have had discussions and meetings with many of the scientists. You don't even know—I donated half that hospital."

Andre ignored the proclamation; it ashamed him before all of the community that his son should make such a donation through foreigners into his own town.

"…And I am friends with the lady whose son got injured," JJ bent the truth a little, knowing the Loxton police would have called in his meeting with a dark boy back to his father. He was furious with his father over the sinister probability of his involvement, and intended to torment the man by not disclosing everything he knew, as custom dictated he should. "I wanted to see how they were doing."

"And you take your little sister too?" Andre accused, "So that she can get mixed up with these *skelms*."

JJ shook his head, "Where do you make up this stuff? *Skelms*? What makes them *crooks*?" He already knew what his father would answer would be, but wanted to draw his father out.

"This is *our* land and they come here stealing it... bringing their ungodly selves and ungodly machines with them. That's why they're *skelms*! Why didn't they go to Australia like they said they would? Why here? In this blessed place, between our Godly people? Why?"

"Because it is the future, father, and because it is not ungodly. Because this area needs to be uplifted and because this is the best place on earth to build it.... Because through science, it will put Africa on the map."

"Well we don't care about science in Africa or uplifting anything... if that is how they uplift—by taking away our farms, blocking our communications, trying to break our economy and calling our beliefs into question?"

"They have not called your beliefs into question. You are paranoid and injecting issues where none exist."

"You watch how you talk to your elders! I am still your father," his father stood up, a challenge, looming over a son who had grown bigger, stronger and faster than him.

JJ didn't flinch. He stayed neutral, his hands palms down on the table between them. He'd been forcing them not to fidget and now he kept his voice low and steady, "*Pa...*" he blinked a slow and deliberate blink of confidence, "...sit."

They locked a mutual stare for long moments and then, slowly, his father sank back down, fists like hams still clenched, remaining in front of his son's open hands.

"I will *never* trust these atheists... these... these... *antichrists*!" Andre spat it out, deliberately, provocatively, ".... these... *satanists*."

"You mean 'these scientists', *Pa*?"

"Satanists, scientists? Yes, they're the same ungodly thing!" Andre asserted.

"Well, yes, of the leading scientists in the world, nearly a hundred percent are atheists, sure." JJ dared twist his father's meaning to make a point. "And what does that say...? It certainly doesn't make them Satanists."

"It says they're against God and that makes them Satanists in my book."

JJ ignored the attempt to draw him once more into the empty old argument on the topic they'd had too many times.

"...And now you talk for them hey?" His father challenged, "You count yourself with the scientists?"

JJ reminded his father that he was a student of many things, among these things he leant toward proofs and rational answers over philosophical ones.

The argument, as always, drove his father blind with rage— Andre would dogmatically insist that atheists and scientists were synonymous with Satanists, and they remained one untrustworthy blanket collection of immoral communists in his mind.

"You forget why we were thrown out of the Garden of Eden!" Andre accused, still niggling for confrontation.

"Because a talking snake said a woman shouldn't eat an apple," JJ couldn't resist the ridicule in his words or tone.

"You're a very funny boy these days..." Andre snapped sarcastically. "Forgotten all you have been taught. The snake was Satan—he wanted mankind to seek knowledge that God had protected us from knowing."

"And you believe this, *Pa*? You really believe it? That knowledge should be avoided? That looking for answers is a sin? Is that why you and the old *manne* are so *bedonnerd*—so insane with anger about the SKA...? Because once again it shows Genesis is unscientific nonsense? I hear there are real problems the installation is causing... why not argue those rather than this nonsense?"

Andre glowered at him but said nothing; the *Dominee* had explained that the Americans would fight this fight, but he wasn't going to arm the enemy through his son with that important knowledge.

JJ sighed, shook his head and pulled his laptop from its bag, flipping the lid open.

"And that," Andre pointed at the computer, "Wasting time with people who know nothing.... I have the only book I need. It is filled with everything I must know—love and obedience to our Maker. I will not deny Him, I will always do his work."

"I used to say the same thing *Pa*, until I met people who were perfectly good without any God, and I read books filled with *actual* facts not just full of opinions; books that have data that *actually* describes the universe. Books so precise that they aren't open to petty, wasteful, concocted interpretation that cause people to go to war over absurd and childish differences." He paused, "And, they also have the benefit of being true."

"Ja," Andre responded. "And it is as our *Dominee* says—when you are a heretic, you think the answers that come from men are more important than the words of God. Since you met *that* woman, you have become self centered and arrogant."

Andre had never acknowledged JJ's marriage and would never say Morgan's name—"*that* woman" was all the mention she'd get.

"I think it is more arrogant to imagine a whole universe made only for you, I think that's a lot more arrogant than realizing how insignificant we are in the scheme of the universe." JJ bit back, then stopped himself—it would only perpetuate more dead-end conversation. "I know you oppose this development—the telescope—but it is futile, pointless. It is finished. The contracts are signed and sealed. You can't change that."

"We'll see…" Andre scoffed.

"Pa… please… I'm trying to make you understand that this is bigger than Carnarvon. It's bigger than the church. It's bigger than government…"

"Ja… the Government, now that's another story. They lied to bring this here."

"I know how you feel about them, but this development is beyond even them. What do you think you're going to do? Bomb the telescope dishes?"

"We're not that crude," Andre assured him.

"I just don't understand what is going on in everyone's heads around here. Why are you so heated about a bloody telescope? It's built on the bones of the existing *Kat-7* and *Meerkat* infrastructure… nobody had a problem with those, but now there's suddenly a *groot geraas,* all of you howling about the SKA. It doesn't make any sense, *Pa.*"

"Because you're no longer here and haven't a clue what we're suffering. Before it was isolated to a small area, but this… this thing… it's taking over and it brings outsiders," was all he'd venture.

"Why didn't you complain before? Is it really just the *outsiders* that drive the *Dominee* to all this madness?"

"Now you stop with your insolence," Andre warned. "I don't question the *Dominee* when it is a matter of faith. He is a qualified theologian and if he feels that this matter is important, I support him."

"Well I'd like to know from the *Dominee* then, because this is absurd. Is the church behind him on this? I see nothing about it outside of this little town."

The question posed in that way triggered a question in Andre's mind, but he was in no mood to admit it to his son, and he could hardly come straight out and ask the *Dominee* in so many words.

"And what is it you think you're going to do...? I have a very good idea of what it might be..." It was an outright poker bluff from JJ, fishing to see if his father would reveal more than he was saying.

"Is your sister carrying stories to you again?" Andre didn't bite. He'd remembered at that moment how Sonja had listened in from the scullery at the previous meeting in the kitchen—at the time he'd thought there'd be no harm to her hearing how men can get things done.

"Please leave Sonja out of this. She's got no part in anything."

"You'd be surprised!" Andre disagreed. "She's very influenced by the nonsense these people spread... And now you take her to the hospital. I don't want her to have *anything* to do with that boy from the accident."

"The accident..." JJ repeated. "What an interesting accident he had...." He watched his father intensively, and Andre looked down at the tablecloth.

"Ja... riding without a license."

"Perhaps. But it is strange that he was on that dirt road when he lives nowhere near there."

"That's none of my business," Andre asserted.

"And I heard that there was an accident on the main road into town that day.... The dirt road *somebody* diverted him onto runs past the Vermaak farm."

"What are you saying?" Andre looked up with fire and ice glinting in the blue of his eyes.

"I'm asking you if you know of an accident on the main road into town. Nobody seems to have heard of such a thing..."

"An accident... Is that what that little black bastard told you?"

"You and I... we passed one another on the road, *Pa*, when I was coming into town... we drove right past one another; you in a big hurry."

"*I... WAS... ATTENDING-TO-POLICE-BUSINESS*," his father spat out the words with staccato menace. "Is this now a court of law? Do you accuse me?"

"Accuse you of what?"

"I want to know whose side you sit on," Andre changed tack.

"You are my father... but there are facts and truths."

"And what does that mean? Where do you sit when our whole community and our way of life is threatened? Where do you sit?"

"Our community is threatened...? Really? You're just afraid of a culture clash that you'll lose. In your mind your old ways are threatened and you're taking it out on people who have nothing to do with it."

"Nothing to do with it...?" Andre scoffed. "They are *here* and don't belong here, and they want to change everything. Don't *dare* tell me they have nothing to do with it."

"If you speak to the coloureds or blacks they'll tell you that we don't belong here."

"*Kafferboetie* talk... That's the *shit* you learn in the city! I don't think your sister should go to that communist university."

"Pa... stop. Cultures mix, populations move... that's reality. You can't avoid it by pretending it away. The fall and failing of our people has always been our clinging to fantasies, to the way we *want* things to be instead of the way they *are*. We're the champions of not facing facts."

There was a long silence before JJ continued.

"That young boy over at the hospital. His mother is here to do a job in Carnarvon, and he has a right to come with her. As I understand it, he isn't even going to live up here—he's going to Cape Town—and he has only tried to come into the community and fit in. And then we have clowns like that Neels who attack him in the school corridors and probably had something to do with what landed him in the hospital now."

"And that's what you think, my son?"

It was getting close to the time that the *Dominee* would arrive and Andre wanted JJ out of the house; *Dominee* Gert let his displeasure in the boy's fall from his grace be unambiguously communicated.

"And if you want to talk to me, don't keep fiddling with that machine of yours. Rather go work with it somewhere else." Andre waved his hand at the computer.

"That is what I think, yes. Don't worry, I'm on my way out *Pa*, my feelings about the *Dominee* are mutual; I'm just sending something off and I'm on my way."

As he said it, JJ clicked the 'record' button on the computer's built in video record feature, then stowed the recording window out of sight to the taskbar and reduced the backlit screen illumination to blackness.

"And I think it's not going to end here. I think his mother is not going to let this thing with Neels blow over."

"What does she say?" There was a shimmer of concern in Andre.

"She's said nothing to me but she isn't stupid. The facts as I understand them don't match the stories I've heard. I'm not against you *Pa*, but I can't be against justice and facts either. I don't want to be forced to choose, I just think everyone around here better start thinking things through before they run into walls they didn't even know are there."

Andre remained silent.

"And I also think that you should all re-think whatever it is you're planning to talk about tonight."

Chapter 18

"Pa gets so upset when you come... It's always the same, he's always angry... angry that Morgan took away your faith... angry that you don't *believe* anymore," Sonja emphasized.

JJ sighed and shook his head. "Sorry for the tensions," he responded. He felt no urge to defend against the accusation; Sonja understood that the claim that his wife had taken his faith was nonsense. "I always remind myself to ignore him and pretend... but I can't. I get frustrated with the same story—it's not even a conversation I want to have... but when he starts, I can't seem to stop."

"You drive him nuts when you ask why *believing* something without evidence is a good thing."

"I think it's a fair question, *believing* can't be worth more than *learning* or *knowing*."

Sonja nodded, she'd come to the same conclusion but only talked to JJ about it. "He says you must just have *Faith* in order to know that answer," she ventured.

"Faith...!" JJ looked out of the window into the far distance. "...Faith is pretending to know something you *can't* know."

"He says he can *feel* it in him."

"I don't doubt that... Faith is an emotion; of course he can feel the emotion. Faith is nothing if it isn't a feeling... like love and fear are both emotions. But to gamble your life on emotions is dangerous, Sonja. It's fine to live out your emotions, but you don't navigate by them."

They were almost at the clinic now.

"I'm looking forward to Cape Town," she said.

"Your heart still set on Stellenbosch?"

Stellenbosch was a university town on the outskirts of Cape Town. It taught mainly in Afrikaans, making study the easier option in Sonja's first language, but it had a reputation for being relatively conservative compared with its rival university, UCT—University of Cape Town.

"I'm on the fence… Stellies would be easier, but I'm increasingly leaning toward UCT… Dad said I'm on my own if I follow in your footsteps to UCT… he says it ruined you. I think I only wanted Stellies to please him."

"Don't let him bully you, Sonja. If UCT's your choice, I'll back you. You follow your dreams, you have too much talent and smarts to do any less."

She leant over and kissed his cheek and he hugged her head to his, temple-to-temple. Her big brother; the *"Oops… and then get married too young…"* she'd heard her father call him when the brandy had loosened his tongue; JJ always made her feel safe. She was just the *"Ooops… I didn't think it was still possible,"* from the twilight years her parents' passions.

JJ had parked on the opposite side of the road from the clinic and cut the engine. He put his hand on her knee and looked her in the eye.

"I love this small town. I love our family and my people. I love community here. I love the peace, the tranquility… being in the embrace of it all—everyone's known me since I was a child; all like family…. But going away changes one."

She was such a beautiful girl, JJ thought. He saw her future mapped in her eyes, intelligent and kind as they were. She desperately needed to spread her wings on a bigger stage than Carnarvon.

"Whenever I come back I see the small mindedness, the bigotry, the pettiness. When you're done studying, go travel and don't worry about a thing, I'll take care of it."

"And *Ma*…? *Pa*?"

"You can't worry about them, you need to live your life... you can't live it for them."

"Ma... she's not happy, with..." she left it unsaid.

"I can see that. Do they argue?"

"No... it's worse than that; it's silent—*Pa* rants and *Ma* changes the subject... I've given up arguing with him too."

"No point in arguing with him, not while you're under his roof. Don't go down the path I've gone down, bashing heads with *Pa*. He's going to need us as he ages, as the world around him changes so much that he becomes lonely and depressed."

"I think he is depressed... he blows up over nothing. *Ma* can't take it much more," she predicted.

"I understand..." JJ was speaking tenderly, pools of emotion showing in his eyes. "When *Pa* was a boy everything he knew was under the thumb of his church and he committed himself to that calling. Everything's changed... his world went upside down. His career hit the wall of affirmative action... the blacks he'd been taught are children that God put him in charge of, are suddenly now his boss... no wonder he's confused and angry."

"I know," Sonja agreed.

"I want you to be smarter and kinder than I've been. If you have a choice to be right or be kind, be kind to him; I'll take the bullets of being *right*. If you disagree with him, don't lock horns; you're too much of a lady for that. And I mean that, you're no longer a girl—you're a lady now."

She blushed and mewed a small and bashful *"thanks"* for the compliment.

"When you want to make a point, don't use a statement, rather ask him questions. Pretend there's an issue you're battling with; make a question out of it that forces him to think..."

"That's clever..." she agreed.

"Questions can smuggle conclusions into minds far more efficiently than beating them in can."

"I don't think he'll change... he's getting worse, not better," her hands in her lap fidgeted with the stress of thinking about it. It was much worse at home than she'd trouble her brother with; her father's mind more deranged and volatile.

"He's got too much invested in his beliefs to ever change, in some ways he represents our old culture... we represent the new..."

The truth of JJ's words resonated within her and she couldn't hold his eyes for fear that her tears would fall; tears of tragedy and loss for a glorious past she'd been pickled in but never actually known outside of the reminiscence and legends that still burned in proud hearts.

She'd witnessed her father's sharp decline first-hand; his rising bitterness, his shortening temper, and it terrified her.

She dipped her face, her vision beginning to mist, but JJ raised her chin with his index finger just as a tear broke over the lid.

"Don't be shy of your emotions—let them go… If we're gentle and smart, we can bring our family back together, better and stronger."

She knew it wasn't true.

"Our generation grew into these changes," he was saying, "our challenge is to help our parents cope with a very different world to the one they were taught to expect."

JJ felt spent. He'd long wanted to say these things to his sister and somehow this moment had scripted itself.

He hugged her in the awkwardness of the car's cramped cockpit.

"C'mon," he said cheerily, "We're too serious… I've got a surprise for you."

They got out and crossed the street, approaching the clinic.

Through the double glass doors in the lobby was a stylishly dressed man with dark complexion talking on a mobile phone. He'd been watching their car since it had pulled up.

Seeing their approach he ended his conversation and dropped the mobile into his pocket. With a beaming smile and two gracefully fluid steps he snatched the door open for them.

"Good evening sir," the man said in a shockingly cultured British accent. "You can only be JJ? I'm *Alok*—Dara's dad; easy to remember… like the song… you can call me *Al*."

Al was slight of build with very white teeth and a finely chiseled nose. He had an engaging, almost pretty face; the likeness to Dara was unmistakable.

"I'm so famous that you know me?" JJ's hand swallowed Al's. "This is my sister, Sonja."

"You're hard to mistake… and the car."

"She's a beauty," JJ agreed.

Al could feel the power in the man's hands, but also the gentleness.

"Indeed! I'm rightly jealous…"

Sonja greeted Al, liking him instantly.

"Well… Marsha's running late—that was her on the phone, she'll be here in ten. Dara's resting—we can sit in here."

Al led them into a small lounge with low couches, low lighting and low tables.

"They put coffee and tea out for us to help ourselves."

They helped themselves to beverages and quickly covered the pleasantries of strangers who'd heard about one another, meeting for the first time, then settled into conversation;

"I'm really sorry about your boy," JJ looked earnestly at Al.

"Well… bad things sometimes happen," Al shrugged in the manner of British understatement. "Marsha's still rather upset, but Dara's being quite remarkable… Still in plenty of pain but he's darned tough. I'm quite impressed really."

"Sounds like it could have been a lot worse."

"Quite… No offense please, but this whole palaver is, well a bit… *strange*… uncomfortable, you know… a bit odd to talk about it with you." Al covered his lips in contemplation. "I know your roots here, and your father…"

He let the sentence hang, not indicating if it was a statement or a question.

There was a pause and the men studied one another, Sonja looked on, JJ kept silent, allowing Al to make up his mind without interference.

"You're just like Marsha said… I feel strangely comfortable with you," he sighed, judging that he could talk freely. "To be blunt… it seems your father had a hand in some events…"

Al went on to briefly recap and outline the situation as they saw it; the attack at the school, Dara's suspicion's he'd been stalked, the rumours there had been a contract of sorts on him, Andre's part in sending him into an ambush.

"You must do what you must do... the law must take its course," JJ summarized his own position on the matter just as Marsha came into the lobby and Al called to her, "We're here..."

Since JJ had last seen her, Marsha had caught up on sleep and looked once more radiant.

Greetings and more pleasantries were exchanged all around and Marsha went to see how Dara was doing, then quickly returned, "He's fast asleep."

"How're you holding up?" JJ asked with a warmth she appreciated.

"Better as Dara improves," she said. "Thanks for stopping by."

"Sorry it's been a few days but it's always a whirlwind when I get back here—catching up… I must confess, when I heard Al was in town, I made a gap; I'm quite the fan and very honored." JJ gestured a bow.

"Oh, don't be silly," Al responded—"I'm the one honored. I understand you pretty much financed this facility, and in a very timely manner too, if I might say… You're a genuine philanthropist and I'm always grateful to meet one."

"Well, yes… Of course, I didn't have Dara in mind at the time, but I'm certainly glad the timing worked out."

They briefly discussed Dara's improvements; he was bouncing back rapidly. Both sides avoided the details of probable legal fallout, skimming only close to the subject.

"Well, I do hope he's better before I head back to Cape Town in a few days," JJ was saying. "The hour I had with him in Loxton was intriguing, he's got an incisive mind; I was hoping Sonja might get to know him… she's also heading to Cape Town next year."

"Wonderful…" Al smiled, "…To study?"

"Yes, Applied Mathematics." Sonja volunteered.

"UCT…?"

"Uhmm, yes, UCT… accepted and I… I'm enrolling," she blushed, "…Stellenbosch accepted too."

JJ's face cracked into a smile—she'd been hedging but was smoked out.

"Tough course," Al observed. "UCT's got the name for it, Stellenbosh is right up there too, though."

"UCT's easier," JJ's suggested, speaking as an *alumnus*, "…it's just up the road from my main home and office, a stone's throw from Dara's new school."

Marsha and Al looked at one another.

"Dara's school… It's sort of a bit on ice now," Marsha volunteered. "The… the incident. It's soured us, I must confess. We're going to leave it up to Dara whether he heads back to the UK with Al to do his last year there or not."

"Completely understandable," JJ agreed, "I'm sorry to say, but it really pisses me off that you had this experience. I'm sorry… I don't know what else to say. I apologize again on behalf of my community."

"It sounds like you think it's more than just a random incident?" Marsha prompted.

"Well… it's awkward." JJ shrugged, and his shrug was confirmation enough.

"Indeed," Marsha allowed, "but we can't condemn everything for the decisions of a few."

There was the long silence of strangers trying to navigate through thorny issues; where potential unknown agendas might lurk. Each weighing whether or not to invest of themselves in the pursuit of commonality.

"So… What are your plans with a degree in Applied Mathematics?" Al asked Sonja, aiming to break the awkward impasse.

"Google's recruitment are looking at her," JJ volunteered and she frowned to hush him. "But it's true, sis," he explained. "Google identify the brightest…"

"You're good enough to flip a flag in Mountain View?" Marsha asked, astounded.

"She came first in the Olympiad," JJ confirmed it.

Sonja hung her head in embarrassment.

"Be proud of it," Marsha gently admonished her. "Celebrate talent. The SKA is also funding scholarships…"

"I'd love to but my dad would never allow it," Sonja responded.

"I see…" Marsha was calculating the drift.

"It looks like a real hot potato…" Al grimaced. "Why's the project so unpopular round here when I've seen nothing like that in the news?"

"I can't figure it out either… I think it's just a small group… renegade. I don't think *they* even know why, they're just feeling challenged… my people are like that sometimes." JJ shrugged again.

"I'm glad you're saying that, because it's all made no sense to me…" Marsha was frowning, "I mean, the SKA is a telescope, for God's sake…. the *Meerkat* precursor ran for years without a bleat of opposition. Now there's suddenly friction? It makes no sense."

"My friends in the town say their parents are complaining… house prices are rocketing because of the foreigners," Sonja added.

"Really? That's not very well thought through…" Al frowned. "Rising house prices shouldn't breed discontent? I mean, the opposite can't be true… people wouldn't be happy if their house values *fell*, would they?"

"A few of the farmers are upset by the limits on radio transmissions," Marsha offered, "… and the forced sale of their land to host it."

"Ja… well, you can understand them being upset about the sale of land—but that's how it is with big civil projects… sometimes they build a road and if your property's in the way, they can't go around it. It only impacts relatively few," JJ argued. "The intensity of it… something else is stirring it up."

"Probably just media hype then," Marsha suggested. "If the media hadn't sung about us seeking the origins of the universe or extra-terrestrial signals, nobody here would have given a hoot."

"Could be… but that's still not enough for such passion," JJ observed. "My dad's not a news guy, the *Dominee* isn't one either… none of them would even bother to read a report about this."

"And the main church? The NG parent?" Al asked. "Are they behind it?"

"I'm not really plugged into that world anymore, but I don't get a sense that they are. It seems very localized, which is odd because the church organization is very top-down. They follow prescription from the leaders," JJ explained. "Then again, *Oom* Gert—the local pastor—he's a bit of a loner."

"And this is what I'd hoped we could chat about," Al kept talking as he got up and brought the coffee pot over to do refills. "I'm really interested in the psychology of it, the local peculiarities. I've just come back from the US... a book promotional tour... and it's quite insane how issues that I don't even think are issues, are blown out of proportion there. It seems you have the same here?"

"My wife, Morgan... she's from the Deep South... from Tennessee. After going to California and marrying me to make it worse... she's about as popular with her folks there as I am here. Our Calvinists are pretty much the same blood-stock and certainly similarly strung up," JJ pointed out. "I mean... the Pilgrims that founded the US and my ancestors here... they were all of the same Old Testament, fire-n-brimstone flavor. You know... back then, our ancestors got on a boat and either went West to the Americas or South to here; so there's not much at a deep fundamental level to choose between the resulting cultures in America's bible belt today, or this place."

"Sure," Marsha chipped in, "Strange how they were fleeing religious persecution and immediately set up persecution under their own umbrellas when they arrived."

"I think that's a misnomer," Al suggested, "I get your *'abused becomes the abuser'* psychological play, but I don't think they were so much fleeing persecution as unhappy that the shift of the religion in Europe away from conservative values... they left because European religious drift was too liberal for their tastes— they wanted to maintain staunch ideals."

"That makes a hell of a lot more sense," JJ agreed. "Our guys here, and the lot over there, clearly haven't mellowed at the same rate as Europe. Europe been secular for ages, the colonies, by contrast, are still so uptight."

"Indeed... And the irony is," Marsha chimed in, "that the Americans enshrined freedom *'of'* and by implication freedom *'from'* religion into their constitution. Al's been coaching me..."

They all laughed at the light moment and JJ pressed on;

"I was surprised... I lived in the States for a while, and I saw that they drew a theoretical line between government and religion, yet today Americans are more plagued by religious attempts to force their will into legislation than anywhere else on the planet."

"I call it *free enterprise* religion," Al proposed. "In Europe the Old-World religions are state sponsored. They don't need to campaign to survive. In the States, religion is sold like any commodity, the way toothpaste or breakfast cereal are hard-sold. billboards, TV ads, print... it's a profitable business; round the clock televangelists."

They all agreed, Sonja listened intently.

Soft moans came from up the corridor and Marsha was up and out of the room in a flash.

"Just a sec, I'd better go see," Al followed her.

"UCT hey?" JJ beamed.

"Too presumptuous?" Sonja gnashed her teeth and the tendons in her neck stood out for a second.

"No... Perfect. I wanted it to be your decision."

"Dad's going to freak..."

"He'll get over it,' JJ assured.

"Wow... These people are so different from *Ma* and *Pa*... so relaxed... And with Dara... almost like they don't care."

"People handle situations differently... cultures too. You know the Brits, stiff-upper lip. Dara's on the mend so they're dealing with us and the situation pragmatically... He's Indian, but a classic Brit."

Al came back in.

"Everything all right?"

"He's a bit sore when he wakes, the medication's worn off... takes him a moment to orientate, I guess," Al confirmed. "You want to see him?"

"We'd love to but don't want to impose."

"Perhaps just give them a few minutes. The nurse is attending." Al sat down again.

"Sonja suggested that this maybe isn't the time to engage you in philosophical conversations?"

Al shrugged, "What else are we going to talk about? It's a waiting game with Dara; we can only speculate about his recovery so many times before my head explodes. Chatting with you is a welcome distraction."

"Sure."

"So… what were we on about…?"

"*Free enterprise* religion," Sonja recalled.

"Ah… yes… Good point. It's interesting, you know… I mean, in the UK and Europe, we really don't see much of this sort of thing, this fundamentalism."

"I watch the statistics," JJ agreed. "There's a marked difference between the US, the *underdeveloped* or *developing* economies, and the European sphere of influence. Religiosity is pretty much imploding in Europe."

"Except of course for a big migration in from the Middle East and the hair-trigger sentiments they bring with them…" Al added. "Now, that's going to make things… *veeeeeery interesting*."

"No doubt… In Scandinavia they're so tolerant they're tolerating intolerance," JJ quipped.

"Truly. Often it's foreigners who go there for asylum… Actually, it's rather a pun; asylum seekers turning it into an asylum," Al joked. "But the encouraging thing is that where there's good education and Internet access… like they're getting in this region… we're seeing a vast swing away from religion."

"Why do you think a swing away from religion is a good thing?" Sonja challenged.

"It's a fair question," Al responded. "It does sound rather mean-spirited with us sitting around here griping about people's private beliefs, doesn't it."

"No, that's not what I meant. I'm not disagreeing with you I just want to get your perspective," she spoke with ease, like an adult.

"*Practicing the question-technique?*" JJ smiled at her knowingly and she smiled back in accord.

"Well," Al ventured, "One could go off on tangents and draw lists of atrocities that religion has visited on individuals and populations, motivated *entirely* by hoping to appease the notion of what a particular deity wants done."

"Like slavery, apartheid, witch trials and wars?" Sonja proposed, exercising her new questioning technique.

"Yes," Al agreed. "Of course, all of that. It's all quite true, but if you argue that tack with adherents, the whole debate will quickly collapse into mud slinging. The religious will snap back and claim that all of the fascist and communist despots outlawed religion… and, somehow, in their minds these political murders equal blood on the hands of anyone educated enough to have got past superstition. You follow me?"

Sonja nodded that she did.

"But that's a daft point of view, isn't it? Firstly, anyone who knows history knows that Fascism was a conservative Christian movement. And communism merely removed the notion of a God and church in order to set itself up as the supreme deity, its leaders instituting a cult of personality focused solely on them, with no Jesus or other distraction. It's a tactical move. That's why all the communist despots always got a grip on peasant societies who were already primed for totalitarianism by their historic servitude to orthodox religions…

"Sure… very smart," JJ'd never considered this angle, "…easy pickings for a regime to build their own cult—replace one God or demi-Gods with the *Dear-Leader* leering off of every wall."

"Voltaire said," Sonja added, "…Those who can make you believe absurdities can make you commit atrocities."

"Precisely… yes. And, yes… as you said, Sonja, slavery and Apartheid were undeniably both inspired by the Bible… or interpretations of the Bible."

"You know our history well."

"I'm an anthropologist… it's my job. But if a God authored or oversaw the Bible, I'd expect him…" Al's eyes twinkled with mischief, "…or her... I don't want to be accused of gender prejudice… to have had foresight enough to see the room he'd left for these gross *misinterpretations*… He should either have edited those things out, or intervened when they went off-message in competing bibles and sects. But, honestly… those are not the worst atrocities of religion—and here I mean *any* religion. Because…"

"And prayer…?" Sonja asked over him, carried away with enthusiasm for her new technique of asking questions to move the conversation. "…I wondered—when you heard Dara was so critical, did you pray? Surely you did? It's natural to pray."

"I don't know that it's natural to pray," JJ suggested, sorry Al hadn't finished what he was about to say, but also glad to see his sister flexing her mind.

"Oh… I think it is," Al countered. "Superstition is the result of a very important evolutionary mechanism…"

"An evolutionary mechanism?" JJ frowned, "Really…? You're the psychologist, I'm not going to argue it, just intrigued."

"Sure… I'll explain that in a moment, because you need to grasp what I mean when I say that prayer is a superstitious appeal… a begging for a particular outcome—and prayer and superstition come from a common root."

Sonja was surprised by the answer; "I don't see how superstition and evolution can be related?" she posed.

"Fairly easily… we evolved from prey animals, agreed? Our ancestors a few thousand generations back were pitifully weak out on the African plains."

"Yes…" both listeners agreed.

"Those of our ancestors who were not suspicious of every little rustle in the bush or crack of a twig in the dark, well… they aren't our ancestors, because, *Chomp-chomp*, they entered the food chain and became nutrition for predators."

"All right…"

"So we inherited suspicious genes—nature selected for animals, for *our* ancestors, who had a natural suspicion of anything out of place, any small sound… those genes slipped through the filter and found their way to us, made us naturally suspicious. Agreed?"

"Okay…"

"But then, as a species, our brains sophisticated; just imagine it—huddled in a cave with thunder booming outside… or having to ford a river in flood—our ancestors naturally assumed a benevolent or malevolent intelligence that had *intent* in the thunder or raging waters; that's what a more sophisticated mind does, it projects *intent* into inanimate objects—I still do it; I get cross with a nail that won't bang in straight… that nail is deliberately *trying* to be difficult…"

"Makes sense…"

"Humans love to personify inanimate objects. Through this mechanism, that very-necessary *suspicion* we'd inherited morphed into the *superstition* of projecting intent into everything—and this brings us to prayer, because *projecting intent onto causation* is what it is to beseech the invisible to not harm us, or to smooth our path. That's the connection between our evolutionary-driven suspicion, superstition and prayer—we project intent and we beg for clemency."

"Ahhh…"

"But now you have me very excited, you see; it's my field; just shut me up or nod off for a moment if you're hating this," Al went on.

"No… it's fascinating," Sonja urged.

"Okay… So each river or volcano or forest gets its own deity that in the minds of people who must deal with it has this *intent*. Eventually, in our collective mind and culture, those individual gods took on the characteristics of our own projected characteristics; As a species we had adopted farming and settled into communities—so that little clans all fell under a hierarchy of tribal leaders and eventually under kings. In our projected world, paganism had arrived. Not just a new god for each river, but a single god for all rivers, another ran all oceans, yet another was god of all mountains."

"Why did one God triumph if he isn't real?" Sonja posed.

"That's where it gets very interesting because the monotheistic religious concept, the idea of just one single God, is the next step… it just flows from logic:"

"From logic…?"

"Let's say… there's a volcano in Hawaii… *Pele* is the god… even if *Pele* is the god of *aaaall* volcanoes… doesn't matter to you if you don't live near a volcano, right? You don't fear *Pele*? Do you sacrifice to him…? Pay him any attention? No… he's insignificant to you. But one day someone tells you… 'Listen, mate… there's a single God—he's like the emperor over-ruling all the individual gods, and it doesn't matter if there's no volcano here—he's not just a volcano god… He runs it all… oceans, rivers, lightening, fire, famine, plague…. He's the one you have to watch out for! And... he's made me responsible that you grovel to him..."

"I do the enforcing for him..." JJ had got it, "and, if I don't enforce it, I get punished."

"Precisely! Wherever you go from now on; now that you've been warned; whether you like it or not, you're under His spell and *my* authority as his spokesman."

"Very cushy."

"Sure is... It's masterful; It's not just when you cross 'this' river or any river—whether you're sleeping at night in your own bed or walking with your family... He's watching and *I'm* there to ensure he doesn't get pissed off at me—so... fall in line... oh... and beseech him often—pray a lot—we'll come together and pray in a church so we all see we're all toeing the line'!!"

"Fascinating! So it's not long before people hedge their bets and fall in line with that God—the Almighty one..." a light bulb of realization had gone on in JJ's head; "*Voila*! Monotheism... *Voila*! Representatives of that monotheistic deity: Moses, Jesus or Mohamed... *Voila*! Enmity and wars between those that cling to one or another of the all-powerful versions of the story... I mean—thirty thousand versions of Christianity alone."

"Precisely and so, Sonja... did I pray when I heard Dara's situation was dire? No. I felt no urge, none. I've overcome that urge by understanding what prayer is and where it comes from. Instead, I sincerely *hoped* that the medical facilities and professionals were up to the task, and... thanks JJ for your contribution... they seem to be. But, let me explain something additional that is interesting about prayer... a logical fallacy. Is God—I mean Yahweh—is he *omniscient*? Does he know *everything*—even the future?"

"That's what they advertise," JJ agreed.

"How is *omniscient* different to *omnipotent*? I don't know the English words." Sonja checked.

"*Omnipotent* means He's *all-powerful*, can do anything; *omniscient* means he *knows* everything," Al clarified. "So... God knows everything, even the future... before you pray for something, He knows you're going to pray for it. This means that by the time you pray He's already considered your prayer and factored it into the plan ages ago..."

She was laughing at the ridiculousness of it revealed.

"….Think about it; you're *never* praying for something He's overlooked—He's omniscient, right? You're praying for *something He's already decided against*—not just originally decided, but He's seen you through time, and seen you praying, beseeching Him to change His mind! Once you've realized this, you appreciate that prayer is really a nutty concept, just a control mechanism for that 'Let's gather and watch one another all do it together' I just described. So, no… I never thought of praying… I try very hard to not knowingly do crazy things."

"Yeah… there's that comedian who did the skit on it—Carlin… George Carlin. He said 'If you don't get what you want, you say it's God's-Will… So why don't you just forget praying and go straight to God's-Will if he's always going to do what he wants anyway."

"Carlin had great insights, JJ. Funny guys can have more impact than clever ones."

"Loved his skit on the Ten-Commandments."

"Don't think I've seen it…."

"Oh—look it up *'Carlin, Ten Commandments',*" JJ suggested.

"But you mentioned *Omnipotent*, Sonja?" Al went on.

"Yes."

"Now, you're both smart people—and I'd like you to explain to me how God can be both *omniscient* and *omnipotent*…? The two concepts contradict one another…"

"How?" Sonja looked perplexed.

"Well… If you can see the future you won't make decisions that you will want to change your mind about in the future, understand?—or you'd see that you were going to change your mind… right? So it suggests that if you want to change your mind in the future, you didn't see that coming… hmmmm?...! And the only way to get around that is not to change your mind, which means you're not all powerful—not *omnipotent*. They contradict one another."

Sonja started to laugh.

Just then, Marsha came through to say that Dara was ready for them.

Al assured her they'd be through in a minute and finished his thought as they slowly began to move into the corridor.

"You were going to say what the worst thing is that religion has done?" JJ prompted.

"Ah, yes… The worst atrocity of religion in today's world is that it makes people satisfied with not having answers; it allows one to throw resigned hands in the air as soon as the investigations become a little tricky… to declare that some things are just *'unknowable'*… a *mystery*. To teach that attitude to children is a travesty, a crime."

"Our constitution actually outlaws it," JJ pointed out. "A major court battle is testing this very thing in our schools."

"Your country's an enigma," Al shook his head. "I saw something about the case in the media… some kind of 'God' acronym taking the schools on?"

"*Ja*," JJ nodded, "They're called 'OGOD'… it's a High Court case. Pretty much misunderstood, they're not asking for new laws, they're just insisting that the constitution be applied as it is written."

They moved slowly down the corridor, chatting quietly about the impact of teaching religious dogmas within school syllabi.

"It relieves one of the burden to study, to invest, to explore, to seek, to think or to educate," Al suggested. "Religion makes a virtue out of willful ignorance; I say *willful,* because we live in an age when good and accurate information so painstakingly won is readily available. You can only be fearful and willfully stubborn if you manage to keep avoiding it."

They reached Dara's ward and filed in.

Dara's bruising was wicked and in full flush across his ribs.

JJ noticed how he displayed the injuries in Sonja's direction with almost a hint of pride.

She clucked her sympathies, but JJ could see that she was uncharacteristically bashful, not her usual talkative self… there was something there in the way she looked at him that went beyond pity and JJ felt his culture rising within him; old bigotries die hard and it annoyed him that he felt this irrational protectiveness over her.

In a very short time, Dara was too exhausted to hold more than superficial conversation, so they bid their farewells.

As they went through the foyer to the outer door Marsha put her arm around Sonja and hugged her fast, "I've really enjoyed you coming over. I can see that Dara is quite taken with you, will you please come back?"

"I'd love to," Sonja beamed.

They exchanged phone numbers and departed.

JJ took her out to the best restaurant in town for dinner; it was the only restaurant, the choices of venues were limited.

Chapter 19

It was a little before midnight and JJ was back home from the hospital and dinner with Sonja.

The night was eerily still; the stiff breeze that had earlier in the evening forced the men to meet indoors around the kitchen table had abated.

In order to capture the action through the built-in camera and microphone, JJ had set his laptop where it would have the best view over proceedings. That best position; where the computer was neither conspicuous nor at risk of being cleared away; had been atop the fridge. This meant there was no power supply available and the recording had necessarily run on battery.

JJ retrieved the machine and hit a random key to reactivate the sleeping blank; the screen stayed black, the battery was dead. He put the computer on charge in his old bedroom and went for a shower.

The wind had died and the night was still, so he fished in the laptop bag for an earpiece, plugged it in, and opened the recording he'd set up at the tail-end of his earlier discussion with his father.

It was the better part of an hour of wasted recording before the last of the men had arrived and begun to settle. The sound quality was sub-par and JJ had to strain to hear details. He hoped it would improve once all were taking turns to talk and the microphone auto-balanced to the lower ambient volume.

There was a surprise too—a young stranger sporting a beard and, even at a glimpse, a fanatical glint to his eye had arrived with *Dominee* Gert.

He was introduced as being up from Cape Town. He was evidently the founding member of a new group but the noise of the men settling in and their women coming through from the lounge to fuss and ensure that there were sufficient beverages on hand, had obscured both the man's name, his organization and his business there.

It was another twenty minutes before they settled and began to discuss anything of consequence. By now JJ had heard the newcomer's name was *Andy*.

The *Dominee* had produced a news cutting, "The rubbish that they print, only saying what they want people to hear," he read the headline, "'*Religious Communities Embrace Science*'."

He shook his head and read on, "Poor and generally conservative communities are extremely accepting of cutting edge science projects even though they starkly contradict their beliefs, the Science Minister has said. Major projects like the SALT— Southern African Large Telescope in Sutherland and SKA at Carnarvon in the Northern Cape province are actively now looking for the origins of the universe and earth's place in it."

"Because they won't accept the truth, they invent bullshit and lies," Andre grumbled his monotonous mantra as soon as the *Dominee* took a breath.

"The irony is, these installations are being developed amid deeply conservative communities," Gert read on, rubbing the insults in, "…Yet, despite the fact that the science starkly contradicts their faith, the communities are embracing the investments with open arms."

"Embracing?" Andre spoke for them all as his frustration boiled over, "They lie and lie, then lie again," emphasizing each 'lie' with the hammer of his fist on the table. "Are city people so stupid… so gullible to believe this report? Do they think we're all idiots out here in the countryside? That we have a Faith that is so unimportant to us, yet we can be bought to *not* believe it and stand up for it, to *not* defend it? My own son…" He didn't finish his sentence, just looked to the other men in askance and tragedy.

Watching the monitor, JJ felt a lump in his throat. He wanted peace with his father and all these men that he'd known a lifetime but he was unable to get over this hurdle with them.

"Ja, Andre," Jan de Villiers the former army Kommandant agreed, "All the youngsters are going the same way."

"Not all," Gert the *Dominee* reminded them, not wanting this negativity with a stranger present, "There is a resurgence in belief. This is what I'm waiting for… hoping for. Andy will tell you… People are starting to wake up."

"But they are buying our youth, Gert," Andre lamented; under the stress of it, uncharacteristically using the *Dominee*'s name in public. "Buying them with free computers and Internet connections so the children can be fed more lies. Everywhere you hear about the 'economic benefits', and these *mamparras*, these coloured and black fools, they think that they're all suddenly now going to inherit houses and cars from nothing."

"But our Lord Jesus was tempted by Satan in the desert too, my friends," the *Dominee* pointed out, needing to calm Andre. "It is the temptation that makes our faith stronger. We have a strong youth group now. Even with Neels now going away, I have made Gerhard Stander the youth leader and he is very charismatic."

"Neels is leaving?" Jan asked with some surprise.

"He's off on a scholarship program to Kentucky in the USA for 3 months," the *Dominee* disclosed.

JJ stopped the replay and backed the recording up to ensure he hadn't mis-heard it; "*Neels is leaving*"?

He listened to it twice.

"Quite sudden?" Jan observed.

"The opportunity just came from new friends of our church, an Evangelist group in America—*Genesis Is The Answer,* they're called," Gert confirmed.

"I've heard of this group," Dr. Louw, the school Principal spoke for the first time, "The *Genesis Answers* group has that *Genesis Museum*?"

"*Genesis Museum*?" Jan asked.

"Yes… very well funded. Led by an Australian, Kenneth Bacon. They raised nearly thirty million dollars to build a *Genesis Museum*. It displays all the science in a Biblical context… the *right* science." Gert added, emphasizing 'right'.

"An actual museum? A building?"

"Ja… more than a building, Jan. Massive… it's over acres. Millions of visitors already." *Dominee* explained, evidently quite taken with it. And JJ wondered about that.

Dominee Gert was not usually an enthusiastic man about anything that lay outside the firm tramlines of his own childhood faith.

"I've been communicating with Bacon and his group for a while and also with their benefactor," he went on. "His people contacted me through Andy, but I wanted to first know what they were about, so I dealt with them privately till now, to see if they were *properly* of the Faith. They're Evangelists, not our own denomination but as Andy will tell you, in these times when we're under siege, we must not let our differences divide us."

"Led by an Australian, you say? With some of this telescope in Australia, perhaps he will want to collaborate?"

"That's how I'm thinking too. They're going to help with funds for our fight. A delegation's coming to see us soon."

There was a general hubbub of approval and excitement among the men.

JJ paused the recording again to let it sink in. As Gert spoke it was all falling into place, the connections immediately obvious. He caught himself pondering it aloud, "South Africa's Bible Belt cozying up to their American counterparts… all the crazies egging one another along? Shit!"

This was not good news, it would push the whole issue into a new direction and league; it set JJ's mind to racing. These strange bedfellows falling into league was a natural progression, he realized. He knew all too well how, for decades in the US, extreme sects of Evangelist Christians had been agitating in politics, medicine and education to oppose progress, to drive biblical agendas and enshrine biblical governance in all-important matters of regulation.

As a boy JJ had seen the tail end of quasi-theocracy driving South African politics and its biblically inspired *Apartheid;* he looked on it with extreme distaste.

Historically these groups had waged war against Evolutionary Biology for the challenge that its discoveries posed to biblical creationism. The more he thought about it, the more he realized that the SKA and its objective; to uncover the origins and evolution of the universe; trampled the same biblical sentiments.

His mind needed a break, to consider what he had reviewed so he got up to make tea.

The kettle was just beginning an escalating hiss when his father appeared in the doorway. "Hello *Pa*, did I wake you?"

"No, I couldn't sleep."

"Tea?"

"It'll make it worse."

"Ma?"

"She never has problems sleeping. Women… you know, nothing important on their minds."

JJ hated it when his father spoke glibly like that about females, but it was cultural. The older men-folk cherished their women but generally thought of them as children unburdened by 'big' issues; white women were senior children, several rungs above the other races who the old culture thought of and treated as young children. Fortunately, he thought, things were changing rapidly in the new generation.

It wasn't worth challenging though, as he sometimes did, not at this late hour.

"How was your evening?" His father asked.

"Had a *lekker braai"* JJ responded casually.

"Good—Sonja home?"

"Safely in bed, yes."

A *braai* was the traditional way to spend a Saturday evening grilling meat over coals—and JJ had gone on from dinner to the tail end of a *braai* on one of the farms of old friends.

He'd faced too much red meat from his mother's kitchen for the entire week already and needed something less substantial for a change, so he'd delayed his arrival at the *braai* to ensure the eating would be over.

The womenfolk at the *braai* would have insisted on dishing for him and would never allow a man to choose only salad.

Andre had been phoned during the evening by three different parties living in the town who reported his son's car outside the clinic, "*…and now at De Meerkat Pizzeria*"; casual reports of JJ's movements streaming in, woven into other mundane village chatter.

The Ferrari had been at the Pizzeria for an hour and then departed; but JJ had only arrived at the braai at ten-thirty—a ninety-minute gap remained in Andre's mind unaccounted for; nobody in the town volunteering JJ's whereabouts during that period, and it plagued his police brain that his son was not volunteering the details, even after some prompting.

"I'm sorry we have tensions, *Pa*," as all JJ would say.

He knew his father's every expression so intricately that he'd guessed already what information his father had about his movements.

His was the only car of its type the village had ever seen, and he knew full well that his minor celebrity status in the village meant his movements would hardly go unnoticed or unreported. But he was sick of the pettiness of logging and defending his every movement. The time had come to let the tensions exist if they must exist.

"I just want to visit and relax and bring everyone presents, *Pa*," was all he'd offer. "I have enough stress in the city. I could easily rent the best room in town but the best room in town is here with you and *Ma* and Sonja. This is where my heart is—it's better than any plush hotel or mansion."

Andre still looked peeved.

"I don't want you and I to have trouble," JJ offered to neutralize the suspicion still written on his pa's face.

"Ja… we like you here too, my boy," there was a momentary gentleness to the big craggy man; he so rarely let gentleness or emotion breach through his tough façade.

Then almost as if catching himself Andre hedged against showing any more weakness; "…These are stressful times… not stress we're making, stress pushed on us from outside by the *rooineks* and their Communist government. We don't want this stress."

"It's too late to get into it again, *Pa*. I just wanted to say I'm sorry for earlier. I want you to know that I'm not the enemy… I understand everything you feel, I just want to give you a perspective… I know is not easy."

JJ could feel his father's mood switching into a battle mode, the big battered shield rising before him, covering the slipup of momentary emotions that had exposed his soft underbelly.

The more vulnerable Andre felt, the more he overcompensated with an offensive;

"There's another troublemaker in town…" Andre prodded, "…that little black fucker's father."

"How to react and play this?" JJ's mind was suddenly bolting in every direction, as if a bucket of ice water had been thrown over sleeping cats.

He knew his father was studying him for his reaction, so he didn't react. He knew it was a test; his father would know through the rumour machine that Al had been at the clinic this evening, and that his own presence at the clinic had most likely boomeranged straight back to his *Pa* the instant he'd cut the engine outside it. It was a trap that JJ couldn't help walking into, "He's a really nice man, *Pa*. Educated and very polite."

Andre snorted and shook his head denying the possibility, a seep of distrust for JJ and his secrets now unmasked in his eyes.

"Pa… at this hour…? Really… I don't want to go there. I met with the man because I admire his work, and because it's an honor, and…"

"And you take your sister there again, to those type of people after I asked you not to? Expose her to such rubbish?" The old man was quickly becoming volatile, his elephantine memory delivering them right back where they'd laid off earlier in the evening.

"Pa..."

"And you don't bother to mention it? You don't volunteer it? I get from you *The braai was lekker*? But where you *actually* ate dinner and went *before* the braai... that..." he left it there, frustrated with himself for not holding back as he'd promised himself he would.

"You're going to wake *Ma* and Sonja. Please let's just go to bed."

"Wake *Ma*... wake *Ma*...? It's better to tell your father to shut up than to be honest and straightforward like you were taught before the city."

JJ felt anger beginning to grip within. The frustrations of small-town living crystallizing—everyone knowing everyone's every move.

"I'm not going to argue with you *Pa*, not at this hour. If you prefer I'll go home tomorrow, but I'm going to bed now."

Andre glared after his son but did not follow down the corridor. JJ did not look back.

JJ sat on the edge of his bed, his hands shaking and vision jumping with each pounding heartbeat.

He began to breathe, deliberately, drawing breath in through his nose, his hands raising an imaginary weighty load up to his chest, his fingers held rigid... *hold*... and released the breath with a sigh, the imaginary weight gone, his hands falling away in a controlled push back to the floor. Then another breath and another.

A recent adherent to yoga, he took a firm grip on his galloping emotions and began the mantra that he had practiced; *"Bhaja Man Mere Hari Ka Nam, Hari Ka Nam Sat Nam."*

As he repeated it, the hypnotic nasal rhythm of it took him to the palm dappled shade of his oceanfront bungalow's wooden deck. Now he could hear the gull calls and the rush and wash of the waves, the burble of laughter meshed with the clap of tennis balls meeting wooden bats; the wafting subtle whiff of sun cream and salty air drifting up from the throng of towels and sun umbrellas arranged close below his wall; *"Bhaja Man Mere Hari Ka Nam, Hari Ka Nam Sat Nam"*, he repeated, *"*"Bhaja Man Mere Hari Ka Nam…"*

The irony dawned on him and he began to smile, the adrenaline gone, calm restored: "Oh my mind, meditate on God's Name, God's Name is Sat Nam—Truth," the English translation of the mantra that he parroted in the Gurumukhi language of Punjab.

Punjab was, he realized, ironically a relic of Al's and Dara's own bloodline; the 'black devils' whose arrival into the little world of this community had caused such heated friction. That he should have spontaneously retreated to this foreign technique under his father's roof, after his father's outburst… *"Serendipity!"* JJ said it aloud to himself, a chance occurrence, indeed.

"God's name is truth," he said it to his father as if his father were in the room with him.

It conjured a God that JJ no longer took to be literally true and certainly not the God, the Jehovah, the Yahweh of his father and his own youth. The mantra, he understood, was nothing but a tool to trigger the psychological Pavlovian conditioning to whisk his mind to a healthier place for the moment.

His father would be outraged, JJ contemplated; that his son was violating the second commandment; *"no strange Gods before me,"* under his very roof.

It was too late now to review the recording of his father's cabal meeting any longer, so he closed the lid on his laptop, swung his feet onto the bed, and snapped off the light.

In the dark he lay and contemplated it, "…*'no strange Gods before me'*… What a strange echo," he thought. "From a time truly not long ago when this was my childhood bedroom and that sanction seemed so deadly serious and important."

Twenty years ago, JJ was the youth leader in the church under *Dominee* Gert. This environment was his home.

"I think, *Pa*, it's time I go to my real home," he told himself out aloud.

Chapter 20

The next morning JJ's mother, Johanna, was in the kitchen. He kissed her good morning then went to take a shower.

When JJ returned he found her in his bedroom, the bed made the travel bag he'd packed and left on the floor now standing accusingly on the foot of the bed.

"You're leaving so soon?" His mother's eyes were misty and near tears—it was always like this when he left, Johanna always wanted the family together.

"It's been almost a week, *Ma*. I have business to attend to and Morgan's flying to the States for Thanksgiving…"

"You said you could do most of it with your phone and computer. You said she didn't mind?"

"Yes, but only for so long. There are overdue meetings and site inspections… I need to spend some time with her because it's going to be an awkward trip for her. I promise I'll be back soon, as soon as she's gone."

"It's because of your father, isn't it…?" She went straight to the truth of the matter; they both knew she'd named the real reason.

He could never lie to her when she looked at him like this.

"I want peace with him, *Ma*, but when we're in the same house it creates friction… he won't even say Morgan's name. It's been years and it's time to get over it. This creates so much unnecessary friction for Sonja too. *Pa* thinks I'm influencing her."

"It is a worry," his mother was frank. "But I believe she has her own mind… your father does think she's completely under your spell."

"We think so much alike because we're the same generation—almost the same generation." He paused, "We have different influences now to what you lived through… and that is what changes us."

Johanna was going to stop him to point out that every generation has different influences to their parents, but JJ forestalled her before she could.

"What's different now, *Ma*, is the communication. When you and *Pa* grew up there were rigid structures; you mixed with the town, you seldom met strangers. The coloureds and blacks stuck to themselves. Maybe you read a newspaper or some popular books—that's it. But Sonja sits at school next to all races, she has access over the Internet to the whole world—not just spoon-fed media but social media where she interacts two-way… not only consuming what she reads but interacting with others who have very different ideas. Her friends in social media are from all over… from the Middle East, America… from Europe. They're friends because they have the same interests and intellect, not because they're neighbours. So it's completely different for her than it was for you… even different than it was for me just ten, twenty years ago; it's all moving and changing so fast."

Johanna was nodding—she couldn't argue it.

"She's such a smart girl, *Ma*. Maybe a lot smarter than you or *Pa* or anyone in this town realizes. She has a big future…"

"You're telling me she's also going to leave?" His mother knew it, but saying it choked her.

"There is nothing for her here after she's done with university. She's not the kind of girl who's going to finish a degree and then come live in a small town," JJ put it simply. "But with the developments that are coming there's a good chance she might be able to come home…. With what they're building here… with the…."

"With that cursed machine?" She cut him short.

"You call it a 'cursed machine' and I know you mean cursed literally, *Ma*. And I cannot blame you. I have not forgotten all I learned growing up under the *Dominee*. If you take all that nonsense to be literally true, then, yes… it can seem like it's cursed."

"It is! Look what it's doing to our family" Johanna said emphatically.

"Ma... We can't have this conversation when your frame of reference remains rigid and dogmatic... when you rely on just one source... on the *Dominee* for your information."

Johanna's face was a mask; fierce and unblinking, her son attacking her very foundation.

JJ saw it and softened his approach;

"Please, ma... please know that I have studied psychology and I fully understand the conflicts and fears you are feeling. Your certainty that you are right, that our traditional culture is always right... That is hard to shift inside of yourself... I understand that. You are the matriarch, the mother figure... you cannot afford to be vague in the things you hold dear if you are to be a rock to us all. I can only say to you that while on the one hand I respect that, the world beyond this town is moving fast and you cannot avoid that change coming here too. I want to act as the conduit to help you and *Pa* to adjust through this difficult time... I am not challenging or insulting you, your culture or your position as my mother. I am just trying to be a good son and give you a different perspective."

She was listening to him intently trying desperately to subdue the voices inside that screamed at him not to be a foolish young man and to listen to her, the elder.

It was the same rebuke every elder in every generation in every culture through all history of time has felt bursting from within. But Johanna was an intelligent woman and she had a vast respect for her son's character and integrity.

She used this respect now to remain silent and at least try to meet him on the even ground of reason where her deep emotions were held in check.

"This machine you call *cursed*—the SKA—it is a telescope... It's nothing more than that. I think the *Dominee* is making a big *geraas*... such a big noise about nothing. I really don't know what has got into him."

'*Dominee*' was a trigger word; nobody could criticize a *Dominee* without his adherents leaping to his defense, but before she could react JJ held and squeezed her hand warmly to quell her.

"… that is all the SKA is—a telescope. It will only read the facts about the universe. And whatever those facts and data say is the way things really are. If there is a God who put those facts and data into the universe and we are made in His image, then our curiosity and ability is all to His Glory. Our discoveries then belong to Him."

He was deliberately using language that would win her over. She was a much more reasonable person than any of the men— "Come to think of it," he thought, "most of our women are in the Afrikaner culture are more reasonable… probably because they're excluded from the hierarchy and so less indoctrinated."

"I know you have accepted for a lifetime that the universe and mankind came into existence one way," JJ was talking earnestly, careful in his choice of words, purposefully avoiding saying anything more that was vaguely negative referring to trigger words like '*Bible*' or '*Faith*', "…but there are countless ways to interpret stories; to take them literally or dodge ridiculous claims by calling them figurative metaphors. But the data is not vague—it is precise. What can be wrong with precision?"

"You are too clever for me," his mother said.

She didn't want to argue either—not if he was leaving now, but his words had reached her as they always did and she would think them through.

She dared betray none of it even to herself, but over the years he'd been winning her over with his persuasive arguments.

"You're calling the project 'cursed', yet it has the potential to bring Sonja home. It will give her an opportunity to come home if that's the path she chooses…" he paused, looking to clinch it by hitting his mother in the sweet spot; "If I could find opportunity here and through it, I'd come home too."

His mother looked down and swallowed. There was nothing she wanted more.

"And…" he went on, "…it's becoming possible… the new airport, the fiber-optic communications. Calling it 'cursed' ignores these facts." He paused, "And *Ma*, it's just the pursuit of knowledge… I must say it again… what is 'wrong' or 'cursed' in looking for knowledge?"

Just then they both heard the police van pull into the driveway—*Pa* was home for coffee.

Neither of them wanted to be having this conversation when Andre came through the door.

Johanna went out to put a pot on the brew and JJ threw some traveling clothes on, hefted his bag and came out to the kitchen.

The atmosphere in the kitchen was brittle; *Pa* sat at the kitchen table and eyed JJ.

"Morning *Pa*," he greeted his father.

"Were you not going to say goodbye?" His father gestured at the packed travel bags.

"Pa…?"

His father shook his head slowly as he looked down at those hands that had once held this boy to his breast, spread on the table, dwarfing a steaming coffee mug between them.

"You are my *Pa*. Why would I leave without saying goodbye?" The silence returned no answer. "This is so unnecessary, *Pa*. I have no argument with you. We have so much in common… this is nothing for us to trouble over."

"Ja…" Andre grunted in non-committal disappointment, his mind comprehending nothing of what was being said; only the pain of reaching an impasse and decision walling up his emotions.

"Can we not just be a father and a son?" JJ asked, "And leave all this outside influence outside?"

The awkward silence crackled. Slowly, like a gunfighter of the old West his father lifted his head and a lightening storm of danger threatened in his expression. His heavy-set brows met in the middle, dragged together by the frown of a weighty decision already made, "I wish for my only son to leave my house and not return."

His voice was a low rumble, only just audible; it sounded like the angry God of old talking through him.

Johanna walked out the back door into the garden and the fly screen crashed closed behind her.

"As *Pa* wishes," JJ stood and picked up his bag in his left hand, offering his right to his father.

Andre looked at the hand long and hard then slowly he raised his gaze from JJ's hand to look his son ferociously in the eye, his own hands never moving from the table "Will my son give me my wish?" he asked throatily.

JJ's jaw bit and clenched, his face shot through with anguish. He blew a shaft of heartbreak out through his nose, a slow heavy tragic expiration of air, "I love you *Pa*," he said, turned and went out through the door, closing the screen so that it did not crash and exaggerate the tensions.

He found his mother down by the weeping willow near the bottom of the garden, her body heaved and choked. She could barely breathe and could not talk.

JJ held her to his chest and she was immobile, stiff as a pillar of salt, shivering with tension. She sobbed softly until the front of his shirt was wet and he held her tighter.

A few minutes later the screen crashed again but Johanna kept her head buried against her son. His own tears were running, one at a time down his cheeks, soaking into his mother's hair.

There was a light crunch of gravel approaching but neither of them looked around, and suddenly arms wrapped around them both, small delicate arms that held with a furious strength. Johanna went limp at the touch and JJ braced to hold her up as her legs began to buckle.

The three bodies stood in mutual embrace under the coolness of the willow, knotted together as one.

A short time passed.

"Sonja...!" came Andre's voice from within the house, it sounded mortally wounded. Shock shot through JJ's body, he'd never heard his father's voice sound like that and he braced for the worst, not beginning to fathom what that *worst* may be.

Always-obedient, Sonja was gone—off to hear her father's whim—a moment later the fly screen crashed. There were no more sounds but the light rapid-fire tugs of breath from his mother, the sobs giving way to the wounded agonies of accepting fate.

"I must go, *Ma*," JJ said softly, "but I'll be back and I'll fly you down to Cape Town for a holiday."

He felt her nod, just felt it. He would return, he would come fetch her; he never lied, but something unexpected and precious had died here today.

She felt aged from within, to JJ she felt desperately frail.

For an age they stood together, JJ feeling the eyes from the house on them. Slowly he coaxed her in an edging waltzing embrace onward toward the garden gate that would take them both off his father's property as requested and around the public sidewalk to the driveway where his car stood.

When they reached the gate they heard the police van's engine turn. The reverse gear sang its signature yodel and JJ could see the flicker of the van over his mother's head through the bougainvillea hedge as it backed out and halted in the street.

The van pulled away changing up through the gears—and his father was gone.

In the far distance, they heard the fly screen crash again and moments later Sonja was with them.

"Pa says goodbye," she said. "He asked me to tell you how sorry he is. Ma… he said we must get ready for church now. He'll be back to fetch us."

JJ felt his mother's head move in denial—shaking with tiny movements of resolve, side to side. It was easy to misinterpret but her whisper to herself confirmed her intent *"Nooit weer"*—she'd never again attend the church.

Chapter 21

Andre arrived at the church only just in time for the 10am Sunday service.

Thankfully, he thought, most people had already filed in and were seated. It was the first time in living memory he was there alone—without the family he was so proud of—his beautiful wife and breathtaking daughter.

That the congregation knew JJ was in town and hadn't attended last week and again today was more embarrassment than he could bear—but now his wife and daughter had refused too.

Sonja had not outrightly refused but her mother had done so on her behalf, insisting that she needed the girl there to take care of her, sick as she had suddenly been overcome. Lately, Sonja had been seeking excuses not to attend but even laying down the law this morning to her had not won her submission.

Getting that girl to submit to many things these days was harder and harder, he pondered. "In a time not long ago a good hiding on her backside would do it," he considered. Though, he had to concede to himself, at seventeen she was a little old for that; besides Johanna forbade it; "It's not the done thing anymore, Andre."

"Just another *blerry* problem the *rooineks* and their Communist government have forced on us," these frustrations were without end.

The last of the worshippers were funneling into the building as he approached. Mercifully they only had a chance to nod greetings and had no time to quiz him as to why he was attending all alone; but the question in their eyes was a nagging accusation; the questions were there and would come when tea was served.

When the service began, he heard little of it but a drone, his head so full of voices as it was; of arguments with his wife, stubborn as she was; with his son, rebellious as he was; and, with his daughter, impressionable as she was.

He fought each of them a dozen times and then another dozen—he heard every argument they put to him and combated them.

Amid his internal dialogue, he'd see one or another of the parishioners chance a glimpse in his direction, trying to make it look as if they were casually scanning for friends; but he was a policeman with an eye for motive, they'd instantly truncate their casual scan as soon as they saw him eyeing them back.

Throughout the service his humiliation continued to grow as whispers went all around the flock behind hands; the gossip telephone was in perfect working order this morning.

As *Diaken* he'd normally take his seat near the front and at the right hand of his *Dominee*, but with his police uniform donned this morning he was on duty and this gave him the excuse he desperately needed to sit at the back and beat a hasty retreat just before adjournment.

His gaze ran over the crowd, out of habit doing a roll call of familiar heads and profiles.

Many of the pews stood open these days, more open spaces than people. Sitting at the back of the church today as he hadn't done in years, this truth was plain to see; gaping holes of empty benches between the small family and social groups that sat together in clumps.

There was a time he recalled when one had to be inside and seated early to ensure a seat, when the throng stood all out the door and hymns raised the roof. Today for him, the choir was more a collection of individual voices than its usual solid chorus of overwhelming and enveloping beauty.

And, he admitted to himself sourly, that kind of full house was even before they'd let just *anyone* in—blacks and coloureds had their own churches back then, and the laws of that time aside, non-whites would never have dared to come interfere with the time-honored patriotic mood of the whites celebrating their God-given land as they now did.

But now even though this was *the* major church in town, attendance was so pitiful that the darker people threatened to outnumber the whites.

What to do about this dreadful situation?

This new voice now joined the other arguments in his head, also conspiring to keep his mind out of what the *Dominee* was roaring about; his accusing finger jabbing down from the high pulpit, here and there, into the congregation at anyone known to be involved in nefarious deeds.

Then, a little relief and hope for a better future as he picked out Neels Vermaak's block-cut hairstyle in the second from front row, his father's head alongside his son's, the pair cutting an identical silhouette and Andre felt the pang of this morning's loss all over again.

"A good boy," Andre mulled to thwart the cacophony of miseries of his morning. "Much better to send him on the American holiday and let this nonsense with that *prrrrretty* boy blow over."

He heard the *Dominee* talking about *"die Hemel"*—the heavens and that the new foe, the SKA, trying to pry them. Talking about the help that God would soon send to them from America; the *Genesis Answers* organization, his new soldier in arms, Kenneth Bacon; *The Revelations Institute* and delegation from the *Templar Foundation* too; just the need-to-know information given to the community that he'd said he would share at last night's meeting.

Just as Andre finally disciplined his concentration to the important task of participating in the prayer, the heavy grumble of the Ferrari went slowly past outside and his mind chased it down the road like a dog off its leash.

With the sound's departure, his heart sank for the son he had banished and it boiled with anger at the boy's stupidity in forcing his hand.

He tried to bring his thoughts back inside to help raise the rafters with the beautiful hymn being sung, but his mind would not obey—it was a bloodhound out on the trail trying to sniff where that car had come from and where it was going to—passing the church was not the route back to Cape Town and his son had clearly not departed directly for Cape Town as he should have an hour earlier.

JJ had been elsewhere… making trouble—of that Andre was certain.

Chapter 22

JJ had left the desperate embrace of his mother and sister locked together in the old family driveway. He hadn't looked back as he let the engine burble away at an idle down the street without allowing it its head.

In the cockpit the phone call he'd made rang through the speakers and Marsha answered.
"Could I stop by? It's quite urgent," he'd said.
The good news was that Dara was discharged and Al and Marsha would pick him up on their way home after some shopping in the town.
"We could have a quick coffee if you suggest somewhere," she'd offered.
They'd met at the only option—where he'd had dinner with his sister the night before; *Meerkat Restaurant*.

Meerkat was surprisingly stylish as small-town establishments go. Its décor and menu already anticipating the expected growth of a more discerning market of inbound professionals.
JJ had been a few minutes early and chatted mild pleasantries with the proprietor until they'd arrived.

Over coffee he'd briefly recounted to them the information he'd gleaned from his secret recording the night before.
"Jesus… They're getting *that* lot involved now? We should probably have seen this coming," Al had said, referring to the organizations that were planning a delegation out to discuss a resistance movement with their church counterparts. "They picketed some of my book and speaking engagements last

month, with their *'Burn in Hell'* placards. I do have to tell you, there's just no reasoning with them."

"It's the old story," JJ had agreed, "if you could reason with fanatics, there would be no fanatics."

"Question is, what to do?" Marsha posed.

"I don't think there's much to do until they make the first move. I get a sense that your locals don't grasp the magnitude, that it runs to billions of dollars and international influence," Al suggested. "But the Americans will and they'll throw plenty of cash at a fight too."

"I woke early and skimmed ahead in my video recording, sampling; and something is up with a land claim they're planning," JJ had confided, "but I haven't had a chance to really detail it—I'll do that in Cape Town. I've got to get back as things there are unraveling… Unfortunately things here unraveled completely this morning with my family too."

"Sorry to hear that," Marsha said and JJ briefly outlined it before Marsha asked, "Land claim?"

"They've got some notion the Bushmen can get a bid in and tie this all up in red tape."

"Sounds ominous," Al had said.

"Could be…"

After the meeting, JJ wanted one last chat with somebody. He could have avoided the road past the church but burned to see if the police van was outside, which meant *Pa* was inside.

His car slid down the road, it's engine grumbling moodily to itself at the indignity of walking when it could run.

The van was there—but ma's car was not. If she'd gone to church on a day *Pa* had duty, they'd have come separately, of that he was certain.

The issue gnawed at him and several times he resisted the urge to turn back for home to check in on her. He did not want to violate his father's wishes, but he also did not want to re-inflame her agonies—or his own.

He knew that below the exterior of her gentle spirit lay a rod of iron—that she would right herself and immerse quickly into the mundane of being a policeman's wife in a small town full of minor intrigues of major importance.

He'd call Sonja later and catch up on news from the home front.

When the asphalt ended the gravel began and JJ nursed the thoroughbred over its well-graded surface at a crawl. *Oom* Willem Bauer sure ran a tight operation JJ marveled, his roads always the best in the district, his storage sheds, livestock pens and staff quarters betraying his 2nd generation German roots, down from Namibia.

On the fork leading to the laborer's housing the road suddenly degraded; the roots of the Australian blue gums making the surface severely uneven, so JJ halted in favor of caution.

Etiquette held that he should first take the main route to the farmhouse before visiting the farm laborers—to give greetings and at least hint at what business took him to see staff. But it being church time, the entire Bauer family would be absent till noon or beyond, and he reckoned if ever quizzed he could claim he'd undertaken the ritual but nobody was home to witness it.

He parked away from the shade of the trees, preferring the superheating of the sun to bird droppings that might corrode his precious darling's paintwork; it would be hours before he could wash it clean.

The walk from the car was a pleasant three hundred meters in the shade of the trees, and a small delegation who had heard the unaccustomed rumble of the performance engine edging toward them had already gathered, their ears and instincts for changes in their environment tuned at uncanny levels of sensitivity. Some of the kids came in a racing gaggle heading directly toward him—several of them steering old bald car tires with planks of wood.

"Hello *Baas JJ!*" They exclaimed in excited unison when they recognized him, long before his dulled city eyes could pick them out as recognizable individuals.

"Hello *kinders...*" he replied, and he could see that as the road curved, their attentions were already past him and on his car in the distance behind him. This strange beast of a vehicle needed their expert attentions and they barely checked stride as they flew past and onward.

"...kyk, maar moenie aan die kar vat nie... hou daai tire ver van die kar af!"

Looking, but not touching was never going to happen and JJ didn't mind; but he was genuinely concerned about the tire scraping the car.

"Jaaaaa baas!" They sang in unison over their shoulders as they tore off bare-footed, galloping down the thorn-laden track.

Most of the girls not interested in the car had whirled early and were running with hitched-up dresses howling like town-criers back in the direction they'd come, heralding to their elders—*"Dis Baas JJ! Baas JJ."*

JJ arrived to an almost celebrity enthusiasm from the small group. Although it was still pre-noon several of the adults were already well inebriated and stumbled and tottered about, trying to fix a focus on JJ so that they could touch him—the sober ones scolding them away.

They all liked JJ—he'd grown up between the farms and most of the older generation knew him very well from when he was a rough and tough farm-boy with a good heart. Even then, as a boy, he'd had the uncompromising Calvinist ethos on the sports field and as a taskmaster; when their *Baas Bauer* had hired him to help oversee lambing season.

Oom Karel lay where he'd always be found if he had time off, under his favorite tree—an ancient battered FM radio producing tinny treble-rich renditions of tunes popular six or more decades earlier.

On seeing JJ he made to get up.

"Sit.... Sit maar Oom," JJ gestured for him to stay put.

The old man gave him a *haasbek* grin—a single last tooth visible—his face disappeared into folds of delight, "Jaaaa my boy," he said in Afrikaans. "I've been waiting for you."

The reference to *waiting* caught JJ a little by surprise, "It's kind of you to say so, *Oom*."

JJ made to sit down cross-legged in the dirt but Karel forestalled him and yelled for his someone to bring a blanket. It was hurriedly folded for comfort and laid down with humble apologies for its threadbare state. JJ knew it would be the best in the house.

Some of the youngsters milled close by trying to remain inconspicuous yet within earshot to soak up whatever portentous news might promote their standing in the community if they heard it first-hand from this visiting luminary.

There was some small talk about the ongoing drought and distressed state of the farm and its livestock, and then JJ smoothly moved into the matter he'd come for—the snippets he'd gleaned from the video recording of the secret meeting in his father's kitchen the night before.

"Ja, my boy. I know about this thing coming to us," the *Oom* was just cagey enough for JJ to pick up that there was more afoot than what he'd get in one meeting. "My boy—my grandson Dawie, he tells me what they tell him at his school."

'*Dawie…?*' JJ knew that name and then it hit him—the boy's name had come up in discussions with both Dara on that first day and then through Marsha subsequently. By all accounts he was a bright boy. This connection was quite fortuitous.

"Is Dawie about?" he asked the *Oom*, "I'd like very much to meet him."

Karel sent a runner to go fetch the boy who was off playing with a slingshot. Such an important errand caused some squabble among the boys, each wanting the honor—two took off racing one another out into the heat.

"I'm glad the kids are learning about this new development," JJ was saying. "It is going to bring a lot of good here."

Karel frowned, weighing this sudden turn of events.

"These *ears* are going to bring *good?*" He asked of JJ in a testing manner.

"Yes," JJ volunteered, "…more work, more money to the town can only be good, no?"

The *Oom* began to worry at his chin with his nails, thinking… scheming what this meant.

"*En Baas,*" he inclined his head, "the *Baas* thinks it is not listening for the Devil?"

JJ chuckled—*"They've gotten to him,"* he thought. "No, my *Oom*. I'm certain the devil has nothing to do with this... But I heard some stories, *Oom* ... that the *Dominee* came to talk to you."

"Ja", the *Oom* responded simply—his eyes now betraying no direction of his thoughts. "Didn't the *Dominee* send you?" he asked tentatively.

JJ was confused by the question and frowned—Karel saw his genuine puzzlement.

"*Baasie*... you are a law man now, in the big city?"

"Yes, *Oom*—I'm a lawyer...?"

"And did the *Dominee* not send you then?" The old head was cocked to the side, shrewd suspicion in his eye.

"No my *Oom*, why would the *Dominee* send *me*?"

"Because, excuse me Baas—but the *Dominee*, he said that *lawyers* will come—you know... to help with our claim."

It all began falling into place—the old man thought he, JJ, was here at the *Dominee*'s behest to fight the case for the land-use claim.

"Ah... yes, *Oom*—now I understand. No... no-no... The *Dominee* and your *Baas* Bauer don't know I'm here; and I don't *want* them to know I'm here," he pointedly looked at the children close by who were eyeing him and straining to hear.

Karel tracked his gaze and understood.

With colourful expletive language and threats, *Oom* Karel promulgated JJ's request into law to be disseminated to all others by everyone in earshot.

Enthusiastic nods accrued and the whites of eyes showed with earnestness that the insistence was agreed to.

"Ja Baas," said the old man—his eyes twinkling now with conspiratorial cunning; he and his people loved a good intrigue—in the absence of television, it was their living soap opera. "Nobody will talk, I'll see to that," he assured JJ.

"Good," JJ knew Karel wielded power beyond his frail appearance. He was a living representative not just of the surviving elders, but the departed ones too and nobody would cross that line; the wrath they'd face went several steps past the mere judicial law of the courts.

"Another lawyer will come," JJ predicted, "...and I'm sure he'll come with the *Dominee* and papers. They will tell you how much good putting your name to those papers can bring to all, but you must say that you need to think on it—don't let them have your mark immediately."

"Ja *Baasie*," it was what Karel had decided to do anyway.

"And you have Dawie ask his friend—the new boy, Dara, to arrange a copy for me. I'll arrange for Dara and his mother to get them to me," he paused a moment, not leaving anything to chance, "Nobody.... absolutely *nobody* must know what we've talked about," he emphasized.

"That is the right idea, Baas," Karel agreed, the cogs whirring behind his canny old eyes. And then he shouted out, "Where is that boy? Did those other boys fall asleep looking for Dawie? Somebody go find them!"

Another small delegation ran off into the sun and the bushveld.

"And I'll be back soon to come help," JJ assured. "I'll bring something nice from the city." He winked at the old man; "Now, when I leave here, *Oom*, send one of the boys, a trustworthy boy with me—I have something in the car for you."

Karel's face imploded into delighted wrinkles again and he cooed and swooned—it was sure to be tobacco. "Ooh... I hope it is very special," Karel hinted, "*Veeeery* special... Some *wild* tobacco maybe?"

JJ just smiled. *Wild tobacco* was local code for *dagga*—marijuana.

In these climes low-grade versions of the plant grew wild and carried no social stigma; it had a long cultural legacy and a short legal sanction.

JJ chuckled, "Ja, *Oom*. That stuff will make you slow and stupid."

"This old bushman is happy to be slow and stupid if it turns off the cold in his bones."

Just then, Dawie came puffing up the dirt drive barefooted and dusty.

"*Hello Meneer*," he greeted JJ and held his gaze with uncharacteristic assurance. The boy's eyes were alive with knowing.

"This one is Dawie," Karel said with great pride, his eyes sparkling with love for the boy.

"I'm very pleased to meet you," JJ offered Dawie a handshake.

The lad's grip was firm and dry, his small bony fist like a knot of hardwood.

"Thank you *Meneer*. *Meneer* is a friend of Dara?"

"Yes," JJ confirmed. "I believe you spent a lot of time with him."

"*Ja Meneer. Meneer*, how is Dara?"

"He is going home today, you can call him."

The lad shuffled and looked at his feet, offering an unconvincing "I will."

"Our phone *eeees* broken, *Meneer*. We need a new phone because it doesn't work anymore," one of the other boys on the fringes chipped in.

"*Jy... voetsak....!*"—*Get away from here*—Dawie's backhand gesture emphasized as he scolded his peer. "*Moenie kom staan en bedel nie,*" he laid into his peer, warning him with several rapid versions of colloquialism to *not come stand around begging*.

JJ saw Dawie's leadership role accepted from the others who all jumped with fright. He instantly liked the boy's pride; his anger at not wanting to betray to an outsider their impoverished state that left them without even a phone between them.

"Let's see..." JJ said to himself rhetorically when Dawie was done.

"Meneer?"

"*Niks nie...* nothing... You go to school every day?" He quizzed the lad.

"*Jaaaa, Meneer!*" Dawie replied with grave emphasis on the affirmative, "I *never* miss a day!"

The sea of little spectators who were pretending not to listen, as they most certainly shouldn't have been, all nodded agreement as earnestly, two or three of them verbally chipping in positive murmurs confirming Dawie's diligence.

"You have told your *Oupa* about the SKA? The telescope?"

"Every day!" He declared. "I am very excited about it. They have told us all about it at school."

The old man was nodding sagely, leaving JJ relieved that sense was prevailing in this unlikely little corner of the region.

On a whim, so taken was he with the boy, JJ said something he hadn't planned to say, "Do you want to come to the city?"

It was out before he even understood why he'd said it.

The boy's eyes looked startled and he vigorously agreed without hesitation.

"A visit when Dara comes—we can arrange that—and then we'll see..." JJ left what was on his mind unsaid.

"It would be good if he went to the city," Karel chimed in. "A boy like this... he must learn so that he can grow and make us all strong."

"I will look into it," JJ promised. He knew Marsha was thinking along the same lines and on a whim had effectively offered to collaborate.

JJ stood up and the old man battled to his feet too—refusing orders to stay seated, "I must move these old bones," he chuckled, "or they'll take root."

"I would like to stay, but it's a long drive to my home still."

JJ put out his hand to shake but the old man used it as a pivot to pull himself toward the big man. It was a first time ever—*ever*—that he had hugged a white man, but something in the moment commanded him to do so.

The act came as a surprise to JJ in whose culture men did not ordinarily hug—they certainly did not hug across a colour bar. But it was a natural moment, one he was glad for, allowing him to push another silent hidden artifact of a miserable legacy dormant within, away and behind him.

"In case we don't meet again, Baas," the frail old man was saying.

JJ could feel the truth of it in his bony shoulder blades, which seemed at this instant so much like angel's wings.

"No talk like that," JJ scolded him. "We all need you too much... your wisdom."

"Any wisdom I have is in this boy now," the old man retorted.

"I'm back shortly," JJ assured, inclining his head for Dawie to follow. He turned and walked away toward the car.

The two made their way past the others doing Sunday things. Many farewell greetings later the giant and the urchin were rounding the gentle bend and obscured from sight by the trees.

Karel lay down again to think about this very strange turn of events—the son of the policeman, the *Dominee*'s once-favorite, taking a stand against them.

It made him laugh.

"You look after your grandfather," JJ told Dawie. From his wallet he peeled a sizeable wad of notes, folded them and then surreptitiously slipped them to Dawie so the ragtag band of curious followers couldn't see. "I want you to buy a mobile phone with that and some airtime. I'll give you my number and email—you have computers at school—we'll stay in touch. Your grandfather is going to need special attention—I am going to arrange that he gets properly assessed at the clinic on a regular basis... And, Dawie... there is some serious business going on here, I need you to be my agent."

The boy was beaming—deputized as an agent, he seemed to have grown vast in stature; taller and walking like a giant next to one.

"You know who my father is?" He asked Dawie.

"Ja Baas."

"When we're alone you can call me JJ," he said, and the boy looked abashed.

"Ja Baas... JJ," Dawie responded coyly.

"All right... it will take some getting used to..." JJ reminded himself; the formal respects beyond the cities were still ingrained. "My father is a very good man," he explained. "He sometimes seems angry, and as a policeman he is always suspicious—he is paid to be suspicious."

"Ja Baas... JJ."

JJ looked at the last few stragglers still nosing close by and they read his meaning; they fell back slightly, out of earshot. "And I love my father like you love your grandfather... But a father can be wrong, I can still love him and know that he is wrong."

"Ja..."

"I don't want to hurt my father in any way. I don't want to embarrass my mother in front of the *volk*," he paused to let it sink in. "But there is a little trouble coming that will put me against my *Pa* and others. This can't be helped. But the longer you and I... the longer *we* can keep this secret, the smaller the trouble, and the happier everyone will be."

"Ja Baas... JJ, I understand," the boy said with nodding resolve.

JJ opened the car and began to rummage in his bag for something. He found the package and held it as he spoke.

"I need you to control the others. Like your grandfather, you will become the clan leader one day—and this is where your leadership begins. Here, today."

He handed the package over to Dawie.

"Dankie Baas..." he hesitated and repeated with much effort, *"Dankie..."* the *baas'* name resisted leaving his lips without its respectful title, *"...JJ."*

They were alone afterall, he thought, just as the *Baas* said it should be.

JJ squeezed his shoulder like a friend, surveyed up and down the road as if to check for prying eyes and stooped down into the bucket seat. The door shut with a precise-*'thunk'* and the muscular engine barked into life.

The other kids startled and shot back several paces. Dawie stood his ground. He had never seen such a machine close up and his heart matched the beat of its engine—his knees felt like boiled spaghetti, so he turned and began to walk, turning back to wave, walk, wave, walk.

JJ put the car in gear and eased away, careful to not disturb dirt or flick stones.

He saw Dawie sniff the bag in his hand and smile.

JJ wagged his finger and shouted after him, "If you want to come to the city, *that* is for an old man's pain *only*."

Chapter 23

De Villiers Prokureurs—Attorneys was uncomfortably close to the Carnarvon Police station.

Then again, Marsha reminded herself, everything in Carnarvon was uncomfortably close to that building and the man she had developed an aversion to.

Before leaving, JJ had given her some pointers and made a call to someone he called *Pieter*, the attorney who would assist her. He'd spoken on the phone in front of Marsha but he might as well not have, as the entire conversation had been in Afrikaans.

The building was drab; the carpet inside grey utility tiles of the nonexistent-pile variety. The waiting room was depressing; the cheap plant in it fake, the magazines on the high-gloss lacquered pine coffee table incomprehensibly in Afrikaans; by the look of their well thumbed pages, they were far out of date and concerned with farming and gossip.

The secretary who greeted Marsha did so in Afrikaans also.

"I'm so sorry," Marsha apologized. "I can't unfortunately understand."

"*Oooh*, sorry," said the tubby lady with hair styled in another era, "You're that American from England. I'm Beatrice. Meneer de Villiers… he-*is* called in and *says* he is almost here."

She made up for bad dress sense, turgid looks and an unfortunate stumbling accent laced with odd sentence structure; and words directly translated from her native Afrikaans; with an engaging smile and vast welcome. "Can I get you some tea or *koffie?*"

"That would be very nice, yes—uhhmm coffee please."

The lady rambled a litany of questions and observations from behind the kitchenette screen as spoons clinked cups and what sounded like tin too.

"You do take sugar?" Beatrice asked as she handed over a steaming mug, advising that there were already three in and it was stirred.

Marsha looked into the swirling muck just placed in her hand and wished she'd asked for water—which would be harder to ruin. But Beatrice was telling her all about the hairdresser in town that was introducing a fantastic new system for affixing fingernail extensions; or that's what Marsha thought she could glean from the broken English and even more confused specifics that Beatrice had only just *herself* heard about this morning from a Mrs. Vermeulen.

Marsha's reservations for pursuing Dara's issue through this law firm were peaking. On the other hand, JJ had warned that the only other attorney in the town would be hostile to her, "He's an elder in the church," he'd mentioned and by now she realized that no more need be said.

Beatrice was just getting going on some problems she was having with a tooth and the difficulties of getting it resolved in such a backwater, when Marsha saw a latest model SUV pull up outside and park alongside her own. By now she'd expected *quite-what* sort of vehicle she did not know.

The man who alighted was stylishly dressed, stylish at least for what she'd also thought might appear—by this stage of her acquaintance with Beatrice, a blue Safari suit with high socks carrying a comb for a crew-cut hairstyle and steel rimmed glasses had seemed most probable and likely.

He came in through the door with a smile and apology for being late. "I'm Pieter... Please come on through, Mrs. Martin—Beatrice, can you organize coffee please—would you like?" He looked askance at Marsha.

She'd only managed a single sip of the over-sweetened dishwater and had bravely managed to swallow it only because

Beatrice had kept a close eye on her, so she declined Pieter's offer, "Please call me Marsha," she added.

"Thank you," he said to Marsha. He'd seen the liquid misery in her hand and rounded on Beatrice, "*Agghh nee, Beatrice!* You gave her that rubbish you drink." He took the mug from Marsha's hand and passed it to Beatrice. "And you put three spoons of sugar in it I'm sure?"

Beatrice hung her head mournfully and admitted with tiny nods that he was right.

"I can't seem to train her," he said to Marsha in front of her. "She's so good with filing and on the phone but she thinks everybody else's taste buds are as bad as hers."

Marsha found herself intrigued with this strange little office, its internal dramas and over-zealous idiosyncratic receptionist.

"Now you make us some proper coffee—the one I bring from Cape Town. And use the new machine, not that old drip filter!" Pieter was gentle but firm. His tone sounded weary. Evidently this was a long-enduring skirmish.

"Is your husband joining us?"

"I'm afraid not. He's supposed to be leaving soon and we felt that it's best if I take it from start to finish. He's getting as much time in with Dara as he can."

Pieter ushered Marsha into his office and shut the door behind him.

Inside, it was much more lavish. A new laptop sat on the desk and a row of bound legal books filled the walls. The carpet was plush and the *Herman Miller* office chairs straight out of any leading I.T. company. The whole experience of the starkly differentiated division between the two rooms was bewildering.

Pieter saw her confusion and began to explain.

His expression said, *"I know what you must be thinking, but there is a good explanation."*

"This little town is changing fast—it's a work in progress... I took over the practice from my father—the reception is still as it was... if you change things too fast you scare away the old-timers; I just couldn't look at it in here all day long."

"I was wondering..." Marsha agreed.

"And Beatrice came with the deal—she's dyed in the wool, and it's a slow process to change her. I'm sorry about the instant coffee—it's more chicory than anything—it seemed delicious in our past too... tastes in all things are slow to change, hey?" He grimaced and she liked him.

"I understand. A small town like this—the people don't like change."

"The older people hate it, but the younger generation are all for it. I was a year behind JJ and also moved to Cape Town; he went abroad and married a foreigner. I wasn't coming back till my wife fell pregnant. She's from around here... and, you know…"

"I'm sure. It's a lovely lifestyle if you've got roots."

"It is. But it is also quite challenging once you're exposed to a different perspective."

"Which brings me to my son."

"Yes, how is he doing?"

"Not quite well enough to travel but he's mobile again. He's in a lot of pain."

"I'm sorry."

"It's been a rough time. Out of our comfort zone, so much to take in and then… well…. this."

Beatrice came in and the cappuccinos she brought smelled and looked perfect.

"It's one of those capsule machines—automated," Pieter had seen Marsha's relief. "Now isn't that easier and nicer, Beatrice?"

"I prefer my *Koffiehuis* Meneer." She went out muttering about the outrageous cost of the cartridges.

"I'm hellish sorry about the welcome our little town's given you and your boy."

"Please—I'm not blaming the town, that would be irrational. But I do think there's a real problem here. I think there are a few people here that are dangerously fanatical. Dara has paid a price he didn't deserve—nobody can *'un-pay'* it." She paused and shook her head, pragmatism wrestling bodily with emotion. "It really is outrageous... it's only my idealism to be sensible that has kept me from packing up and heading for home."

"I appreciate and thank you that you didn't," Pieter agreed. "Let's get to it and get you justice."

"I want to be honest," Marsha replied. "I don't think we'll come close to seeing justice. On the other hand, I'm not going to let the incident just slide. I don't want Dara to see me quit."

"I think you'll be pleasantly surprised how much justice we can get. How does Dara feel about taking this on?"

"He's very upset and that's upsetting to me. He's gone through a lot for a sensitive boy. He shrugged off the attack at the school amazingly well; I was very proud of that... He turned that proverbial cheek." She fidgeted with her keys.

"If I may..." Pieter interjected. "It's interesting... your use of the term... *other cheek*."

"Oh... you mean it's biblical roots?"

"Sure, yes... *'Atheists in our town'...*," his fingers framed the words in the air, "*...*you're all the buzz."

Marsha smiled, appreciating Pieter's subtlety in pointing out how an opposing attorney might aim to mangle anything she said; "I don't think there's a monopoly on the sentiment," she suggested. "To be a pacifist is the cornerstone of humanism. I think that welding pacifism to a theology is simply a habit for those who haven't thought it through."

"Interesting. You're right... and you're quick," Pieter smiled. "I prefer clients who understand why they're saying something... plenty don't. I distracted you, you were saying about Dara?"

"Well, after this attack, with his injuries so severe the doctor kept him heavily sedated for the first few days. Dara's also suffered quite a bit of post-trauma... nightmares. My husband's very British. He's been an absolute pillar, helping us all stay objective. And, I must say... JJ's sister... she's been visiting regularly, and... oh, please keep that to yourself it's apparently a... a bit of an issue with the father."

"I know," Pieter declared, "JJ told me. Lots of drama on the home front."

"Yes. Well, she's been fantastic. Poor thing, she can't come over in the open... she has to keep the visits very covert. I really don't want to know what will happen when the father gets wind of it—and I'm sure he will, he seems to know everything around here."

"I've known the family a long time. *Oom* Andre is something else. He's a nice man, just some very strange idiosyncrasies. Very bitter about the new political dispensation, doesn't like outsiders or change."

"Scares the hell out of me." She watched Pieter carefully as she went on; "What scares me more, and I'm sure JJ has spoken to you about it, is that he seems to be implicated in this whole affair—caused Dara to divert onto the road past the Vermaak farm... I hope I pronounced it right?"

"Pronounced well enough." Pieter shifted uneasily in his seat, he picked up his pen and fidgeted with it. "From what I've heard... yes, uhmm... it doesn't look good for that involvement. But if we start making a noise about it it's going to... well, you know..."

"Be *awkward*?" Marsha suggested, raising an eyebrow.

"Awkward would be a good word," Pieter agreed. "Small town... he's got a long family history... and police anywhere in the world..." his voice petered out hopelessly, "...hard to challenge. But you're my client and if you want to go there I'll go there. But it will be, yes... awkward."

"Well. I'm not sure how we can leave out something that to me seems to be a cornerstone... material, but let's see where we can go. I'm not being a mum now. Don't get me wrong, I could easily become unhinged when I let my emotions run and they want to run right now, that won't serve us. I'm being a rational scientist if you will... keeping my objective hat on. I'm trying to deal with the facts as they lie within the context we find them."

"I'm grateful for that. As I say, I'll take your case and run with it and take you wherever you want me to take you but I'd be remiss in my duties if I didn't point out the pitfalls too."

"Fair enough... and... sorry, Dara... we were talking about his state of mind. He's going through a lot of sentiments; to get out of here back to England, next thing he gets angry and wants justice. We're playing everything by ear."

"Granted. Well... let's dig in and see what we have. Start with the case against Dara. This morning I was over at the police station speaking to the Captain... He's not remotely interested in it, didn't even know *Oom* Andre was pursuing it."

"Really?" Marsha was amazed, "That constable said the Captain was up in arms... wanted to make an example out of Dara!...?"

"He said there's an open docket; there can be no question Dara was riding underage and without a license on a public road—a secondary one, but he also needed by implication to have traversed a National highway to have got there. He's not denying he was in Loxton?"

Marsha nodded agreement.

"Good… the Loxton police and the owner of the coffee shop where he met JJ have confirmed someone of his description in their town earlier that day."

"Now, this is interesting," Marsha cut in. "I'd like very much to know when and how the Loxton police made the connection to the Carnarvon police—especially if the Captain is disinterested."

"I think I see where you're going but I doubt anything like that is actually logged."

"Are there no recordings of radio traffic?"

"Indeed, but I don't think we have a prayer of getting them released to us. If this were a murder case—maybe."

"So you have to actually be murdered, an attempt is not enough?"

"It's an imperfect system," Pieter agreed.

"It's a frustrating one."

"Sadly, I think they all are, the world over. Yes… again, small town… things are going to work, well… differently."

"You're preparing me for something."

"I am, yes, it's something we have to deal with, circumstances we have to face without emotion."

"I'm a realist," Marsha assured him. "Much as I'm pissed off and perhaps even frightened, I don't want a vendetta, because that's what I think you're getting at. I simply want resolution and to bring this situation out into the open so that we can put an end to it."

"That all my clients were so rational." Pieter opened his palms in praise to heaven. "We're going to get a resolution."

"You were saying, about the police's case?"

"Yes. I'll massage that… It'll go away."

"So, nothing to be concerned about?"

"Not in the scheme of things. No… And from your side we are alleging that there are two incidents concerning the same individual… the attacker… that are somehow connected? I just want to spell it out so we're on the same page."

Marsha explained in detail all that she knew, adding something unexpected, "Sonja, JJ's sister told Dara she feels responsible."

"How so?"

"Evidently, that boy… the perpetrator… he considered Sonja his girlfriend."

"I pretty much knew that. Again, small town stuff—he's the *alpha* lion, she's the prettiest girl around. And the connection to Dara? Sonja only met Dara at the hospital, I thought?"

"Yes they only *officially* at the hospital, but she was there when he attacked Dara… it looks like a racist attack made worse by jealousy… the things he said and way he ambushed Dara… Neels—that's his name?"

"Yes."

"Sonja says Neels was incensed by Dara's introductory talk at the school. Neels wasn't even in the class, but she said it was like wildfire through the school… like Dara had been set up by the teacher… by the preacher stoking *xenophobia* in the kids. They all knew exactly what Neels was going to do coming in from the fields, and when Sonja tried to intervene, he accused her of having a… a *'thing for a darkie'*."

"Hmmm…" Pieter nodded encouragingly, knowingly.

"After the attack Sonja split up with Neels, and that sent him over the edge… set him to bragging around town what he was going to do to Dara. The school principal turned a deaf ear."

Pieter let out an agonized sigh, "I can only say it fits a pattern. But courts don't judge on patterns, they judge on facts, and so far we don't have any."

Marsha nodded, appreciating a truism the world over.

"What exactly did Neels say to your boy?" Pieter quizzed.

"It was in Afrikaans so it meant nothing to Dara, but Sonja wrote it down for you."

Pieter read the note, "*swart moffie duiwelaanbidder,*" his eyebrows lifted. "That's a hate crime, she'd have interpreted for you I'm sure—*black homosexual devil worshipper*. You prove he said that and he's in deep water. If he was the other side of eighteen when he said it, he'd be even deeper."

"We could scout around for witnesses. I wouldn't want to put Sonja through it even though she's willing, I think there are too many implications for her."

"And for everyone," he sighed, "…Honestly Marsha, it's worth a try, but I think you'll meet a wall of silence, nobody'll speak out. If I'm wrong, this changes gears and it goes to the Equality Court, and that hits the press. Nobody round here will have that staying power to testify against a prominent family."

"And the significance of that court? I can guess but I'd rather ask."

"The Equality Courts were created by the Promotion of Equality and Prevention of Unfair Discrimination Act 4 of 2000, which was promulgated as a direct result of section 9 of the Constitution of the Republic of South Africa."

Pieter stood up and ran his finger along the spines of the books on his shelves as he was talking.

"So it's a proper Magistrate's Court?" Marsha asked.

"Oh, no—it actually falls under the jurisdiction of the High Court, the Supreme Court—it's a very serious matter."

"A Supreme Court?!" Alarm was in Marsha's voice.

"Don't stress—under the Constitution, South Africa is one of the few countries in the world where a layperson can use the machinery of State, at the State's cost, to test the constitution in the High Court if they feel they have been violated."

"This country is a real enigma," Marsha remarked. "In some ways so locked into the past, in other ways… if only in theory, so progressive."

"It's not just theory, it's very real. If you have the evidence, we can bring the matter and it will be expedited. There is very little case law in this regard so that the courts are hungry to test it, to animate the law and develop jurisprudence and precedent. First, we need the evidence and the witnesses."

Pieter pulled down a volume from his shelf and now read from it, "The purpose of Equality Courts is to adjudicate matters specifically relating to infringements of the right to equality, unfair discrimination and hate speech, with a view toward eradicating the ever present post apartheid specter which essentially has divided the country along racial, gender and monetary related lines.

Equality Court proceedings are more akin to civil proceedings as opposed to criminal proceedings in that the onus of proof of a claim is on a balance of probabilities, and there are no prosecutors present at inquiries."

"What this means is that we don't need to prove *'Without a shadow of doubt'*—it does give us a powerful case, so long as we can find witnesses to testify."

"And the… uhmm… what lawyers call the finding?"

"Remedy?"

"Yes—the remedy? What's the outcome if a judgment is upheld?"

"Depending on the circumstances—a fine, community service. Prison is unlikely but not out of the question."

"As you say, it's speculative unless or until we get witnesses?"

"Precisely. What we ought to do is cast around. I know this boy's reputation, people either love or hate him, he's very abrasive. There's a lot of talk around town that he's a real bigot, it's hearsay unless someone credible steps forward with a specific gripe and I don't know what it will take to make that happen. Ask Sonja if others will come forward and meanwhile, we concentrate on a civil case."

They discussed the type of evidence Pieter would need and Marsha came up with the best she could think of.

"Dara's bike is in perfect condition after the incident, except for a small damage to the crash bar. It looks like it fell over at a virtual standstill but he has injuries that the doctors say would be consistent with a very serious high-speed fall."

"That's a lot closer to the kind of facts we need. That can form part of a deposition from the doctor and an expert in crash forensics."

"There were no skid marks and I didn't expect any because Dara's clothing and the bike showed nothing like the injuries his body had taken. I took a ton of photos at the scene… The two farmers who helped out were brilliant. Jakob van Breda—he's really my landlord, we stay on his farm," and she read from her notebook, "Frik Hen-something-or-other?" Her pronunciation was poor.

"Frik Hendriks?" Pieter guessed.

"Yes—that's him. Frik, he's the one who found Dara the night of the accident. He was very helpful. Says he's a hunter and he sure seems to have an eye for detail."

"I think you're in luck then because he's the closest thing to a forensic specialist in this area. Not university trained but he owns a game farm and is a very well known hunter. You're especially in luck because he hates the Vermaaks. They've had a feud for two generations already. They've got adjacent farms and have had countless trips to court and probably the doctor too from the dustups they've had. If he's got something, we may have something."

"So—finally… our first breakthrough," Marsha rolled her eyes comically.

She had a sense of humor and Pieter really liked that in a lady.

His wife had lost her sense of humor when their income took the knock of leaving the city. She nagged incessantly and found fault in most everything he did these days; he consequently was finding almost every woman attractive… But Marsha didn't need a man to have a difficult spouse in order to find her attractive—she just was.

"We took some pictures of the place and position Frik found Dara in." She handed Pieter the prints from the day the two farmers had posed to reenact the discovery.

He looked them over.

"Frik seemed to have a pretty good eye for all kinds of things. He pointed out tire tracks behind a low thorn bush, I took several pictures of the proximities and the tracks on the ground."

"They're clear, they're tire marks for sure, but it proves nothing."

Then she handed Pieter another sheaf of prints, "These ones are of the helmet, different angles."

He looked through them slowly, back and forth. The tire marks were clearly imprinted. "You still have the helmet?"

"Yes… in a bag, put away in my cupboard with strict instructions to the staff not to touch it."

"To my naked eye those tracks are the same or bloody close to the same," Pieter put the best of the helmet and the dirt tracks side-by-side. "I'm no forensic specialist, I don't know how many variations there can be on tires but to me this is pretty hard evidence if my instincts are correct." He laced his fingers behind his head and rode backward in his office chair, staring into the distance past Marsha.

"The helmet has stress fractures. From what I've learned that would take quite an amount of force."

"Now that sounds interesting…" he kept staring, then stopped and sat upright and examined the prints. "Look… these aren't official police photos and there are no official police measurements of the scene, so far as I'm aware."

"Then how can they charge Dara?"

"Circumstantial. They're not charging him with crashing they're charging him with riding. The crash is inconsequential as far as they're concerned. Honestly, it's petty of the cops, it's nothing; they're just being difficult."

Marsha nodded agreement.

"If that's all you've got… the pics… it's a hell of a long shot. I doubt you'll get that boy on criminal charges—the burden of proof required is higher. You may get something though on a civil action."

"What does that translate to? Precisely I mean. What does it translate to in practical terms."

"Well—on a criminal case… on attempted murder, it's very sketchy, I don't think a local prosecutor will touch it. You can sue for damages, the civil evidence requirement is less."

"Well I think a damages case is appropriate. There are some hard costs—medical…. insurance has picked up most but that's not the point."

"This isn't America, we don't have a jury or a history of big awards."

"I'm… we're not looking for an award, it's not about money, it's about right… about justice and about responsibility."

"Then I think we've got a case. What I need you to do or I can do, is bring in a forensic expert on the tire tracks. It's going to cost you out of pocket, and we can sue for costs."

Chapter 24

JJ felt torn by conflict.

Intrigue and distress now wrestled one another within his mind—the review of his secret video needed completion; though he wanted its insight, he hated the inevitable wedge it would drive into his family.

Throughout the long drive back to Cape Town the arguments with his kin were a litany inside his head so that he'd decided to take a few days to let the whole matter settle. He distracted his thoughts of the awkward trip with the pressing executive duties that had mounted in his absence, contracts needing review and points of new negotiations requiring his input.

He'd of course romanced his wife and topped her up with attention and affection, before packing her off to see her own family for Thanksgiving. Then he'd gone to his beach house to find some solace.

All night he'd tossed and turned, the sound and smell of the sea just meters away was a comfort made of white noise.

For all the family tensions, the embrace of community in those few weeks of his visit back to Carnarvon had made his beach house seem a lonely place; his yammering TV now created some atmosphere—News, sport and re-runs of old 1960's Star Trek episodes that he loved for their simplicity burbled away— old human dramas that dealt so innocently with the convolutions of integrity juxtaposed with the unfolding dramas of mid twentieth century perceptions of modernity out in space.

Before dawn he'd woken and spilled out of bed to go jogging. Five barefooted laps at the water's edge, back and forth across the beaches that girded the bay, gave him a short but intense workout; the soft cloying sand made his lungs and thighs scream for mercy.

The South Atlantic was a bath of ice. Diving into it felt like a slap across his face, the crushing tourniquet of cold mincing his brain. He jogged back up to his house and took a cold shower that felt warm in the rising dawn.

Martha, his housekeeper, emerged from her quarters, "Morning sir, breakfast on the deck?"

"Hello Martha. Please… Two eggs sunny side and bacon, no toast, but tomato, mushroom and fried banana out here please."

Twenty minutes later and the first rays of sun had clawed up over the mountain behind the house and begun to explore the rocks at the southern extremity of the crescent bay with its headland jutting out to sea.

JJ sighed and closed out the morning papers in the browser on his electronic tablet, then opened the video where he'd left off back in Carnarvon.

The grumbling cantankerous aging men in that worn old kitchen of his youth immediately came to life, battling imagined monsters from his forgotten past. The scene came flooding from the screen into his modern haven and it instantly sullied the prosperity he always felt here in his paradise setting.

The grimness of that suspicion-laden negative world of his father, family and community, self-imposed for countless generations, was like a heavy gravity of despair; a mean thing pulling the light and happy mood of his morning into the shadows, into the morose myopic place that is the siege mentality of his people.

He dabbed the *play* button; "…Our friends and visitors from America will be arriving in days. They're first on a Mission to Uganda to have meetings about the reversed legislation on the death penalty for homosexuals," the *Dominee* was saying and it struck JJ like a crowbar over the head to see the connection between Evangelist hysteria over homosexuality and its vicious homophobic implementation in Africa so plainly revealed.

"They need to start that good work here," Andre grumbled, and all the others nodded in grave accord.

"They will," Gert the stern old *Dominee* assured them. "When our new friends arrive here, they're going to meet with *Religious Freedom SA—RFSA,* Andy's group in South Africa." He turned to the stranger, "Maybe it's a good time to introduce yourself and the details of good work you're doing for us all, Andy."

Andy thanked the *Dominee* and briefly recited his resume.

As he began to speak the penny dropped for JJ. The initial glimpse of the man's face had been vaguely familiar to JJ, but he'd sat with his back to the camera and JJ had forgotten he was there. But the more he spoke, the more his nasal whining became unmistakable. He had recently been featured on a national TV news magazine, drumming up cross-denominational support for his *RFSA*, claiming that his biblically inspired rights to beat children and to keep women in their place were under attack.

By all accounts, according to what Andy was relating, they were already getting support from America… It was alarming:

"…And, because we are going into this fight as one," Andy was saying, "I want you to know that we are not alone; let me expand on that from our charter."

He cleared his throat and began to read in his thin voice; "God is calling to all Christians to put aside doctrinal differences and to stand up together against the ungodly laws that threaten to overwhelm our nation. God insists that together, we halt government in its attempts to systematically remove our freedom to believe and to teach and to live by the Word of our God in its fullness and in accordance with our interpretation of the Bible. The enemies of God want to make man's laws above God's laws. We declare that this is a proclamation that we will die to defend. There is no option for any Church that holds its God as true to watch from the sidelines as the secular forces drive an anti-religious doctrine against us. As they presume to tell each man what he may or may not believe and how he should act according to those beliefs. If you fail to speak out now and join our cause you may soon find yourself in a land that implements a freedom *from* religion rather than freedom *of* religion."

JJ shook his head, mouth agape at the claims. He'd recently seen the hysteria over the trumped-up issue being drummed from many angles in the press.

The *Dominee* then added his own piece, *"Isaiah* tells us that 'When the enemy comes in like a flood, the Spirit of the Lord will lift up a standard against him'."

"Add any gospel that vaguely fits, Gert, why don't you," JJ spontaneously challenged the video.

"This is great news," Dr. Louw the school principal was saying to general approval. "I have just had a letter from one of our concerned parents about major attacks against schools teaching biblical lessons."

"That OGOD organization?" Gert asked.

"Yes… they're making big problems for us… but we have a right and an obligation to teach scripture in our classrooms."

"This is what we're fighting against," Andy asserted.

The issue skirted the same territory, as an argument he'd had a dozen times with is father. JJ recalled how well even Dara had argued it in published blog under his *'Memes'* pseudonym; Dara had cleverly first made the case that religion is nothing more than "superstition dressed up in a funny outfit and wearing a ridiculous hat." And he'd underscored his claim with dictionary definitions that closed the case on it:

"Religion is the worship of a superhuman controlling power, especially a personal God." He'd expanded the definition; *"God is a supernatural being, and superstition is the belief in supernatural causation based on belief."*

Dara had gone on to argue that definitions allowed the words *religion* and *superstition* to be transposed, one for the other.

Dara's *Meme* character had argued a point that now rang true for JJ as these old men grumbled about their authority being eroded; that it is nonsensical for religion to be given any say in education:

Meme's had said; "It sounds acceptable that "Religion has *this* or *that* view in education; it sounds acceptable only because we're accustomed to people hearing it, but let me use the other word—*superstition*, and listen to how absurd the same sentence sounds:

'Superstition has *this* view in education'; and, 'superstition insists on *that* right'; or… 'we must approach a particular problem in education from some other superstitious viewpoint'."

That superstition must have its say in what children think and learn is indefensible, JJ could only agree; the change of word revealing the madness of it; "My superstition is the superstition of peace!"—"Well… my superstition is superior to your superstition, because…"

Now in the video before him, JJ was watching a man with a Doctorate in education extolling the virtues of why he should be allowed to beat his own brand of superstition into impressionable kids. It made him want to hurl his reading tablet over the wall onto the beach below.

Dr. Louw was still expanding on the details of the various actions being brought against him as an educator that he felt were his biblical right to ignore, "This nonsense about not hitting the children? This country is in the mess it's in, because we can't hit them anymore. But I do; I know my Bible and I know my rights to my beliefs and I know my obligations to my Maker; so, if the kids entrusted to me step out of line I *donner* them like I was beaten—It did me no harm! And, they appreciate it too, when they're older, they appreciate it… they come and thank me."

JJ's head involuntarily shook side to side; "I don't thank you, you brutal old fuck," he snarled at the screen. He was finding it difficult to rein his emotions in. The insidious connections and maneuvering and outmoded mindsets all revealed in such quick succession.

He'd grown up under a regime of beatings; beatings from his father and beatings from the *Dominee* and beatings from this same principal.

His blood surged and boiled in his ears and he cut the video for a moment to regain his wits. In spite of a Constitution against it, it was all still going on in the dark corners of the country; obsolete thinking in teachers too lazy and locked into an old-fashioned mindsets to find an alternative to violent resolution.

Andy was giving the principal rousing praise; "We do the same through our church. We are not going to back down to their laws. We follow the laws of God, first and only."

There were grunts of agreements and vigorously nodding heads.

"And you, you sniveling little turd…" The whole unpleasant business of listening to these men planning a regression for the country was making JJ intensely angry.

Andre suddenly appeared at the camera, his face filling the screen. He looked for one quizzical moment at close range directly into the camera and unnervingly into his son's eyes, then the whole image rocked violently as he looked down and stooped—the sound of bottles within the fridge clinked as the refrigerator was pillaged.

Martha had brought coffee out and heard the tone of JJ's fury and looked at the screen; the man she saw there she'd met only once and instantly disliked.

"Is it your father, Meneer?" she asked.

She was very fond of JJ and thought of him as a son. In many regards he let her act like a mother; a strange cultural interaction that had grown up between the master and servant classes over the century or two of their interaction across the sub-continent.

"Thank you Martha. Ja it's my pa; some unpleasantness from home that I need to understand and deal with."

He'd paused the video.

She nodded sagely, "But they're a long way away, this is a different world… you mustn't let them make you angry."

JJ knew that she had an uncanny ability to take in at a glance an entire volume of interpersonal strife or gossip. He smiled at her, "Yes, it's a different world but every day our worlds get closer, more entwined. They don't want our world, but they don't want us to have it either."

She went about her business and he took a lingering sip from the mug and a long hard look out over the ocean. Dogs romped, lovers held hands and a family with a toddler were making sand castles and laughing together.

"I can't take much more of this shit," he said to himself, but he wanted to get the review over with so that he could put it aside and not return to it.

He hit *'play'*.

"...it's not stopping there, Deon," *Dominee* Gert added to their gathering mood of perceived oppression. "Our synod is coming under pressure over women's rights. They want us to let women become *Dominees* now. And we must have homosexuals in our church."

Andy confirmed and reinforced what had just been said.

"And I told you all twenty, thirty years ago when they wanted us to allow *hotnots* to come to the church that it was just the start," Jan, the old army *Kommandant* chimed in.

JJ bridled at *hotnot*—an ugly racial slur so easily used by men he used to respect back in a time when he was infected with their madness.

"Ja, Jan, we all saw it coming, but what was there to do? We got sold out by that turncoat *De Klerk*." Andre added.

"Fok, Pa!" JJ spat back at the screen, "Are you never going to let it go?"

In the 1990's, the Afrikaner, South Africa's President, *FW De Klerk* brokered the end of apartheid, South Africa's racial segregation policy. De Klerk won a Nobel Peace Prize for his support of the transformation of South Africa into a multi-racial democracy by entering into the negotiations that resulted in all citizens, including the country's black majority having equal voting and other citizenry rights.

"*Manne*," the *Dominee* declared on the screen, "these matters are all urgent and they are draining to us. We are all agreed and hundreds of groups like us are at this moment wrestling with all of these matters. We are lucky now that God is waking groups like us up all across the land and the world. I don't care if you call your God Allah or if you pray in a Synagogue—our God is the same God and our enemies are the same enemies. It is time for us to put aside our differences now and fight for our rights and our history."

The agreement was not enthusiastic, but it was unanimous.

"We have seen the faithful splinter over the decades into many churches; now the time has come for us to join back together. This is the moment our God has chosen to bring his lambs into one flock. Ours is an old tradition, the Americans are bringing a new tradition—their way is too much noise and drama and howling for me, but it is perhaps something that the younger generation will respond to. It is something I will learn from when they are here; they will encourage our youth service to use their format. I say we embrace them, we focus on our similarities and put aside the differences."

He shifted into a preaching mode, his voice mesmeric with melody and prose:

"I want us to be *paaaart* of this Global movement," he sang. "*Nooooobody* can deny that we sit in a backwater to the cities, but as *Gawwwd* did not deliver His own son into a royal household or a city but instead to the poorest of the poor and most downtrodden, so too is He now allowing the Devil to deliver to us… to His people in this dry land… the opportunity to hold His sword and rise with it and cut the head off the beast."

JJ almost expected to hear a roar of approval from a vast crowd so intense and consuming had been the speech; but the *Dominee* was not yet done.

"We will return our people to their roots. We will embrace the black and brown men as our children; we will make them God's true servants and once more do our bidding on His behalf. This machine the outsiders wish to build, they say it is to find how the universe 'evolved'—now I ask you; they can't explain to us how their own evolution is supposed to work… how a monkey can give birth to a man, and before they're finished with that lie, they want to make the lie bigger and say that even the universe evolved… from what… I ask you? From what?"

The passion of it all overcame him and his voice caught in his throat.

The old man, JJ thought, looked about to suffer a stroke. Strangely, the words didn't sound like his; they sounded repeated… contrived and learned.

Things were turning decidedly interesting; the *Dominee* began laying out the strategies they'd adopt in using the Bushmen for the land claim.

"I have been advised that under no circumstances should we suggest to them any form of Land Claim. Under the Act, a Land Claim becomes very messy; it will take a lot of resources and create a mess of unintended and definitely unwanted consequences. Our aim—the aim they must want—is a Cultural Heritage site."

He went through his files and pulled out a stapled sheaf, "Now I want to read to you the basis on which the claim will be made," he cleared his throat:

"In his State of the Nation address 2014 the President uttered a promise that provisions would be made *'for the recognition of the Bushman Khoisan communities, their leadership and structures.'* It is important to remember that the Khoisan people were the most brutalized by colonialists who tried to make them extinct, and undermined their language and identity…"

JJ paused the video; the irony of what he was seeing unfold too staggering to believe; These sentiments being read aloud by the *Dominee* had, over decades gone by, so many times been roundly condemned and damned by this same man from his pulpit.

JJ marveled at what treasons the *Dominee*'s mind must have been screaming as he read these truths, trying to make them palatable in pursuit of his current agenda;

"…Apartheid mythology taught that the first settlers entered a religious vacuum when they landed at the Cape and encountered its indigenous inhabitants. This is manifestly untrue. Far from being an 'empty container' into which religion could be emptied, Khoisan culture was already religiously rich."

As the *Dominee* put the paper aside, JJ saw the sheaves of it betraying a palsy, a shaking with fury; the words that spoke lies against his people were a poison chalice that circumstance forced the *Dominee* to drink from;

"We know that those are all propaganda lies, but using them is critical to our cause—it's the academics' own lies and the *rooineks'* own laws that we'll use against them."

"*Fantasties!*" Jan the *Kommandant* exclaimed.

The *Dominee* picked up the sheaf and continued, "While the early settlers included a small number of Catholics and Jews, only the Reformed faith was officially recognized. The passing of the *Voluntary Act* in 1875, while recognizing the importance of religion in the Colony, effectively re-constituted faith communities alike as voluntary societies, and to these ends..."

Infuriatingly the screen suddenly went blank mid sentence. JJ checked the progress bar—the recording was over—the rest of that meeting far away in another time now lost to him.

"FUCKIT!" he cursed, and Martha stood bolt upright at her mop. "Sorry Martha."

The entire recording had exceeded three hours—the battery on the computer had died on the recording.

Chapter 25

Dawie checked again for traces of blood. Every few minutes he'd wipe his nose with the back of his hand and peer in the dim light of the single naked dust-laden bulb for any faint smear of it; at last it seemed clear.

Though it felt like his throat had been ripped out, his vision had returned. He could see up through the bars to the outside that it was twilight; his family would be ferociously angry with him by now. Probably, as would be usual for this time of evening, his father would be blind drunk and there'd be hell to pay when he got home… if he got home.

The muted distant voices along the dingy corridor suddenly popped from the background to full volume; the door to the charge office had opened and he could hear the click and squeak of approaching boots. He was the only inmate in the cellblock; the footsteps could only be coming for him again, and he cringed to the back of the cell, praying in sniveling fear to slip into a crevasse in the old fractured plaster.

The apparition appeared at the gate, a key bunch jingled merrily as the selected one metallically clinked against steel frame, finding the slot, and the bolt shot open. The gate swung heavily aside with a resounding CLANG! and the bulb within illuminated the giant constable who filled the doorway.

This time he did not step inside.

"*Staan… weg met jou!*" The order to get out was barked.

After the ordeal of the past few hours Dawie didn't trust his own ears. He thought it a trap, another ploy for the policeman to extract secrets he was not keeping.

"*Luister jy nie, boetie?*" The rumble of his voice suddenly encouraging with a psychopath's gentleness to it.

Dawie was listening all right—it was his legs that weren't.

"*STAAN...*" the policeman encouraged and then erupted—"*en... FOKKOF...!*"

Terrified, Dawie found his feet, his knees sagging with fear. He approached like a whipped dog, hunched to offer the smallest target for a crippling blow that must surely come.

"*VOETSEK!*" The constable boomed after the fleeing boy as he would to accelerate any escaping mongrel.

Like a scolded hound through a doorway past the knees, Dawie was into the corridor and scooting for the doorway and freedom beyond it.

He heard the footsteps striding up from behind as he came into the glare of the charge office.

One black officer was seated, he inclined his head rapidly at the door to liberation—the universal signal to go '*that way*' in a hurry.

In a flash Dawie was out and running—running for his life, like a jackal pursued by the hounds of his deepest fears. He was listening for a yell to return, listening for the brute to challenge him, straining for the snicker of a pistol's slide; and then, when he was beyond gunshot range, expecting the inevitable turn of the police van's engine and squeal of pursuit.

Instinctively he avoided the direct route home, jinxing instead into a side street and then an alley. Like a hyena slinking along fences, blending into the background of oncoming night.

Mid afternoon, he'd been on the phone, walking back from school. It hadn't been *Baas JJ's* airtime either, it had been airtime he'd bought with extra money he'd earned by washing the car of one of his regular customers; Dawie had a business doing odd jobs in the town.

He'd been so proud of that phone and guarded it with his life, keeping it in a woolen sock so that it wouldn't get a scratch. Curiously it had refused to work on the farm and only worked in town. When he'd brought the older broken phone to town, it too began to work. The problem had vexed him, and being a bold lad he'd asked *Baas* Bauer, his farm's owner, directly why the Baas' phone worked, but his would not.

"The phone network is blocked on the farm," the *Baas* had told him. This is why my people don't like this SKA. My phone works because it has Wi-Fi and I am using my computer Internet router, not the phone network. Your little phone doesn't have Wi-Fi."

Dawie understood the difference between mobile signal and Wi-Fi, but when he tried to explain it to his people, they were having none of it, laughing at him for being duped. The *Baas* was lying to them, *again*; more of the white man's tricks to keep them at a disadvantage they concluded.

The community also wanted to know how he'd come by the mysterious new phone he'd acquired. He'd of course told the truth to his people; that *Baas JJ* had given him the money to buy the phone, so that he could help grandpa and that he could also take care of important business. He'd regretted betraying his word so readily, but it was impossible to hide the phone, and he had no better story to explain how he'd come by it.

Most believed him, though a few were deadly jealous; they'd begun the rumours about theft. He'd ignored them, not dignifying lies with more than the minimal truth.

The phone had already been very useful and Dawie was constantly contemplating by what other ways he might exploit it. Because he had the phone, from a spot he'd jogged to along the road closer to town, he'd arranged for Grandpa to be picked up by Dara's mom and taken to the clinic in two days. One of the goats Dawie kept in a private arrangement with their landlord, *Baas* Bauer, had been sold for meat to a laborer on another farm whome Dawie had heard was getting married; and his social life and opportunities to meet up with Dara were taking good shape with this valuable asset in hand.

Indeed, the phone had quickly become a central pivot to his life. With his own investment into airtime he'd begun to make a tidy profit renting use of the phone to the other families that lived and worked alongside his family; it entailed them taking a hike until there was sufficient signal to make a call. But unless the receiving party was standing by off of their farm at a location where there was signal, no call would connect. It was a huge step backward for everyone who had become accustomed to the free access to signal that had for a decade and more become widespread; and then suddenly cut to accommodate the new SKA infrastructure.

He was certain *Baas* JJ would not mind—the *Baas* had not said he could *not* use it in these ways.

In the few days since he'd acquired this asset he'd become so comfortable with it that he had it out of the sock and was talking into it when the police van had pulled up alongside.

"Nou waar kry jy dit?" JJ's father had asked him as he got out of the van. The constable's question was rhetorical; he'd already heard it was stolen.

A surge of adrenaline had pulsed to every extremity and Dawie had babbled, not making sense. And the less sense he made the more skeptical the policeman had become as he'd opened the cage on the back of the van.

"Klim maar in," he'd invited Dawie in a friendly manner, and the phone was relieved from his hand as he'd stepped into the cage.

During the trip back to the police station, Dawie had slunk down as low as possible; terrified somebody would recognize him in his school uniform.

His mind had been a barrage of angles. *Baas* JJ had said his father was a good man, just suspicious. But he could not betray the *Baas* and reveal how and why he'd come by the phone, because the *Baas* had specifically linked the necessity for the phone with important and secret matters that had to do with his own father—the man now arresting him.

"I'll tell them a rich *Baas* from the city has given me the phone to help my parents and neighbours," he hatched the story during the short trip; it was the truth after all. It just didn't have all the facts and he had assured himself that it should clear matters up.

There'd been no more time to think it through as they'd pulled up outside the station and the van door had unhitched. He'd been quickly ushered through the charge office where a member of the public had been making a statement to the black sergeant.

As they disappeared into the gloom of the cellblock, Kruger had offhandedly mentioned catching a *"hotnot dief"*—a little coloured thief—and the stranger making the statement had nodded approvingly.

As the open handed slaps had come, he could feel that they were just hard enough to hurt, not so hard that their sound would carry to ears that might help. The handcuffs to the bars had bitten into his flesh with each blow that had sent him reeling.

He repeated his story between cracks against the head, but was quickly cornered in its details; he'd not thought far enough through to concoct an identity for the mysterious and benevolent stranger he alleged had funded the gift.

"So you're a hard boy?" Andre had said in a cruel mien. "…I know how to make a hard man humble."

The gate had clanged and bolted. Ten minutes later Kruger had reappeared carrying a section of car inner-tube and a spray can. Dawie's mind exploded in terror, he knew what was coming.

The big man had grabbed him and with practiced deftness pulled the section of car inner tube over the boy's head.

The rubber had sealed Dawie's eyes and breathing. He'd instantly been locked into a claustrophobic world of terror—the rubber extinguishing his ability to breathe.

Ten seconds felt like a minute, twenty felt ten times longer.

He'd felt the blackness of suffocation coming and started to taste terror as his throat clutched spasmodically; his chest had heaved, his body straining with futility against the biting cuffs that had unforgivingly held him.

Kruger had picked the precise moment that the boy would black out; he'd lifted the cloying rubber from the boy's chin just enough for him to suck air—and with that desperate clutch for breath the Constable sprayed a measure of pepper gas, then dropped the rubber seal back in place.

Dawie had exploded into an insane rage and his haunting growls had fought against the muffle, desperate to be heard.

Five seconds passed, then Kruger had stepped forward and rolled the rubber back, enough that the boy could breathe again freely, not so much that he could see.

"Now I want you to tell me the truth…" he'd spoken very gently but firmly, almost like a father might.

Dawie had cried like a baby. Choking on his own vomit and pouring saliva, his resolve to protect his new friend, *Baas* JJ—the torturer's own son—broken.

"Dis Baas se seun, Baas"—your own son, he'd disclosed. *"Dis Baas JJ wat dit vir my gegee het."*

Andre had ripped the tube from Dawie's head with a ferocity Dawie could scarcely believe. Dawie could see nothing for the tears and the burning, but he could hear the constable's breathing—snorting with each breath like a ferocious bull about to charge. He braced himself to receive a clout that never came.

"My own son hey?"

The cell door had clanged to a close and the footsteps had retreated. The door into the office had ripped open and slammed shut and he was left in his private hell, hanging from the cuff attached to the bars.

After fifteen minutes, Dawie's eyes had cleared, he could see again. The black sergeant had come and unlocked the cuffs through the bars. He'd said nothing, just took the cuffs and left.

It had been many hours before Dawie was given his release.

Now, as he ran he wondered about the phone—about the dashed dreams it's confiscation meant for him. About the anger *Baas* JJ must surely have for him losing such an expensive device and betraying whatever 'serious business' it was that he'd embroiled Dawie in.

He arrived at Tjaardt's house when it was almost dark.

The family were eating and the doorbell rang six urgent times before Susanne—though everyone called her Sussie, Afrikaans for *Sister*—reached it, irritated by the insistent intrusion.

She peered out through the peephole at the swollen, distorted face with terrified swiveling eyes urgently begging a sanctuary. The doorbell rung a seventh and eight time before she realized who the haunted stranger was.

"TJAARDT!!!" She involuntarily yelled as she ripped the door open and fumbled for the keys to the security gate, "DAWIE...! What in God's name happened to you...? TJAARDT!"

The whole family arrived as one, cramming the doorway to take a look.

Dawie began to cry. He knew a big boy should not give in to public tears, but the relief of finding a safe harbor broke over him like a wave and he sank down where he stood and sobbed.

Sussie swarmed over him like a blanket, enveloping him in her ample bosom and effortlessly plucking him to his feet in a single lift with the adrenaline shock of his appearance.

In quick order he was laid out on the couch, wetted cloths were rotated quickly through a bowl of warm water and used to douse the chemical sting that still raked his eyes. Milk was brought for him to slake away the burn in his throat and he was consoled and caressed by everyone from every angle as they craned and cooed over him.

Dawie related his ordeal.

"Die fokken vark!" Sussie growled; she'd always hated Kruger and habitually called him a *fucking pig*—today she spat it with boosted venom.

She kept saying it, devising between the oft-repeated cusses, every manner of threat that ran from outright vigilante reprisal to a Constitutional Court application.

Eventually Dawie's condition was stabilized and the next step put into practice.

Dara was called and Marsha was put on the line. The address was given and she promised to be there without delay.

By the time Marsha arrived, Bennie Pieterson, the town's mayor, Tjaardt's uncle, had been in attendance for some time. He lived three doors down and was hailed in the first few moments as soon as Sussie knew it was serious.

Bennie had ordered everyone to leave the room and they did so, retiring to the kitchen, keeping uncharacteristically quiet there as they each tried to steal snippets of what Bennie was saying to Dawie a corridor away.

But Bennie wasn't yet saying anything of interest, Dawie just told his story over and Bennie grunted and said encouraging things to keep the flow and details coming.

When Marsha and Al arrived, Dawie was just about complete with his story, and Sussie took the opportunity to re-join the action; she admonished all of the others to stay in the kitchen and busy themselves with bringing tea for the guests.

Bennie and his credentials were introduced and he took the lead now and retold the story in summary, careful to include those legal issues of abuse that were damning—and there were many.

"I'm just overwhelmed with what's going on in this little town," Al said when Bennie had finished.

"It's not always like this," Bennie assured him.

"I'm sure—for an outsider it's a lunatic asylum," he went on. "I mean; my son… now this. I thought this sort of thing was left decades behind us? If the press get hold of this in the context of what the international community aims to do to transform this place, it's going to be dynamite."

"That's a concern, but I can't deal with anything but this. I'm going right now to lodge a case against the police."

"I'm coming with you," Sussie was already pulling on a sweater.

"No. I'll go alone. I don't want to inflame this any more than necessary."

"How do you walk into the police station and ask the policeman who just violated the law to open a case against himself?" Marsha asked.

"Calmly," Bennie replied.

Chapter 26

"Die fokken hotnot… kont," Andre raved.

He was home in the kitchen, beginning to explain to Johanna why it was already 10-pm and he'd not called to say he'd miss their habitual 7-pm dinner. He'd never normally utter words like *fucking* and *cunt* in front of his wife, but he'd descended several rungs past rational thought and decency.

Moments earlier, clinging to decency by a slender thread, he'd stormed through the door and ordered Sonja—sitting with her mother at the kitchen table, fretting why father was so late and not answering his mobile phone—to her bedroom.

As he was about to leave the shift three hours earlier, the Captain; Andre's black Station Commander; had come in through the door in a black mood.

The Captain had snapped at Andre that he was to immediately hand over his service pistol, which was summarily confiscated to the Captain's private safe.

"You are on suspension… wait here until I call you!"

Sitting where he was told to sit, Andre had seen *that* troublemaker, Bennie Pieterson arriving and disappearing behind the Captain's closed door.

"Fok!" He'd said to himself.

A few minutes later the door had opened and Andre's co-worker, the duty officer, had disappeared in and the door had shut.

Another few minutes later Andre was called in but not offered a seat.

"*Burgemeester* Pieterson called me at home. I think you know what this is about," the Captain had snarled at Andre.

Andre had stood and endured the worst tongue lashing of his life. Never had anyone spoken to him like this, and now from a black man. It took all of his will to not reach across the table and throttle the life out of the Captain.

Now he was home and on suspension, pending investigation.

How stupid, he admitted to himself, he'd been to pick on the nephew of the Landdros. But he'd heard rumours that the boy had stolen a phone, and the boy had flaunted it so openly; almost challenging Andre. The perceived sleight had driven him mad with rage.

On the drive home he'd dreaded this moment, telling his wife—their relationship so strained of late.

"JJ called me," Johanna said. It was all she'd needed to say; her eyes said everything else—her disgust and disappointment in him.

After Dawie in the cell had claimed that JJ had given him the phone, Andre had stormed back to the charge office and gone over the numbers stored in it, and there, under simply "J" was a number; he'd pushed dial and after 4 rings his son's voice was like fist slamming into his ear, "Dawie my boy, have they brought the papers yet?"

On impulse, Andre had cut the call and a minute later the phone had run on the desk—"J" was accusingly on the screen.

"Ja?" Andre had answered, "I'm investigating something here," he'd said to his son.

"Pa...?" JJ had fumbled a response. "Why are you answering this, *Pa*?"

"I picked this boy up with the phone—he says you gave it to him?"

"I did. Why did you pick him up? Where is he?"

"He couldn't tell me where he'd got it... gave me a long bullshit story. There's so much theft these days from these little *donners* so I detained him till he could remember."

"What have you done to him?" JJ's worst fears were at an instant panic. He knew too well that his father was a disciplinarian of the old type. He believed that the only language these local kids understood was brutality.

"He's all right—now that I've cleared it up, he can go."

"Pa, if you have done anything to him…"

"Nothing he didn't deserve," Andre assured sternly.

"For fuck sakes, *Pa*," JJ boiled over and he lost his temper, "… Fuck you, *Pa*, if you have hurt that boy…"

He'd never spoken like that to anyone… now he'd said it to the man who had been his guide and hero for more than half his life.

"I see…" Andre had sounded calm and distant. "Now I see how an atheist treats his father," Andre had blurted his deepest disappointment. "A boy who had God and respect."

"You are really losing your mind," JJ had told him directly, not caring anymore for keeping the peace. "This has nothing to do with the horseshit you're constantly trying to swing on me. This has to do with your bigoted miserable self, and your inability to learn and to change. The world you inhabited is dead, *Pa*. It is dead. It is rotten. It is rotten and I have walked away from it and my mother and my sister will walk away from it too…"

In the silence of the moment that had followed JJ regretted having added his last utterance. It was not his place to disclose what he knew was coming in the family, but years of kowtowing had peaked and he no longer cared to guard his tongue.

"Ja, well… you have chosen your path then," Andre too had crossed a boundary of caring. "You are with the enemy now… equipping the enemy. *Tot die bitter einde, seun*," he'd spat out the declaration as though it was a lash to JJ's face, and he'd cut the call.

To the bitter end, son—it was a challenge dredged through a century and more since the British and the Boers had fought a vicious war, a sore still festering in the heart of the most unyielding in Afrikanerdom. It meant that JJ had become a detestable *verraaier*, and a turncoat was worse than a *rooinek*— there could be no turning back, no surrender, all out war… again.

Andre saw in his wife's eyes all of those things from the final conversation he'd had with his son; the final conversation he would ever have.

She turned her back on him, serene and composed; the familiar squeak of floorboards marking her passage as she sailed out of sight in the direction of the bedrooms. Andre heard the single knock and turn of Sonja's handle, the door tapped lightly closed.

A moment later the handle, the light kiss of the door in its jamb, the footsteps Andre knew so well disappeared into their bedroom. The door reported it's brutal closure.

He sat at the kitchen table for what seemed hours while sporadic footfalls travelled lightly up and down the unseen corridor, the opening and closing of doors reporting their business.

His prison was silence, his mind caged by culture, by unyielding pressures inherited from a father who had reaped it from his father before him. Back through endless time, strength demonstrated, no pity for self or others expected or given.

Now the shame at facing deeds he'd called his obligations became phantoms leering at him, taunting from the shadows of his boyhood home.

The weight of being a man came down on his shoulders, smothering his wish for life out of him. Conflict. Nothing but conflict marked the memory of his adulthood as he sat, crushed under the immensity of circumstance.

Sonja didn't say goodbye, but out of sight and in the gloom Johanna said her farewells. She was leaving that instant for Cape Town. She would never come back. She'd said it and he knew it was true; Johanna never made an empty promise.

The car started in the driveway and, as the sound of the engine faded and died into the still of the night, Andre began to cry.

He had not cried since he was a boy, but now the emotional drought was broken and the tears came like dollops of hot rain ahead of the thunder; first one and two, and then three-four-five. It was possible to count them at first, and then the storm burst and the heavens of his tears opened. He cried as he never thought he could.

When the tears were done, he went to his rifle safe.

Chapter 27

As Johanna arrived in Cape Town, JJ was preparing for their return to Carnarvon.

The call had come in well before sunrise. It was the *Dominee* and he was sobbing. JJ didn't know that the *Dominee* could cry, but Gert had howled so hard that he could barely talk. He'd called from the scene. He'd been one of the first to witness it.

The sound of a shotgun carries a long way across a small town in the dead of night.

Andre was at the kitchen table when they found him. He had arranged the family around him; their pictures in frames like an amphitheater of spectators come to watch him leave. Pictures from the early years, before the children came, before the first "*oops…*" when he and his Johanna had squinted as school sweethearts optimistically into the lens. And then the small family emerging in the story, concluding their triumph with JJ in graduation regalia—so proudly the first of the family university qualified.

Nobody knew where Johanna and Sonja were in those first horrific hours, the frantic hours spent searching and fretting the worst… so many police families extinguished by the gun.

Mother's car was gone from the town, and as she eschewed a mobile phone—Sonja had been JJ's only hope. He tried and re-tried her number; terrifyingly, Sonja's phone relentlessly going directly to voicemail without a ring; threatening the worst.

He'd alternated the frantic and fruitless calls to Sonja with calls to Morgan. She was ready to fly back to be with him, but they'd decided there was little she could do so she would remain on call to support him.

It was well into the morning, a leisurely ten-hour pace from Carnarvon, when Sonja appeared at JJ's door.

He grabbed and embraced her with ferocity of relief that drove the air from her lungs.

He'd been crying and she saw it.

"Where's *Ma*?" he asked urgently.

"On the stairs."

"Come inside… sit down," he flew out the door to fetch mother.

When the women were both seated he came and knelt in front of them, taking a hand from each he held on firmly as he told them plainly what had happened.

They fell in unison into him and his arms swallowed them to his chest.

The clutch of embracing misery heaved together, agonized wails of tragedy ricocheting off the walls, overwhelming the room.

Martha came in and silently slipped back out. She already knew about Andre and had already cried for JJ's pain for many minutes in JJ's arms. She listened from the kitchen until the timing was right and then she made tea, hugged and cried with the women and quietly withdrew to her quarters, occasionally returning to see if there was anything that she could do.

By the end of the afternoon JJ had begun to implement practical steps. He had a plane of his own but wanted to offer his mother more comfort and a faster transit, so he chartered a jet from a friend.

He called his doctor who made a house call and delivered sedatives.

In spite of the pharmaceutical assistance, none of the family slept.

Johanna degenerated into blaming herself and JJ was forced to admonish her firmly—"Pa did this to himself, *Ma*. He has been driving you away for years. He loved us all but he could not get over his fears and frustrations."

Nothing helped.

It would take years for her to recover; if she ever could, and JJ knew it.

Sonja was silent, her eyes rheumy and far away in a different place in time.

After that last call with his father, JJ had wanted to call Marsha. The urge had been there but he'd decided to let the situation play itself out and not trouble her unnecessarily with yet another embarrassing fiasco exploding in his community, perpetrated by his father.

But after Marsha had been called by Sussie to come to Dawie's assistance, she'd called JJ.

It had been awkward; JJ had once again been put in a compromised position; compelled by deep cultural urges to mitigate the indefensible, yet revolted by his father and the old ways the man represented. With his worst suspicions of what his father had done to the boy realized, he'd told Marsha to spare no expense seeking medical assistance for Dawie and committed that he would support a legal case, even though it went against his own blood.

When Marsha had hung up, JJ had called Dawie's number hoping the phone had been returned so that he may talk to the boy—or, failing that, talk to whoever answered it in the police station. But it had gone directly to voice mail.

He'd called his father's mobile, but after two rings it too had cut and gone to voice mail. He'd called the number again twenty minutes later and the same pattern played out; his father was screening.

He never did reach his father again.

Chapter 28

Marsha's keynote speech in which she'd touched on the Kardashev scale and its Type 1, 2 and 3 Civilizations had prompted a vigorous debate in the town during the final days of school.

John Fiske, the new science teacher whose employment had been afforded by recent donations from the SKA fund, had found the notion of the Kardashev predictions utterly fascinating.

Informed by them, he'd delighted in contemplating the vast cosmic drama that may be unfolding in the heavens, a drama whose radio emissions might well rain down into the telescope dishes to be centered around the little town.

After Marsha's address, John had spent a few minutes sharing his enthusiasm with her and she'd given him her personal email address.

He'd then taken the discussion points he'd gleaned from Marsha back into the classroom where it had quickly become a vast and passionately fought debate among the kids that the long-time old-guard teachers and Doctor Louw watched with rising distress. John had kept a stream of information flowing to Marsha, detailing interesting points raised in discussions.

The debate had re-ignited the same rumblings and schism in the community that the Dara incident had prompted months before.

But, year-end exams were upon them and to the relief of Principal Louw the debate was ended; Louw hoped, forgotten.

Then, to his fury, with the school year officially over Dr. Louw discovered that John had gone over his head to secure permission directly from the education governing authority to use school facilities to continue the discussion for anyone who wished to participate.

Louw was furious.

The next discussion group was scheduled for 10am Thursday, a public holiday. It was anticipated to last two hours.

Worse yet the black devil's mother, Marsha, had agreed to open discussions about the viability of achieving *Inter-Stellar Travel*, while the boy's father, Al, had agreed to give a presentation on *Ancient Aliens and Gods*.

Andre's funeral was set to begin at 3pm that same day. It was a disgrace.

Dominee Gert had, for the record, officially lodged a complaint through Principal Louw's authority to have the presentation cancelled on the grounds that it insulted the community by violating Andre's legacy as a pious man.

"With all respect, sir," John was in heated debate with Deon Louw, "That is a *non sequitur* argument. It…"

"It's a non-nothing…" the Principal snapped back, "Don't come in here at this sensitive time for our community and throw around your big words."

"It is not a big word. It simply means that the conclusion you're making does not logically follow-on from what is at issue. We have planned a morning of discussions with preeminent scientists—world-renowned scientists—who we are fortunate enough to have available. Under normal circumstances we would not even get a reply from people of this caliber let alone their time—they'd never even come to Carnarvon. And there are dozens of people who have RSVP'd positively—many of them parents."

"I don't expect you can grasp this John because you don't come from a community," Louw's voice stung with implied insult, "but this topic at this time is a slap in the face of a well respected and deeply religious man who was a cornerstone of our Faith."

"I am afraid that you are right, Doctor. I don't grasp it. We will be finished a full three or more hours before the service begins. Hell—the late man's own son and daughter are coming to our event; evidently then they find no insult in the two events occupying the same day when divided by lunch… Indeed, the holiday specifically commemorates *reconciliation*, it is *National Reconciliation* day so that I think it is appropriate."

The Principal snorted with mockery and disdain. "*Reconciliation*… We don't need any reconciliation we only need respect for our Faith."

As John was about to respond, *Dominee* Gert barraged into the Principal's office; he was in an evil mood and glared lightening bolts at John. John nodded a cordial greeting, "Good morning *Dominee*," he said.

Gert did not reply, his mouth pencil thin.

"Well?" Dr. Louw asked of Gert.

"Daai f-ken Kaptein…" Gert hissed through pinched lips, minutely indicating to The Principal that in John's presence, *now* was not the time for details, *"…hy skop vas… ek sal jou later sê."*

John knew next to no Afrikaans, but it was clear that Captain had been uncooperative, and John guessed he meant the Captain of the Police. He shook his head in amazement that they'd take the situation that far.

The Principal glared at John, "So you remain unwilling to accommodate us… a whole community… and put aside your ungodly agenda for just this one day?"

"Sir, we are discussing interesting scientific topics—there is no intention to mention your God," he responded evenly.

"Ahhhh…. *Our* God… it's *our God* is it? Is 'God', not enough?" Louw interrogated, dripping in sarcasm, trying to draw the *Dominee* in, trying to goad John into an open confrontation.

"Well yes, sir—I've heard you say often enough *'Our God'* and I am merely providing you with the respect and honor that it is your God," John welcomed a blow-out for tactical reasons but felt no emotion for the contents of it. "And, if the *whole* community wants to be accommodated, they will simply vote with their feet and not attend."

There was a moment of silence and the two men had a stare-down.

"That will be all then," Dr. Deon Louw said curtly, "You can go."

"Thank you, sir," John said cheerily, "*Dominee*..." he nodded the greeting and left.

The two men stood in silence until they could no longer hear John Fiske's footsteps disappearing to the convention room up the corridor.

"*Onbeskof!*" Deon spat, "If I could only fire him I'd do it on the spot."

"Why don't you?" Gert asked.

"Because he is forced on us. Forced from the education governors. It's politics," he shook his head, just a rapid dart of frustrated tension. "What happened with the Captain?" He asked of the *Dominee*.

Dominee Gert van der Nest had taken his complaint to the police station. Had Andre still been alive, lowly Constable or not, the *Dominee* would have called him privately and he'd have followed the request without hesitation, delay or paperwork; none of this degrading begging for decency in the charge office.

And, Gert had noted, this arrogant pretender in the role of Police Station Commander had not even had the decency and respect for the *Dominee*'s standing to invite him and his gripe into his private office. Oh, no!... He insisted on taking the complaint out in the public and open charge office where all the other coloured and black officers could hear the business.

Without Andre, the last of the old guard were now gone. And Gert felt the crushing weight of doom against his people and his culture beginning to squeeze the hope from him.

He'd asked the Police Captain very reasonably to accompany him back to the school to impress upon the new teacher that today was not the day for dissention. And the Captain had asked if he should go in his official capacity as a policeman.

Gert had not expected the question and dithered with it, undecided, his mind racing to weigh the implications if he committed either way to a reply.

"What is the difference," he'd asked of the Captain.

The Captain had said that if he did it as a colleague of the dead man he could leave to the task immediately and without further ado. He would of course be happy to conduct the complaint in his uniform for whatever impression that might make.

But if he did it as a policeman, as an official demanding compliance, he'd explained, for *that* he would need a contravention of a law and an official charge to be laid.

Gert had been unable to come up with any specific ordinance or law that would be contravened if the symposium went ahead.

"How about trespass?"

It had been clear to Gert when the Captain suggested it that it had not been a genuine suggestion; far from it, it had been highly disingenuous, the Captain's tone mocking, toying with him.

"I have already explained to you when I laid out the issue, Captain," the *Dominee* had said with a bitter timbre to his voice, drawing himself up to his full height and authority, "that this is not a question of trespass because the teacher concerned has permission. It is a question of decency and respect for our culture."

"So there is no actual law being violated then, *Dominee*...?"

The *Dominee* had clearly seen the ridicule in the man's eyes.

"...But you would like me to come with you and make the request...? Because, you see *Dominee*... this is where I'm confused; a request on my official behalf as a policeman or a request on your behalf as an *ordinary* member of the public?"

The police juniors had all been sneaking open smirks at the *Dominee* as he was being moved around like a pawn in chess; maneuvered into a checkmate. And Gert had seen how they openly mocked him with their smug smiles without their commander saying a word against it.

It had been a call of 'check' in the checkmate game and whichever way Gert could have answered he'd look like a fool.

"If you will *not* assist then I would like for you to make a statement to that effect, please." Gert had tried to divert from the head-on defeat.

"A statement?" The Captain had grinned openly.

"Yes. A statement. I would like you to make a statement." Gert's voice had risen, becoming shrill.

"A statement saying?"

Gert knew he'd been outmaneuvered. He'd been so goaded he'd blurted, wanting to make a statement without thinking through quite what its thrust should be, but he was too deep in it now to back down—he'd needed to force the Captain to refuse to take the statement so that he could share the insolence of his refusal with the community.

"I *insist* on you making a statement, Captain. Kindly get your pen and write down what I say, so that it is on the record."

"It is unusual for you to *order* me as an officer to make a statement, but I will consider it as a courtesy for you, sir, if you'll please just tell me what aspects of our discussion you wish for me to record."

There was a long pregnant silence. The only sound had been one of the policeman's ballpoint pen skidding over the foolscap sheet on which he was pretending to write, but Gert knew he was just doodling.

The *Dominee*'s face had been swollen and red with indignation. He'd taken charge of his voice and delivered his final plea with force, as if from the pulpit;

"The man I am burying today, Captain, was a friend. He was a pillar of this community." He'd halted, searching the Captain for any shred of humanity. "His father… his father before him was this station's commander. He was a policeman just like you… Do you have no respect for the uniform and what it stands for?"

"It stands for the Constitution of the Republic of South Africa," the Captain responded quietly.

The *Dominee* had turned and walked. As he went his grumbles about incompetence, corruption and lack of honor were said loud enough for all those in the charge office to hear.

The *Dominee* had heard the Captain saying in a voice measured to reach him too, "I remember Kruger's father from when I was a young boy and neither he nor his son were a policeman like me… or a policeman like any of you."

Gert had explained it all to Deon, and the two men were outraged, but they had played all of their cards. There was nothing to do now but put this matter aside and prepare to bury their friend.

Chapter 29

Dr. Louw was not comfortable with technology. In fact he hated it.

His misgivings aside, he had discovered that the new CCTV system at the school, donated recently to oversee the security of computers donated by the SKA project, was quite a useful instrument.

With it he had solved some small mysteries around the school—minor pilfering by pupils, some graffiti culprits, smokers and other anti-social behaviors. But he battled to operate its menus.

Frans van Doorn was one of the less popular of the boys. Introverted and disinterested in sports—a very real social disability—he occupied the lowest rung of social hierarchy among the learners; but he was a whizz on computers.

Ahead of the science fair meeting, Deon had spotted Frans in the corridors and asked him for a quick review of the CCTV system—how to switch between the camera frames and a few other useful details.

Dismissing the boy, he'd watched the monitor with growing alarm as the parking lot filled up and overflowed, multitudes streaming into the lecture room.

He cut to the lecture room and saw that it was extremely full already, no more seats available—and there were twenty minutes to go before the talks were scheduled to begin.

Among the familiar faces he saw a divide—a polarization of those who upheld traditional values and those who were enamored of boastful human pride as he thought of the delving into the higher sciences.

Then he saw the police Captain arriving in plain clothes. Tall and arrogant, with a confident swagger that made Deon smell the acrid sweetness of his own sudden adrenaline-fueled armpit sweat.

There was no sound on the CCTV pickup, but now he needed desperately to see if the Captain had relented and was going to do the right thing.

He made some adjustments to the settings that the boy had taught him and then hurried down to secure a seat for himself.

"My boy is very enthusiastic about the project," the Captain was saying to John Fiske, the science teacher and convener. "He's in the tenth grade and comes home every day with fantastic facts. I heard that our guests here today do our small town a great honor and I wanted to hear for myself…"

He'd noticed the school Principal close at hand, sidling closer, straining to hear what he was saying while pretending not to be listening or to even have noticed him. And he knew too that the *Dominee* and the Principal were in conference and aligned on every matter. In fact he knew about every secret meeting the men had ever held with his now departed colleague.

The Captain raised his voice a little to ensure that Louw would hear him, just to rile the man;

"…I wanted to hear our guests explaining truths that we so rarely get the chance to hear out in such a backwater. They do our town a great honor," and then he grasped Deon's elbow and Deon whirled with genuine surprise to face him, "Hello Dr. Louw—Malusi Motsoaledi, you probably don't recognize me out of uniform."

"Oh… uhmm… yes, yes… Captain Motsa…" he stammered the name badly and gave up mid way through; the expected confrontation robbing him of his poise.

"Oh, please, call me Malusi," the Captain said in measured and modulated accent, "it's easier on the European tongue."

Motsoaledi had worked hard to lose his African accent in favor of a cultured one he intended to exploit as his career took him onward, and this presumption ate at Louw and all of Louw's peers too.

"An *uppity kaffer*," they called him.

"We are very honored and grateful that you are hosting such an event with such esteemed dignitaries at your school today, sir," the Captain goaded.

"Thank you," Louw replied without meaning it, his lips pulled into a hard thin miserly line that only grudgingly gave up the terse response—he did not invite the Captain to call him Deon.

The presumption and insolence of the man was too much to take. And without another word he wafted into the crowd seeking a familiar face; the familiar face he saw was his former pupil and son of his late friend, JJ Kruger. And right next to JJ stood the boy who'd started all the trouble at the school, Dara.

A testing tap on the microphone sounded through the amplified speakers, and John began introducing the speakers and the topic inside the hall;

"...we're especially honored today to enjoy not just one but *two* internationally acclaimed scientists from quite different fields—and they're related—I mean that it's all related, both the topic and the talkers."

There was a light chuckle from the audience.

"And, much as our experts study aspects of reality that are quite apart from one another, the nature of science is that they intersect in some extraordinary ways, so that the topics chosen for this morning are not arbitrary, but intended to tell a cohesive story."

Both Marsha and Al sitting in comfortable lounge chairs nodded agreement.

"The initiative that brings our small town such vast knowledge and talent is of course the point of departure for these addresses. As most of you will already know, the SKA has its focal point here in Carnarvon, and its findings will have vast implications for humanity well into the future. From it, we expect to uncover not just the origins of the Universe but the patterns and evolving elements, molecules and chemicals that make it up—and of course, the nature of Dark Matter and Dark Energy."

He paused momentarily.

"So, there is one unbroken chain from the Big Bang, through quantum mechanics that gives rise to physics, and physics gives rise to chemistry, which in turn is the basis of biology, and of course biology ultimately works through natural selection on this planet—and most likely across the entire cosmos—to give rise to complex evolved life and civilization as we know it. And in turn, civilizations build cultures… our culture has built technologies that are delivering staggering results… results that contradict our oldest philosophies and confirm our least believable imaginings."

He paused another moment.

"And then there is us, here, today. Our lives full of all the exciting and sometimes mundane realities that make up what we call 'being alive'. For me personally, being alive goes a step further than a paycheck, bills, taxes… romantic dates, having children… entertaining or even planning my holidays. For me to *feel* alive I actively and daily have a regime of marveling at the vastness and the intricacies of that which we glibly call *reality*. I hope that our guest talkers here today can infect you with some of that same appetite for wonder. So without further ado, I hand the microphone over to Professor Marsha Martin."

A vigorous round of applause pounded out a confused rhythm from seventy percent of the attendees; the remainder sat stoically, unmoved, stony faced, arms folded or hands pointedly in laps.

"Thank you John," Marsha adjusted the microphone to her mouth. "Some of you may know that my colleague and co-speaker here today, Alok, is also my husband. And, that our son, Dara, is with us today also. Africa is an exciting place and coming here has been challenging and exhilarating all at once."

From the audience, Dara beamed at his mother. He was on crutches and still moved gingerly.

"My family is unfortunately separated to different parts of the world… it's a symptom of our careers that we must accept. There is perhaps a perception that scientists are tremendously wealthy, and although it is true that we feel very wealthy in that our work rewards us in non-monetary ways, alas, for the most part it attracts pay no better than a tradesman. This means that we live apart and when we're in the field we're quite far from easy commuting routes. So I am especially happy today to have Al here and visiting us for a short time. I am especially pleased to share this platform with him today, the first time in our careers. I wish to thank John and the school for facilitating this and ingeniously devising a topic that ropes us both in."

Seventy percent of the audience smiled, the rest did not.

"And, I am aware that the town has, in these past days, experienced the tragic loss of a beloved citizen from one of its longest-standing families. I invite that we take a minute of silence to contemplate in our own way this tragedy, and send our most sincere condolences to his son, JJ and daughter, Sonja, who have so kindly and bravely taken time to attend."

Deon, the Principal, was disgusted by the sham of her concern. He made some show of using the silent moment to leave—some of the thirty percent who had folded arms got up, tapped wives on shoulders and left too. Their vacated seats were gladly taken by others who had stood and clapped a few moments earlier.

As the silence came to its end within the lecture room and the distant microphone's muffled voice began laying forth that there would be a talk followed by question and answer sessions, the small group of deserters met in the foyer outside.

"The impertinence of it," Louw told them. "I thank you for taking a stand by walking out with me."

"We only came here to give them hell," one of the men said, and others nodded their heads.

"The *Dominee* and I both asked them to kindly not hold this meeting today... they couldn't be bothered. There is no dignity and decorum in these people. They're without decency."

As he spoke, they began to drift together away from the meeting, down the corridor; furious and unsure of their next move but happy to have registered their discontent.

"...so I will try to give some brief idea of the challenges we face when we consider interstellar travel. Alas, some of you might find it tedious to stay focused and I won't blame you for nodding off..."

A good chunk of the audience were smiling encouragingly.

"...but, if you manage to stay away, when I'm done, I'll turn you over to the real star of the show—to Alok. The reason I must go first is that I'll set up the necessary foundation of facts that will make his speculations that much more interesting...."

"I've got some facts too, you know…!" Al chirped in from the sidelines, and a ripple of chuckles ran through the crowd, and John felt vindicated for standing his ground and letting this proceed—the lighthearted banter was proving to be the ideal tonic a grieving family and community might need to take their mind off of tragedy.

Marsha smiled warmly; "Trust me… I'm the boring nerd in this family," she assured the crowd. "Al will dazzle you with the wild and crazy possibility that human beings are some product of a space faring race out in the cosmos. No doubt you've all seen the television documentaries about *'Ancient Aliens'* who, according to the pundits, allegedly came to earth and seeded it with life; or at least fast-tracked human evolution in a technological direction away from our basic ape cousins. I'm not accusing him of believing it, but it makes for a fun speculation."

Like a tennis match, the grim-faced remainder of the thirty percent shook their heads with irritated vigor. The arguments and questions they had prepared to tackle these two scientists with needed no speeches or lessons to precede them. In their opinion, it was a monumental waste of time going through the speeches in order to get to the Questions and Answers session.

"So…" Marsha began, "Space. It is rather well named, because there is quite a lot of it…"

It was met with a sea of smiles and a proportion of set faces, hardened to resist any attempts to woo them.

"I think it's quite hard to gather just how much space there really is. Let's start like this. The earth is forty thousand kilometers around, that's its circumference, so it has a diameter of just less than thirteen thousand kilometers—step back into space and you're looking at thirteen thousand kilometers from side to side. But the sun has a diameter of nearly one-comma-four *million* kilometers diameter. To give perspective, if I have a ball that is one meter high at my knee—a gym ball that represents the sun, the earth is smaller than a marble. One million three hundred thousand earths could fit into the sun."

She let it sink in.

"Now, our sun is just a star close by, and stars are just suns far away. Our sun is quite average, not the smallest, but by a long-long way from being the biggest. In the Milky Way, the galaxy our solar system finds itself in, *Antares* is the biggest, and its diameter is a truly staggering one thousand one hundred and thirteen *billion* kilometers—it has a diameter a thousand times bigger than our sun. This means that five hundred and twelve million of our suns could fit into that one single sun. On that scale where the earth is a marble and our sun is an exercise ball a meter tall—one of those *Pilate* balls at the gym—Antares is a kilometer-high mountain; Table Mountain down in Cape Town is that height… the earth is a marble next to it."

By the look on the faces, it was going to take a lot of pauses just to set the most basic ground to begin discussing interstellar travel.

"Okay—so these are the bare basics to start getting a handle on how big space is… Next fact; as my late colleague, Carl Sagan once remarked, there are more suns in the universe than there are grains of sands on all the beaches of the earth. That's a big number. To spell it out, it is ten to the power twenty-two, or, a one with twenty-three zeros behind it. And ours is just one of them."

She wrote the number on a blackboard, "*10,000,000,000,000,000,000,000 stars*"

"So if our earth could fit into one of those suns one point three million times… *Sheeew*… That's a lot of matter… a lot of *stuff* out there. And then there are dust clouds that probably push the amount of matter in the universe up by a significant figure again."

"Come on Marsha…" Al chimed in and there was a murmur of amusement through the audience; even the stony expressions nodded in agreement. "I'm only here for 3 weeks," he teased.

"We have quite a way to still go, I'm afraid." Marsha warned, "I unfortunately have to still hurt your minds quite a bit."

Someone got up muttering about the absurdity of the numbers being discussed, and left the room. His seat was taken. Marsha watched him go, allowing him to leave in silence so as not to inflame his clearly volatile mood. When he was gone, she shrugged, and there were more mild chuckles.

"Okay—so we have all this matter, all this stuff, in stars and gas clouds—but how much space is it set into? Remember, this part of the discussion is about us traveling between the stars, so I'm trying to set the scene here for the magnitude of the universe—so that my complaining husband can give you a sense of whether '*Ancient*'—or more contemporary—*Aliens* have popped by for tea or to abduct the impressionable for a quick medical."

A mobile phone rang and was cut, Marsha stole the moment to sip water. The ringing prompted others to check and turn their phones off.

"If we took all that matter and represented it as a single grain of sand, how large a room would we set that grain containing all matter in the universe into? The answer is staggering"

She turned to the board and drew a cube then wrote "32 km" on each of its sides.

"We'd need a room thirty two kilometers on a side and high… fifteen miles a side… about from horizon to horizon on a level plain… Those of you who know False Bay in Cape Town—that bay is thirty two kilometers in both directions… and, for a sense of thirty two kilometers high, consider that a Jumbo flies at about ten kilometers altitude. So, into such a vast arena you'd place a single grain of sand and smash that grain into trillions…" she pointed at the number on the board—1,000,000,000,000,000,000,000,000—"…of pieces, each representing a sun. Any questions?"

There were no questions but a sea of bewildered looking faces.

"Okay. So, like I said, space is big, really-really-really… *reeeeally* very big. The moon is a little under four hundred thousand kilometers from earth—and it takes light just over a second to cover that distance. It took our fastest spacecraft three days to make the same trip. The sun's further away; one hundred and fifty million kilometers—or around eight light minutes. You'll see that I sneakily introduced a new measure of distance there. The moon is a *light second* away, the sun is eight *light minutes* of distance away. We need this new form of measurement to start looking at the distances to the stars, because kilometers will make no more sense out there in space."

She yawned in playful pantomime, playing to some expressions of bewilderment reflected from the audience. "I warned you… I know it's tedious, but it'll be worth it to stay awake,"

The established split and mix of expressions still suggested that the majority was thoroughly enjoying the details.

"Let's press on to the juicy bits that Al will share… When you look at the *Southern Cross* here in the Southern Hemisphere, there are two pointer stars; the one closest to the cross is *Alpha Centuri*—and it is the *second* closest sun to the earth after our own sun. It is four-point-two light years away. The light you're seeing has been traveling at three hundred thousand kilometers a second for over four years to strike you in the eye. It's a humbling thought, so savor the effort the stars gone through to entertain you. Never look up again without thinking about that, because all others are very much more distant than that."

She wrote on the board again; "*42,000,000,000,000km = 4,2 light years*"

"But, if you want to stay with familiar units, a light year is around ten-trillion kilometers. Alpha Centuri is far away, and, you'll agree that four-point-two light years is easier to work with than those endless zeroes in trillions of kilometers when talking about even our closest neighbour."

She pointed to her freshly written number.

"The center of the Milky Way is around twenty six thousand light years, so its light reaching us now left the Milky Way before humans domesticated animals or planted crops. We're about half way from the center, so there's another that much out to the edge in the other direction, and another twice that to the other side of the Milky Way from its center. Now, I'll try to spare you many more figures, but each star within the Milky Way occupies about seventy eight cubic light years of space, or around three comma five light years—but it varies because gravity clusters stars, so there are pockets and open expanses—like villages here in the Karroo—where each house in the village represents a whole galaxy—except, a whole lot more of them, so maybe the microbes on the dust in the houses…"

She pointed at that latest figure on the board; $42,000,000,000,000 km = 4,2$ *light years.*

"The fastest rockets humans have ever produced have achieved speeds over sixty thousand kilometers an hour, yet they'd take eighty thousand years just to the nearest star, just over four light years away… four and a half billion years, as long as the earth has existed, to reach the Milky Way's center. Even eighty thousand years is a long time; it's almost as long as humans have been humans. Eighty thousand years is too long to sit in a spacecraft breeding generation after generation just to get there. We need something a lot faster than rockets… you can see I'm hinting at Al's speech here."

"Are we there yet?" Someone heckled in a playful voice from the audience.
"An excellent pun," Al agreed, "Come on Marsha, I'm itching to talk."
The easy fun-filled atmosphere was buoyant for most, the hardliners sat, unmoved, like cats with swishing tails—Marsha systematically laying down a solid foundation of established facts.

"Simmer down boys," she quipped back. Not much more from me. But since I'll be testing you on this later, let's just recap distances: If the sun were now reduced to what I'd said the earth was earlier, the size of a marble, the distance from the sun to the Earth, which we call an '*Astronomical Unit*" or *AU,* would be about a meter and a third—four feet in old money. Well… then the Earth would be almost *invisible* because it would be barely thicker than a sheet of paper. So, for more perspective, on this scale, since it takes light eight minutes to travel those four feet, the *orbit* of the Moon would be about six millimeters in diameter or three millimeters from the earth—which is about the size of a pinprick. On this scale, our closest neighboring star, Proxima, is about three hundred and thirty six kilometers away—two hundred and ten miles in Americanese. Call it four hours drive if you don't break the speed limit. Space is big, distances are huge."

She wrote once more on the board, *"900 years"*, and as she wrote she said; "Now I can see I'm losing most of you and my husband wants the floor, so I'll wind this up as quickly as I can."

"Let's say you took Methuselah from the Bible; at nine-hundred years, he's the longest living human ever claimed, so we're using him as our astronaut; we'll stick him on a rocket as a baby and aim it at the nearest star, maximizing speed to get him there before he dies nine centuries later. Just one of the problems you'd encounter to achieve this within a millennium would be the *kind* and *quantity* of fuel. You'd of course also need to accelerate the fuel you're carrying, in order to accelerate you more. The kind of rockets we have right now in the early twenty-first Century use chemical propellant, and, were all the matter in the universe nothing but chemical rocket fuel, there wouldn't be enough of it to make that trip in such a relatively short nine-century transit— So… forget interstellar travel with our present chemical rockets. We need something else… Nuclear bomb propulsion, if we could build such a thing, would be better but you'd still need a thousand million—a billion—supertanker-loads worth of nuclear bombs… so, forget that too. Using fusion rockets… a thousand supertanker loads might do it… thing is, we have no idea how we'd make fusion rockets… Antimatter rockets? If we could make them—and at this moment in time total human production of anti-matter over the last several decades stands at less than a fraction of a gram—we'd need ten railway tanker loads. And when you get there you'd need the same amount again to decelerate on the other side. And, that's without going into how you'd accelerate up to the necessary speed without killing everyone aboard with the G's."

"Star Wars made it seem a lot easier," somebody in the second row suggested loudly, and a few laughed.

"Ahhh…. Hollywood," Marsha sighed. "Oh… that it was so easy…. Yet, Hollywood does *actually* point to something realistic—Warp Drive. If you think you've heard of it you've watched Star Trek. Digging too deeply into the reasons why light speed can't be exceeded is a conference on its own, so I'll spare you the details."

"Please… and thank you!" Al chimed in again and the audience burbled agreement.

"You can't exceed the speed of light for fundamental reasons. However, you might be able to collapse space or expand space faster than light speed… *that* does not violate physics. In theory we can do it but for certain we'll need lots of energy, lots more energy than we know how to access—I'm talking energy levels far beyond nuclear fission or fusion—beyond our H-Bombs… far, far… *faaar* beyond them. But the mathematics is worked out—all we need is the energy and technology. Those of you who came to my keynote speech a few weeks back will recall the Kardashev scale and us attaining Type-One civilization status… well, that's what I was talking about then. In about two hundred and fifty years—give or take—we should be there if we don't blow ourselves up first; we might well have warp drive."

Al was tapping his watch and some were jovial, enjoying the pair interacting. Of course, some were not.

"I know… I know… this is exciting stuff—I hate talking, but once I start…"

"Don't I know… you never stop," he finished the statement to laughter.

"Last point, I promise; a warp drive collapses space in front of you and expands space behind you. If a traveller wanted to go to say, London, rather than traveling the ten thousand or so kilometers in whatever time it takes at a certain speed, you'd collapse the distance in front of you to a meter and expand it behind you to ten thousand kilometers and step across the one meter *'gulf'* in a second without any acceleration issues—what happens to everything in that collapsed space is something we simply don't yet know… but it probably won't please the unlucky residents. The good news for you, though, is that you would effectively not have to travel at any speed, you would not have to accelerate and suffer acceleration's problems. There are possibly civilizations out in deep space that are not just hundreds of years ahead of us as we are hundreds of years ahead of the explorers who sailed in wooden ships to the Cape, but thousands, tens of thousands, maybe millions of years advanced over us. Do they have warp drive? Possibly, yes. And, with that I'm certain you'll be please to know that, I conclude. Any questions."

"Wat 'n klomp kak," came a lone voice from the audience and many turned to look as the big man with a two-tone khaki and mauve shirt who'd called it a *load of shit*, stood up, buttons around is belly straining against his bulk. He shuffled in his short pants and stocky powerful legs past the knees of others seated in rows and then strode to the exit.

Marsha looked at the audience in askance and somebody made a gesture that universally says, *"Forget it."* Marsha shrugged and sat down.

Al rose and came to the lectern, adjusting the microphone for himself, "Thank you, Marsha. Exhausting as it was, it's really set my talk up beautifully… Do we need a break? Stretch the legs; or you want to go on?"

"I think we can use 15 minutes?" John Fiske suggested.

Al agreed, "I believe there are refreshments in the foyer."

John confirmed it.

People gratefully took to the break.

"Wow… quite a mouthful," JJ congratulated her.

"I barely scratched the surface," Marsha assured.

Like a star with a myriad satellites clustered around, Marsha had a throng of admirers all wanting to pose private questions.

"The real issue," she was explaining, "Is that this stuff is hard… it's complex and intricate… very often it's counter intuitive."

"Absolutely, that's why…" JJ gestured toward two or three small groups filling out of the building toward their cars, "…so many are satisfied in the fantasy world and pettiness. Magic's easy to claim and agree with. Children accept it unquestioningly... *'it's a miracle'* answers everything."

"I'm not touching that," Marsha insisted.

"Guess I'm still in reality's recovery room," JJ made room for Al who had joined them.

"I just caught the tail end of that... there's an important realization we must grasp," Al began to explain. "Our brains evolved on the African plains for two primary functions—to eat and to breed. Science... all those facts that Marsha just went... without even touching quantum mechanics and relativity asks way more of us than we're evolved to deal with; it's remarkable that any of us can grasp any of it," Al pointed out.

"Why are humans different to other animals?" Someone asked.

"*Co-operation*... As a species we are co-operative with one another; that allowed us to organize ourselves and to create cutting edge technologies like clubs and arrow... other technologies all flow from co-operation."

"A lot of people don't cooperate..." someone in the crowd, pointed out. "...they exploit."

"Quite right," Al agreed. "I'm not talking about individuals, I'm talking about communities; we're weak as individuals, strong as groups. If too many in a community are out for themselves and stop cooperating—the community fails; the system is self-regulating."

"The Ten Commandments are all the cooperation we need," came the retort.

"Hmm... but the notion of Ten Commandments belonging to any religion is peculiar, it suggest that nobody knew murder and theft and jealousies were wrong before they were *'given'* insight from an external agent."

"If we weren't given it, where did it come from?"

"We're social animals; pitifully weak as individuals—thin skin, no nails, useless teeth for defense or attack. It goes back to group cooperation and self-regulation; codified 'commandments' are not epiphanies, they simply document observed behavior. Cooperation is written into our DNA and the fabric of our societies."

A throng had collected, hands in the air to ask questions; some having only caught tail ends of the latest statement.

"You're saying the Ten Commandments are not valid?" A gruff man challenged.

"Not at all. I'm saying that the basis of them, the *shall-not's* were already operating long before they were recorded. They're the unmentioned fabric of any viable society—per definition they *have* to be there for a society to begin to develop."

"I don't know how you can say that?"

"Groups rely on trust. A group who thinks murder, rape and theft were *okay*, aren't going to survive very long because trust breaks down… In an anarchic society, nobody has trust, nobody cooperates… they're vulnerable to being toppled by those who do co-operate… that much must be obvious?"

"Can you give an example of an *imaginary* group who didn't cooperate?" The man was unrelenting.

"Well, no, of course I can't give an example of a group that was uncooperative and went extinct because… well, they're extinct… you prove the point with your question. They may have arisen, but were gone in a generation…. I clearly can't give an example of something that never arose."

"Very clever!" The man spat the sarcasm at Al, apparently unaware that he had caught himself in a trap; "You clever people always trying to fool us with word tricks."

"It's not a trick of words sir, it is a fact. And my apologies to you if it seems offensive."

"Ja… everything about this presentation is offensive."

"I… I'm sorry about that."

"You… you so clever, hey? You tell the people here; what successful population don't have God in their life?" he altered the angle of his thrust.

"Sweden?" Al ventured. "They do all right with maybe 90% secularists… atheists by another name. For that matter, most of Scandinavia and Western Europe—totally secular; I'd rather live in Scandinavia than… oh… Nigeria or Saudi or Afghanistan."

"Ha! You won't give up will you?!"

"I will if I'm wrong."

"Lots of scientists are God fearing."

"Lots? I can confirm that ninety seven percent of the scientists who make up the Royal Fellows of Sciences, ninety three percent of the National Academy of sciences aren't— they're non-theists…"

"Those scientists!" the man said it as if he'd hit *pay dirt*. "The ones who set off nuclear bombs."

"In fairness sir, The Royal Fellows aren't in the business of setting off bombs... Regrettably, yes, the bombs and all technologies available to politicians and zealots wouldn't be possible without the help of scientists," Al suggested, and added, "But if you want an example of peaceful people who lived without Commandments, most hunter gatherer groups from the Amazon to the Kalahari Bushmen... right here in your own back yard... are good examples."

"You call the Bushmen successful?" he scoffed then laughed aloud.

"Measuring success requires a frame of reference; I agree... they're not successful at making weapons and forming armies, which helps explain their poverty and present condition living on the fringes of desirable lands that we took from them."

The heads were bobbing back and forth; another tennis match of ideas being lobbed and slammed between opponents.

"So... you must bring that up? That we took their land?"

"Well I think the fact's unavoidable... Nobody can deny that the Bushmen had the run of the whole of Southern Africa until us farmers arrived, killing the wildlife and putting up fences. Don't be confused by the current situation; they didn't choose to live in a dustbowl and eke a living from scraps. That's only since *we* came."

"You emphasize *we*?" The man challenged. "How can *you* say 'we'?"

"I think you're talking about my blackness... it's clear I'm Indian... Well... my people like your people are farmers... As a farming culture, we equally share responsibility of displacing all of the *first people* everywhere, the hunters. I'm part of the 'we'—*we* all are; farming made us settle, invest and want to protect our turf. We invented ownership and wiped out and legislated against the threat of anyone who didn't recognize it."

"Who says my ancestors killed anyone?" He took personal affront.

"Lets' stay away from intent," Al played aikido with the man, deflecting the thrust into a political debate. "Farmers are in much closer daily contact with livestock... In China they live *cheek by jowl* with them, and that's why we see most diseases today coming out of China where microbes jump species… Bird Flu… Swine Flu… They're not just names, they're pedigrees."

"And?"

"Let's say your ancestors never intended or actually killed anyone… any of the Bushmen."

"Ja… let's say that."

"Okay… but your genes from Eurasia had hundreds of generations of immunity built in; we Europeans and Asians brought diseases to parts of the world that didn't have immunity… we decimated the local populations without intending to. We also did wipe out the game for our domestic grazing."

The man looked long and hard at Al, almost sizing him up and measuring him for his coffin. His mind dueling with how to handle this difficult skinny little black pixie; then an argument clincher popped into his mind;

"Then that is God's will," he said emphatically to Al. "They're no use to serve God so He gave us the ability to drive them out."

"Sir, I don't want to challenge you on that. I can appreciate that this is your firmly held stance and I only hope to give you some perspective that is borne out by my study in this field."

"So you're saying that these people, the Bushmen, are somehow useful?" He came in at the knees again, battle set in the thrust of his stance.

"All people are useful to themselves, sir. Again it's the frame of reference that is important… might I expand on that?" Al asked politely, not wanting to trigger a showdown.

JJ had maneuvered into a protective position close by. The man looked peeved and JJ smiled; there was chemistry here and it wasn't good.

The man's stance relaxed and he nodded his permission for Al to go on.

"I'm guessing you feel that your *own* utility is anchored in a celestial Being; the Bushmen feel that their utility is anchored in their ancestors and children. I can only say that if we as modern urban societies want to look for utility in Bushmen, we have two choices—to look at their sustainable lifestyles in terms of environmental impact… which is negligible… it's also unrealistic for our industrialized world; or, we can look at the *very* useful lessons we can learn from their social anthropology."

"English is my second language," the man said. "Don't try your tricks to confuse."

"I'm sorry, I've no intention to trick you—I just don't want to insult you either by being too simplistic and appearing condescending," Al told him, gesturing a quasi surrender with his hands. "I'll conclude it simply, and then I must get back inside for the presentation."

People were filling back into the lecture room.

"In the modern world we're at odds with ourselves. For five hundred thousand generations… not years but *generations*… we lived in small wandering groups. We'd rarely see a stranger and if they were friendly we'd trade or mix our genes."

"Ja, sure…" it was a challenge Al ignored.

"If they were hostile we'd move away… When there's no hospital and combat is hand-to-hand—and when there's no ownership of land or animals, and there's abundance of both… it's better to retreat and live peacefully elsewhere."

"As if you were there to see this," the man laughed again.

"It's an archaeological fact… it's what I study. Farming locked us down to a piece of land. It was an investment that paid dividends only if we could protect it from plunder. We've been farmers for five hundred generations, and…"

John tapped Al on the shoulder and said, "Two minutes."

"…and our psychology and how we deal with one another developed for a thousand times longer in a *completely* different environment to the one that we… *every one of us*… are now immersed in. Our psychology is poorly adapted to dealing with large crowds of strangers."

"...and so what? What good is all this *'knowledge'*?"

"It results in stress... stress kills; massive doses of *cortisol*... *adrenaline*... we're bathed in it, and it's not good for us. We spend our lives in conflict and mistrust; these manifest as racism and tensions far in excess of their logical necessity. And for what? For *believing* slightly different things to one another... Most beliefs that we hold are simply accident of birth—where and when we're born; hardly worth fighting over."

"*Aaaaall* this *gedoente*... all your *loooong* story... based on you believing in five hundred *thousand* generations," he laughed out loud again. "The Bible clearly tells us that the planet is a few thousand years old... so you're talking nonsense."

"That sir is not an issue of belief. The evidence supports what I just said."

The man didn't hear Al's response, he was stomping away, through the doors and out to the parking lot.

Al made his way back to the lectern.

The portion of the crowd that had previously been forced to stand were now still standing while many empty seats stood vacant.

John checked the corridor outside, it was deserted so he invited those standing to fill the vacated seats.

"Was it something my wife said?" Al smiled as they took their new seats and the proportion of smiles returning to him suggested that the attendance loss was borne entirely by the thirty percent who'd shown their disdain earlier during Marsha's presentation.

The crowd settled and hushed.

"So... *Ancient Aliens* and *Modern UFO's*," he chirped cheerily. "A riveting and also, I suspect, potentially touchy topic..."

His prognosis validated by pockets of hardened glares.

"In science-speak we call it *The Fermi Paradox*... an apparent contradiction between high estimates for the existence of extraterrestrials and humanity's lack of evidence for these speculated civilizations."

Al saw not just cell phone cameras trained on him by the unsmiling, but a tripod supporting an old-style video camera in the second row; arranged to film between the heads of the row in front of it.

He quickly thought the unsolicited filming through, weighing whether to request no filming that might jeopardize his agreements with publishers, but concluded that there would be nothing he'd say today that would approach a problem.

"I'm going deviate from my script, to start with an important aspect underpinning our endeavor here; a question triggered by someone in the lobby a moment ago. It's a little off the rest of my topic and, strictly, falls out of my area of expertise, but its relevance will become clear when I reach my original brief. If I do make an error, my esteemed colleague here," he gestured toward Marsha, "will surely interject to rescue me from folly."

Marsha inclined her head in acknowledgement.

"I was asked *'what radio astronomy is and why build the SKA here… at Carnarvon?'* Well, optical light—the light we see—occupies only a tiny sliver of the electromagnetic spectrum that starts at Gamma-rays and goes down in frequency and energy through X-ray, Ultra-violet, Visible light, Infrared—which we experience as heat. The spectrum goes on to fall in frequency down to Radio and Microwave. We think of light as somehow 'special', but it isn't. It is just that we have evolved organs—the eye—that can detect and focus it. When we say *'the* eye' it's rather a misnomer since there are in excess of forty different types of separately evolved eyes, and eyes within those categories at different levels of evolvement that present across species."

The man training the tripod camera seemed to be having a lot of trouble focusing between the heads while remaining undetected and Al was amused, wandering why he was going to so much trouble to keep the very obvious contraption hidden.

"So—how did eyes evolve? Our skin reacts to ultra-violet… it burns. My ancestors came from a very sunny place where Vitamin-D from the sun was plentiful, so I inherited high levels of melanin which shows as black. Many here come from northern latitudes where, over many-many generations, limited sunshine would have culled out those with high melanin… with black skins… leaving that population with melanin-poor skins…

with white skins. In those climes and for obvious reasons, your ancestors did not need the protection against harsh sun. This is how natural selection works. My skin in sunless climates would leave me with rickets and other Vitamin-D deficient ailments."

A hand was up from one of the non-smilers.

"Yes?"

"So how do blacks survive England and Europe?" The man challenged and looked around with pride, knowing he'd publicly stumped the scientist.

"Great question. Diet...." Al responded. "Modern diets compensate for Vitamin-D deficiencies from a lack of sun; we've artificially overcome that aspect of what natural selection would normally do."

"And what has this to do with *eyes* and *radio*?" The man asked.

"You're right. It's a minor sidetrack but it does have bearing. I'm making the point that although our eyes can't see infrared another organ, our skin 'can'... can 'see' infrared. It can't see it as you think of seeing but it reacts to the sun—and that's all vision is; cells that react to light, cells that trigger a minute electrical pulse along a nerve that runs to an analytical part of the brain called the *Brodmanns Area* and *Visual Cortex* of the *Cerebral Cortex* at the back of the skull. So modern sunburn and the tan that follows is sort of an analogue for the very basis of the original evolution of the eye. Light travels in straight lines, light and shadow falling on an ancient ancestor gave a crude advantage to the animal that can detect the change. Those animals that reacted, survived predators and found prey more easily. Over time those patches of ordinary skin tended to build up in the offspring of those with reactive patches, and these patches eventually became what we now know as retina."

Heads shaking in protest to his thesis gave Al the impression that the original thirty percent was now closer to ten percent of the audience who were there for altercation.

"The other side of the visible spectrum, infrared, we feel as heat and we react to it too, always keeping ourselves in an optimum zone between cooking and freezing. I'm sure you can appreciate why evolving heat detection mechanisms proved to be a good environmental predictor. But we don't naturally detect Gamma or X-rays. Why is this?"

"Because they're not plentiful in the environment?" A youngster ventured.

"Excellent! Yes. You don't evolve in a direction if there is no pressure to do so. And radio or microwave... why didn't we evolve these?"

"Same reason?" The same lad suggested.

"No. Radio is quite plentiful, actually. But as a wave, radio is too low-energy and has too long a wavelength to be able to move electrons from one energy state to another as visible light does. It's a mechanical issue... Good so far, Marsha?"

"Gold star," she smiled.

"Good. I learned a lot from this lady," and they exchanged a smile. "So I've diverted my speech, but you'll understand why in a second... Well, the Big Bang, the origins of the universe and the stars themselves broadcast not just in visible light, but all energy levels across the spectrum so that radio astronomy is just another way of looking at what is going on out there. And, because as Marsha's lecture pointed out, you're seeing the sun as it was eight minutes ago, and Alpha Centuri as it was four years ago, we're always looking back in time. Radio waves come through the walls of your house and light doesn't—so radio astronomy tells us stories that the light can't when it gets blocked by dust clouds in deep space. And because we humans have developed the technology to create radio waves, our mobile phones and TV stations have flooded our urban environments with so much 'noise' that we need a big quiet corner of the planet to listen to the cosmos."

"So why come here? Why not go to Australia? Why come bother us?" heads turned to look at the challenger who evidently was taking the whole thing very personally.

"That was a decision that I'm afraid is beyond me, sir."

"Well, for my money you can all *fokoff*"—he said and there were a few lonely claps.

"I'm sorry that you feel that sir, we don't mean to offend," Al said. "We're up to where I was going to begin... Radio and Ancient Aliens... what's the connection? Well, the first connection is that if there are advanced civilizations in space, they'll probably be making radio noise. If we listen, we may hear them and *SETI*, the *Search for Extra-Terrestrial Intelligence*, is doing just that."

"Then why haven't you found them yet?" Came a challenge from the audience.

Al pointed at the numbers Marsha had written on the board.

"That's the problem. Lots of potential out there but the distances and time make any signals fleetingly tiny and desperately far away. Turn the issue around... The Milky Way is a hundred thousand light years across—we as a civilization have only been adding our radio broadcasts to the cosmos for a lot less than a hundred years, so that beyond a bubble around the earth that's *at most* a hundred light years in any direction; two hundred light years across... beyond that advancing edge, humanity is 'invisible'... we don't exist yet on the radio hit parade. Our radio has not reached even one fifty-*thousandth* of the stars in just our galaxy, and our galaxy is one in maybe a *trillion* like it. We can assume the same is true for their signals not having had time to reach us... And perhaps those who are a lot more advanced have moved away from radio to other as-yet undetected methods of communication. Am I starting to hint at the problem?"

There was a general murmur of agreement.

"Perhaps they'd need to dig into their museums of ancient history to find a radio receiver to hear us... and that's '*if*' they knew where in the sky to point it," he gestured, opening his upturned hands to an imaginary sky—then focusing to an imaginary point; "The same way that their host star, their sun, is only a prick of light in *our* sky; our sun and planet are only a pinprick of light to *them*... The only way to collect vanishingly weak signals that leak into the cosmos from us or them, is to use an antenna like the SKA, very precisely aimed at that pinprick in direction, and then trying to pick out the target signal from the background radio 'noise' that is everywhere. If that's not a big enough task there are *billions* of possible frequency ranges to listen for. To call it a monumental task, is to trivialize the challenge."

"It sounds like you're describing a waste of time," the same voice challenged again.

"Surely, learning and discovery can never be a waste of time, sir? Almost every item you have in your convenient modern life is the result of an accident of discovery, looking for one thing and finding another that is useful."

"Professor," came a friendly voice, for the first time a female's voice. "Can we move onto UFO's please."

"I'm a lowly Doctor I'm afraid, not a Professor. But yes, and forgive the side-track."

"It's been very interesting, but I'm itching to know. Do you believe in UFOs?" She inquired.

"Is there life out there? Let me start with that. And I'm not just talking aliens driving spacecraft... microbial life will do.... Well; latest estimates put the number of planets in just the Milky way at six hundred billion."

He drew a line under Marsha's numbers and added his own number to the board: "600,000,000,000—Planets in Milky Way"

"The Milky Way is one of perhaps four hundred billion galaxies, each probably containing that number of planets."

He pointed to the number he'd just written and wrote out the next number: ">400,000,000,000—Galaxies in the Universe"

"I don't want to hurt your mind like Marsha did, but these are the facts. The probability of life arising and becoming technologically capable is tiny, but the opportunities for it are huge. I would say 'yes', in my opinion there is not just life but probably intelligent life in the universe. But saying '*is*', is a long way from saying 'is *now*', because 'now' only applies here.... The 'now' as we look at the sun was in all reality eight minutes ago from the sun's perspective... It may have catastrophically exploded seven minutes ago, and we'd say it's still there. In the case of Proxima it's four years ago. Do you see the problem?"

He took the chalk and dabbed a familiar pattern of dots, three in a row with some other prominent points around it, talking as he did so:

"We look out at Orion's Belt in the night sky and pick the middle star—the other two are at different distances from us and their apparent arrangement from our perspective is just an accident of alignment; they aren't really in a line at all... Well that middle star's *now* was sixteen hundred years ago. What was going on in Earth's history sixteen hundred years ago? The Vikings hadn't even arisen... The Roman Empire was just collapsing. So Orion's 'now' occurred *then*; it's all very mind boggling but inescapable. Are you following me?"

The lady said she was.

"So… UFO's. I'll discuss speculations about UFO's in our history when I'm done with the present." He thought a moment, "I'm going to paraphrase somebody some of you may have heard of, the astrophysicist Neil deGrasse Tyson; and I urge you to look him up… YouTube is full of his stuff…. He was asked this same question, 'Do you believe in UFOs' and he looked long and hard at the questioner and said 'Remember what the 'U' in UFO stands for'. It means *'Unidentified'*. So that when you see a light in the sky and say, 'I can't identify it as anything I know, so it must be a UFO from another planet', your speculation really ought to end there; at the point you declared that it is *unidentified*. To leap from declared uncertainty to the absolute certainty that 'therefore it must be aliens visiting from another planet', is not helpful."

"But I have seen strange lights," she insisted.

"There are just so many tricks that light can play and our brains are just so very easily fooled—this is how conjurers and street magicians make their living. Not by manipulating the laws of physics but by fooling your brain—it's much easier to fool your brain than to manipulate or reverse physics. We need to get past this notion that our brains are perfect or even good data receivers. They simply aren't. This is why we have machines to do it, to take the human element out of perception."

"So, yes or no… UFOs visit earth or not?" She insisted on a definitive answer.

"It's possible, but improbable. We just haven't made enough noise in the galaxy to single ourselves out of the… what was it? Other six hundred billion planets that also need to be investigated by aliens before they randomly find us. They may have come, but it's unlikely. And given the problems of travel that Marsha covered earlier, the time and vast energies needed to take a look, wouldn't you expect unmanned probes first? Would you expect them to come bumbling in here… actually crashing? Or would you expect them to obscure themselves and watch? I personally wouldn't be impressed with the ones that crashed. You know… they're the failures of the Cosmos… to come across the galaxy and then fall out of the sky when they get here…"

The audience applauded.

"Friendly or hostile?" Someone else asked.

"Another interesting question. The good Professor Stephen Hawking is on record thinking they'd be hostile… wanting our women and wine maybe. And he does have a point in that we'd expect to see predators becoming dominant civilizations."

"Why predators," a voice in the midst queried.

"It's in the chemistry and biology. There are ratios of how much energy is available at different levels of a feeding chain. Plants are the lowest level of energy—that's why plants aren't all that active—and then energy accumulates as herbivores eat plants and predators eat herbivores. Lions lie all day in the shade and spend a relatively short period acquiring high-yield nutrition. Their prey animals spend all day eating. Herbivores simply don't have the time off from absorbing nutrition to become a technological species."

"So if they're predators, surely they'd predate?" The lady from earlier posed.

"Another great question, but this goes back to that bottleneck that Marsha talked about in her last lecture on the Kardashev Scale and its Type-One, Two, and Three Civilizations. The civilizations that can't overcome their own meanness, their own suspicions—oh… and you see that word again taking us back to where our morals come from…"

He directed his address to the group who'd stood with him earlier, out in the foyer.

"To acquire inter-stellar travel and become a potential hostile threat to another planet or species there, we have to learn to live with ourselves and get past our suspicions and pettiness. We have to see a planet and its hosts of species as holistic and in balance. Those civilizations that may be out there in the cosmos that *can't* get past their own base predatory selves, will tend to implode and wipe their own civilizations out, never becoming a galactic threat. For this reason I think my esteemed colleague Stephen is wrong. I think that any civilization that becomes inter-stellar has gone through the filter of its own predatory nature and emerged on the other side sensitive to environments."

"You don't think they want our resources? To enslave us?" The lady piped up again.

"That takes us into the realms of the Ancient Alien stories. That the Gods we read about in our Bibles and other mythologies were in fact from outer space? Aliens?"

"Yes."

"I hope I was successful in opening this part of discussion by giving you a sense of why modern UFO's are unlikely. I also hope I simultaneously convinced you that visitors who did or do visit will be inclined toward hospitality and nurture? Now let me deal with their motivation to come here."

He noticed JJ nodding and smiling, and he momentarily felt a pang for how he and his sister must be processing all of this cosmic grandeur on the very day that their private universe was so imploded.

"We evolved for the prevailing conditions on this, *our* earth; for its gravity and its quite specific mix of gasses in the atmosphere. The chances that any creature from elsewhere could arrive here and be capable of stepping out as we saw on the old Star Trek series are... well... remote and probably impossible. That they could consume our meat, fruits or vegetables and derive nutrition is unlikely—the enzymes of digestion are just too specific to where they'd come from; I mean... we share a lot with a cow... a lot of DNA and the same biosphere. We almost share the same morphology... body-plan... yet we can't eat grass and cows can't eat meat... So why on earth would one an alien to be able to digest grass or meat?"

"They'd probably want our water," she persisted.

"There is a lot more water to be had with far less trouble than to drop down into what is the gravity-well of earth to get it, contaminated from their perspective as it would be with microbes that are specific to here."

"How about gold?" Some called out.

"Gold's only valuable to us because it's rare, but gold and other useful elements are plentiful in deep space. A Type-One civilization, the minimum level that could travel as we're speculating, would have energies at their disposal that would make it laughably uneconomical to come here. There is no magic involved in making elements if you have the energies as they would have, you'd simply produce them from the raw materials of the cosmos, precisely as they have been naturally produced through fusion reactions in the middle of stars."

A mighty growl of irritation went up in the middle of the group. Three big men wearing the two-tone shirts and short pants with powerful legs that seemed a standard uniform for those who were perpetually grumpy, all stood in unison and shuffled grousing past seated legs and then strode up the aisle and out; followed by a gaggle of women and children.

Al let the deserters go in silence.

When they were gone the persistent lady relented, "Your arguments are very powerful. Thank you, it's a lot to take in. My last question is this; why all over the world do we see the same reports in history of the same sort of visitations and the same pyramids built."

"Human brains are the same everywhere, their architecture is almost identical; their common experience as proto-humans and then humans is six or more million years old; as a species we have only been out of Africa and having slightly different experiences for say seventy thousand years… which is a fraction of that time. We are much more similar than we are different, so that our brains deal with the environment the same way wherever you go; we see lights in the sky and our common origins which are not that long ago, compel us to think in the same way and come to the same conclusions. Because pyramids are wide at the base and narrow at the top—just like a cairn of stones—it's how things pile up and it's why all ancient human civilizations did it this inefficient way—inefficient in terms of material used to useful indoor space created. What would be remarkable is if various civilizations built inverted pyramids that contravene this 'pilling' tendency… Of course, we stopped building pyramids because we figured out how to make more sophisticated structures that are more efficient. And before I'm asked it; if Aliens built the pyramids you'd think they'd have at least dropped a small piece of equipment, something more than a pile of stones to say they were here."

"Just one last question," John had been trying to close proceedings down.

"The gentleman over there," Al indicated a younger man wearing the two-tone shirt and short-pants uniform of the naysayers.

The man stood up and cleared his throat. He had a round and ruddy face echoed by a rotund body. "You people think an explosion caused all of this. This universe and life?"

"I think you mean The Big Bang, sir?"

The man allowed that he did, "Ja—and where's it expanding into? Into heaven? You'll eventually come to God when that happens whether you like it or not."

Sporadic victory laughs sounded in the audience.

"Well, that's strictly a question for my wife but I'll take it and she can score me. I'll do it what justice I can as quickly as I can...though we could spin it off into an entire conference on that question alone."

The audience who had not just laughed now smiled and nodded.

"First—it was not an *explosion* it was a very rapid *expansion*; there's a subtle but important difference. Second—it was not an explosion *in* space and time, which is properly referred to as four-dimensional spacetime, but rather an explosion *of* spacetime—not *in*, but *of*... that's a very important point. It's important because it addresses what we're expanding into—you proposed heaven, sir?"

The man nodded—"Ja."

"I'll agree with that," Al said and the man looked surprised, "I'll agree that we're expanding into a heaven. Let me explain why: The edge of our earth is not toward the horizon, it is 'up'... correct? It is not left or right or forward or back on the two-dimensional surface—that would just send you on a never-ending journey round and round the spherical ball. To find the *edge* of earth you don't find it—like a cliff at the edge of the flat plain—on the surface, you find it in the third dimension of *up* or *down*."

The man inclined his head with suspicion, analyzing the answer for a trick that Al seemed to be gunning for.

"I make this point because our ancestors who didn't know that they were living on the surface of a sphere—a ball—thought that they could find the edge of their flat world by traveling over the horizon... Correct?"

The man didn't answer, so Al pressed him to agree or not.

"Correct," the man grudgingly agreed.

"So the edge of earth is not on the two dimensions we live on—on that we agree. Now, remember I told you we live in spacetime—spacetime is one thing—three dimensions of space, one of time. Yes?"

"Yes," the man said, but it was a hesitant agreement—his hackles and suspicions high.

"Well—the edge of the universe is not endlessly up. If you were to travel forever at unimaginable speed in any direction into space, you would not reach an edge. You would not reach a boundary, you would not cross into heaven; same as traveling over the surface of the earth—you'd find no center and no boundary. What our universe is expanding into does *not* lie in the three dimensions of *space* but in the fourth dimension of *time*. The center of our universe is our *past* the edge of our universe is our distant *future*. So—we are forever expanding toward your future, perhaps a heaven in the distance of time? I'd like to make it so."

"I rate that a ten," Marsha suggested.

"Aggghh…" the man made a guttural throaty sound, "you *blerry* scientists think you are so clever but it's all bullshit."

Chapter 30

Dominee Gert felt many years past his age as he shuffled up the steps to his pulpit; he had become an old man overnight, withered, tired and worn by tragedy and conflicts, broken and depressed by the loss of a brother in arms and dire realizations.

He surveyed his flock and there was not a seat to be had. It was many a year since every pew was crammed as it was today; even the aisles were overflowing with a crowd standing to the doorway, straining to hear.

A sea of silent somber faces, mainly white, watched him worriedly; he looked like death hovering over the casket of his dead friend. It pleased him that the few brown faces peppering the throng were respectfully well away to the back of proceedings, out of the fold as he thought they should be.

But in that entire crowd two faces leapt at him—the black of their skin drawing his eye and ire—the boy, the devil-child from his school class—the Indian and his father, and alongside them his mistress, the mother of the child; Gert could not bring himself to recognize that they had been married in the eyes of God. With impertinence and no shame they occupied seats that could have been had by good people, by the Godly; they'd seized seats near the front—only a row back and sickeningly close to the bereaved widow, her daughter and the dead man's mother; a pitiful trio alone on the empty plain of the front row bench.

With a surge of nausea the reason was clear—they were at JJ's right hand; JJ, the son who had driven his father to take his own life… the unrepentant prodigal with no shame who now brought the instruments that caused this tragedy right into the holiest place; not just under God's roof but almost up God's very nose.

The insult of it all made him want to clear the entire church hall. This was a service for the eyes of his Lord and for the heart of his departed friend... And then it struck him; this was God's will that he should endure this provocation and prevail.

"I want to go," Dara had insisted.
"But what on earth for?" Marsha had responded. In her opinion it was an exceedingly bad idea.
"To support the living, my friends," he'd said simply.
"I can't fault that," Al had shrugged. "Funerals are for the living—to say goodbye and to help the family say goodbye."
And so it had been arranged.
Marsha had spoken with JJ and he had agreed that it would be a nice touch, he'd agreed with the point of a funeral along the lines Al had suggested.
"Frankly JJ, I am rather concerned though. We are going into a hornet's nest," Marsha had fretted.
"I'll take care of you. The first two rows always stand open for family and close friends. You are about my closest friends in this town right now so you walk in with me and I'll seat you close at hand. I'm coming to your address at the school beforehand, so we can go out for lunch and then straight on over to the church if that works for you."
Dawie and Dara had discussed it and Dawie had wanted to go too, to make the statement of solidarity that Dara had explained to him; but his family would not allow it, not even with JJ's protection.

"We are gathered here today to say our goodbyes to a great friend and pillar of our community. He was a brother to me..."
Uncharacteristically—in all his decades of preaching it had never happened before—Gert's throat clammed tight and his voice fluted an octave too high as he dabbed at a tear that broke over the rim of his eyelid.
"...A brother... A brother and a husband..." he looked at the widow, Johanna—so hunched and small on the hard wooden benches; "...a son and a father," he looked from Andre's ancient mother in the family row to Sonja, his eyes passing over and through JJ as if he was not there.

"He has gone home to his Father and will for eternity remain in his father's Grace. Andre was a man of uncompromising justice. Like the Lord Jesus who was his model and guide, our brother Andre was a protector of the poor and a shield against evil. We are born in sin and many die in sin. And some are born in the Lord's favor but become prodigals who leave and return in glory…. And then there are sons who take the devil's path and refuse to yield." He glared at JJ long and accusingly, and JJ held his stare unblinkingly as if nothing had been said.

"There are many who cannot be with us today," he said, "…they have sent their apologies and condolences. I want to read from some of these for the family."

He began to read them, one at a time, skipping past the condolence from Morgan for her estranged farther-in-law in favor of more deserving messages:

"To my father; *Oom*, since I was a small boy your name has rung in my mind as more than an ordinary man. For me you were like God. You were so big and so powerful and so scary that I really did think that perhaps you secretly knew God personally. That is foolish I know; but it is not a blasphemy: To a small boy your uniform was so impressive and your gun and authority… the confusion was easy to make. But as I grew in the Spirit and you became my guide as an Elder, I could see for myself how the Lord can work through a man and raise him above his circumstances and cruel fates that hold him back, to give him the character to be better than those earthly ones who have oppressed him. I know I am now only a young man, *Oom*, and perhaps many will call me a foolish one for saying it but you were like a prophet to me, lifting my mind to a higher power and urging me to be all that I could be. I wanted to be like you; I hope some day to be in your shadow when we walk together again through Paradise."

It was signed off *Neels Vermaak—Petersburg, Kentucky, USA.*

Once more Gert's voice caught and he teetered near the edge of tears, his voice failing him, becoming threadbare and undisciplined to his most urgent insistence that it should obey, slow its cadence and deepen its tone.

Hymns were announced and sung and extracts of scripture recited. On and on the service went, reminding those present that they were sinners, that Satan, the *Duiwel* himself, was among them and that God was watching—testing and watching.

More hymns and more praise and more assurances that the only way to avoid a miserable eternity was to make the commitment today to follow *Almagtige God*.

Then the *Dominee*, coming to the end of the service, did something that nobody expected; he threw down a gauntlet:

"Too long have bad people ridiculed us here in our own home. To take one's own life is forbidden, but the Lord knows that this is not the case here. Our friend is a martyr, his life taken from him by outsiders determined to destroy all that we hold dear. Only this morning," he looked accusingly from JJ to the black-faces, "they saw fit to besmirch our friend, Andre's good name by holding a service in praise of their beloved science, their mammon."

The despair that had shrouded him until this moment suddenly lifted, his voice began to soar.

"In honor of my fallen brother and by his blood I will send a challenge to these newcomers and their ways of error. My challenge will be that we turn the other cheek... to stand on a podium—to share a stage with them and address my people and allow the false prophets to reveal their faults before the living God."

As his fury of loss and passion for retribution built momentum, his white knuckled fist clung to the rail of his pulpit like a sailor in a tempest. His other bunched fist began beating out a rhythm, thumping down again and again onto the lectern, punctuating his words. And then the old gesturing from his zealot youth began, his accusing finger scanning and tracking over the sea of faces, poking and singling out all those known to be wavering in their faith.

"We will hold a debate... here... in this church. A debate to expose all the lies once and for all—we will debate about morals and ethics, we will show them that they cannot live a moral life without our God."

Gert paused, raining a withering stare down the row of heretics who had dared defile his church and this ceremony with their presence. He felt the surge and power of the Lord rising even higher within him, confirming that he was right to follow these suggestions prompted to him by others abroad, to make this challenge.

"We will challenge those who want to see us change our ways, and we will *fight* the heathen as we always have fought. I choose this topic for my friend, the man who was my right arm… for the man and his forefathers who tirelessly stood by me and by us for generations; fine men of morals and ethics.

Let us show these interlopers for *who* and *what* they are—they are men of paper, driven by the devil. They have come here to challenge our Lord and His work, work of devotion that we have tirelessly offered and given so freely to the poor and wretched for generation after generation."

Chapter 31

The service and days preceding it had exhausted the *Dominee*. He felt emotionally wrecked, yet duty still called.

He'd received a message from Kentucky in the USA, from the Pastor with whom Neels was lodging, and it sounded ominous. The lad needed to talk, to talk in his own language to his own people.

Neels had wanted to see the *Dominee*, so Dr. Louw the Principal had arranged for Johannes van Doorn to bring his son Frans into school at 7pm and set up a video conference call on the new SKA donated computers and high-speed line.

Gert still marveled at the prospect of seeing the person he was about to talk to half a world away, not quite believing it possible. He'd never imagined he'd live to see the day.

"Ja Neels, en hoe gaan dit, seun?" He was startled to see how gaunt and tired the normally robust boy looked, but he tried to keep the shock out of his greeting.

"Alles goet, Dominee."

It was always like this between men in this culture; though they might ask for help, when it came, they'd declare from outset that all was fine and there was nothing amiss; a strategy to cause the other party to draw it steadily out of them, step by step—leaving them feeling vindicated and light—as if they'd never needed any assistance.

"Is it a good place there? Are the people being good to you?"

"They are good people here *Dominee*, very good. Very Faithful."

"Good, my boy."

There was a long awkward silence.

On both ends of the line observers were milling and both men used body language to ask without the other seeing for the watchers to give them room.

Neels in the home office nook of his hosts half turned but did not look at the listeners in his room and they got the message and melted away. He could have kept talking as they spoke in Afrikaans, but he could not relax his mood with spectators.

A few moments of silence, Neels' head bowed to the camera, then his shoulders convulsed once.

Gert used his hand in the universal *'leave us'* gesture; Dr. Louw steered Johannes and Frans out.

"Oom... *Oom* Andre..." was all that the big lad said in a whisper and another tremor racked through his shoulders; a moment later they shuddered a third time, and then the spasm grabbed him and he began to collapse onto his own lap.

Gert just watched, a tear of his own ran and leapt from his cheek; he wiped the warm tickling trace away—it was hard to watch a man cry, harder to watch a hard man sob.

"He has gone to a better place," he eventually assured Neels tenderly.

"I know, *Dominee*..." the voice was muffled. "... but *why*...? Why?!..."

Gert knew there was no answer to the pleading question; it was not the question of why Andre had done it, that much was obvious—*they* had driven him to it. No. He was asking why God had *allowed* it.

"We can only accept that his work was done here my son."

"But taking your own life is a sin, *Dominee*... it is a *deadly* sin. You yourself have said it many times before. You have preached it. Why would the *Oom* sin? He was not a sinner. He was a man of integrity."

Neels was in anguish far beyond mere sorrow, he was in the anguish of *doubt,* and this the *Dominee* knew to be the most *dangerous* of turf. It meant the Devil was about.

"The Lord will make His reasons known in good time," he told the boy carefully. "It is not our place to ask *that* question. It is only that we know and remember the man that Oom Andre was, and that the Lord allowed this to happen."

Neels kept sobbing, becoming incoherent.

Gert's concern grew, yet he dared not let his fears show.

"Have you prayed?" He asked tenderly.

"I have, *Dominee*… I've done little else."

"Have the people there prayed with you?"

"They have, they have been beyond hospitable. The whole community has come to my aid. They are good people, *Dominee*. They are like us in so many ways but still… they… they're not our people. I did not know how far away my heart would feel. I did not know how lonely I could be in a crowd."

"I am sorry my boy, I am sorry that this distance is necessary. I am sorry that it is so necessary at this difficult time."

"I want to come home."

"You can't, not now."

"Why? Surely…? Under the circumstances… this tragedy…?"

It was an immature view, the *Dominee* knew that; as if it was all a game, a game in which the legal jeopardy that Neels faced was not real.

Like a child with a game or prank not going his way, Neels was appealing for his version of *fair play* to govern; as if this dire hurt to the community's core were a scapegoat that could be traded to mitigate those lesser injuries that he had perpetrated.

"This tragedy only means something to us, to our people; outsiders don't care, Neels. They are pursuing this, making more and more trouble… in spite of the tragedy."

Gert was aware, sickeningly aware, that awkward and ugly questions were being asked about Neels around town; a witch hunt afoot to ferret out anyone who had ever had friction with the boy, an urging to bring them into one single legal appeal to bring him to book.

"You must remain there until we can clear these matters up for you."

"Matters, *Dominee*?" Neels' question was almost childlike, discounting the private admissions he'd made to the *Dominee* in confidence before he'd been bundled off.

"It is not wise that we talk about the details now Neels, not openly like this. I don't know these machines and I don't know who is listening or recording."

"Yes, *Oom*." Neels understood.

"It is more difficult now, Neels… now with *Oom* Andre gone. Now we cannot get justice from our own police anymore. They are against us so we must be careful. Careful and vigilant and clever."

"Yes, *Oom*."

"Now—Let's put this aside. Are you exercising? Your mind will be strong if you keep your body fit." Gert angled to get the boy onto less introspective and questioning topics, onto areas he was certain to dominate.

"Yes *Dominee*!" It lightened his mood. "I went to a practice of their football game, but all those helmets and pads get in the way; I don't know why they wear them. These *ouens*—these Americans… they're *soft*. They're big, but they're soft," and he laughed, "… I hurt them if I just run past. They're so scared of me now so I have no trouble. They won't tackle me and don't want me to tackle them."

"That's my boy," the *Dominee* was buoyed with pride and relief that he'd so quickly stemmed the slide of Neels' uncomfortable emotional drift.

"You stay away from the girls," he warned Neels. "They're different to us. I know they're pretty but we don't know them… we don't know their accents we can't read the foreigners and that means you don't know the… uhmm… the *breeding* of the girl or *how* she is."

By *'how'*, the *Dominee* meant promiscuity and Neels fully understood it within context.

"Yes *Dominee* … they *are* pretty though."

"Pretty can be dangerous… the Devil can appear pretty, Neels. Their culture is different. If you make a mistake there I can't help you. I can only instruct you to behave and know that God is watching."

"Yes *Oom*."

Approaching footsteps and voices got suddenly louder in the corridor and a moment later the police Captain strode through the door of the computer room, followed closely by one of his aides and Dr. Louw in a furious mood. A few moments later the van Doorn father and son followed close behind.

"I must go now Neels," Gert told the boy. "We have something going on here."

He didn't want the boy to see or hear whatever it was that might be afoot—not at such a distance and in so brittle a condition.

Neels quickly said his shocked goodbyes.

Unaccustomed with computers the *Dominee* pressed the On/Off LED button illuminated on the monitor in the expectation that it would finish the call. The screen cut off but sounds from the other side kept emitting from the speaker as someone with an American accent asked how it had gone.

The American sounds meshed in an orgy of confusion in the room as Principal Louw admonished the Captain for trespassing into a private conversation.

"Is this not a public institution, sir?" the Captain asked.

He got no confirmation, but no contradiction either.

"Good. Then I would very much like to review the CCTV footage. I believe from this boy that it's housed in here?"

The confrontation had begun in Principal Louw's office, where the van Doorns and Dr. Louw had been waiting so that Frans could close down the call after the *Dominee* was done.

The sun had long since set. The lights illuminating the Principal's office and other rooms in the building, along with the few cars parked outside, had attracted the Captain's attention.

The Captain had personally come out to the school to see if CCTV cameras covered the parking lot where an earlier incident reported to him had occurred. He'd been surprised to see cars parked in the grounds at such a late hour. He'd parked and entered Dr. Louw's office uninvited.

A short and sharp confrontation had ensued during which the Captain, who knew through the town grapevine that Frans was the local whizz on electronics, had asked Frans directly if he knew where the CCTV monitoring was located, and Frans had answer nervously.

"Yes, sir. It's in the computer room."

"Do you know how to access it?"

"Yes sir."

"Come with me then, we need to see the parking lot from earlier today—can you pull that up?" The Captain had asked as he walked briskly, Frans in tow.

"I'm sure sir."

As they approached, Gert and Neels' voice had echoed hollowly through the empty corridors.

Both Johannes, Frans' father, and Deon Louw in particular had been outraged; how *dare* this black policeman address the boy in their charge directly? The proper protocol would be to ask through his elders. Worse yet the boy had been so servile, calling the man 'sir' at every turn; it was demeaning... unbefitting.

"*Onbeskof...*" the Principal kept repeating to Johannes, loud enough so the Captain could not fail to hear.

"It's only *rude*, Doctor, if there is something to hide," the Captain tersely observed.

"Are you suggesting something?" Louw challenged him.

"I won't suggest anything until I have the facts, Doctor."

"Well... what is it you're looking for?"

"I'm quite sure you can hazard a guess, Doctor."

Dr. Louw hated it when the Captain called him 'doctor'—he said it with condescension, it reeked of insult.

Suddenly the American voices over the speakers from the computer went dead; the other side had cut the call.

"Can I turn that off properly?" Frans asked the policeman, further infuriating the boy's seniors who each silently determined to put the boy's priorities in order as soon as he could be taken aside from this unpleasant man and situation.

"Go ahead."

They could all see that the Captain was enjoying this and it made them hate him all the more.

When Frans was done he pointed the Captain to the large monitor dedicated to the CCTV.

"Let's look at the parking lot on the southern side first, that's where the three cars were parked. Start at one-thirty PM, that's when they discovered the problem… then jump back in thirty-minute increments until we see the vehicles are unharmed. Then we can fast forward till we see precisely who slashed their tires."

As the Captain spoke, Frans busily clicked with the mouse on the several dozen camera angles on screen, identifying the camera he was instructed to review. "It's Camera seventeen that will give the best angle sir."

"Okay."

The boy opened a menu and clicked through it.

"I can't, sir…"

"Can't what?"

"Can't seem to access the recording."

"You can't?"

Frans clicked back out and said "Ahhhh."

"You've found the problem?"

"It hasn't been recording."

"What? Why not?!"

"It looks like *Seventeen, Nineteen, Twenty, Twenty Three…* actually, all the cameras out on the front of the building on the parking lot aren't recording."

"And the others?"

"Hang on—no the others are fine, sir."

"The others are all recording… hmmm. Can you tell when last it recorded in the front?"

"Uhhhmm," he clicked at the menu, and a table popped up. "Well, Seventeen was recording this morning at eight… at nine…

ten… not at eleven… There, it's last recording *waaaaas*…. ten-thirty-seven."

"Interesting…" The Captain was looking at the Principal when he asked, "And how do you turn recording on and off?"

"Oh it's easy, very simple," the boy answered in kneejerk fashion, "I showed Dr. Louw earlier… you just click this button here," he clicked an *'on/off'* toggle on the screen, "and when the red light 'R' comes on it's recording. Click it again and it's stopped."

"That's interesting, Doctor. You said earlier you didn't know anything about how these things work and now we didn't record who the vandals are. It doesn't make the school look good when the sponsors have their private property damaged and the system they paid for to safeguard it has been tampered with."

Chapter 32

"Looks juuus' like home t'me," Gabriel Broad drawled in his Texan accent. He was scanning out over the dry flat scrubland to the distant hills.

His small delegation had touched down on the new hardtop runway outside Carnarvon an hour earlier than expected. This put the welcoming committee half an hour late for their arrival.

The hour difference in arrangements had been caused by Uganda's time zone an hour ahead.

"I do apologize for our lateness, Pastor," the *Dominee* had said in the most impeccable English he could muster, "but we *was* set for your arrival at eleven and only got a call after you'd touched down. We made a scramble the *fastest* we could to get here."

"No need for the apology, y'all. That would be my own fault," Gabriel declared, feeling magnanimous for the rare admission. "Jus' didn't think to check if y'all had more than one time zone. But this place is *beauuudiful*," he didn't want to dwell on his folly, "just like my boyhood in Houston."

"We like it, it's a heavenly land," Gert agreed. "How was your flight?"

"*Craaamp'd*", Broad complained, his hand patting the vastness of his ample gut, "But Bud-Junior here he was a-swimmin' in his seat weren't y'all just, Bud. Sure hope y'all can get him a proper meal t' fill him out." And he began to laugh at his own joke at Bud's diminutive size; his jowls—flanges of loose flesh at his jaw—dancing a merry jig to his grunts of laughter.

Bud remained silent. He rarely spoke or offered a facial expression.

They looked an odd pair; the preacher—a barrel with legs—and Bud his understudy, a telephone pole topped by a *Stetson*.

They both wore expensive suits—rattlesnake boots for the preacher, running shoes on his aide.

The *Dominee* had also donned his finest suit for the occasion and he looked rather like an emaciated penguin.

The farmer Willem Bauer, *Oom* Karel the Bushman's employer, had his best suit on too though it was years since he'd worn it and the waistcoat buttons didn't come close to engaging their job.

Jan de Villiers was kitted in his blue safari suit. He'd made it a moral decision; he didn't like Americans. Thirty years earlier as *Kommandant* he'd felt betrayed by the Americans in the Angolan war when their promised invasion through Zaire had not materialized and he'd lost men to the diplomatic miscommunication—or that's what his superiors had told him the issue had been. Regardless, he was determined to hold the grudge and made both men pay when he shook their hands.

"Y'all got a fine strong grip there, son." The preacher said, massaging his hand when he got the crumpled thing back from Jan.

Jan was ten years the Texan's senior but was fifteen his junior in health and vigor; his blanket dislike of Americans aside, he didn't appreciate the man's manner from outset and so had punished him most severely.

The runway lay eight kilometers south of Carnarvon, just off the R63 highway to Loxton and Cape Town. The flight path approach had put them directly over the SKA compound.

"You must have had an early start?" Willem kept up the small talk. At heart he was a peacemaker and wanted to support the *Dominee* who had said this meeting was important to their struggle.

"Up at three," Broad confirmed. "We cleared through your Johannesburg customs and came straight on down... planned to fly past Cape Town first to collect young Andy, but he's up a-ministering to a new congregation somewhere hereabouts. He'll truck in under his own steam later I guess."

"Yes Andy will be here at noon," Gert confirmed.

Fact was, Andy Selbourne was not ministering at all; he was busy acquiring a new church in the town of Kimberley four hours drive to the North East of Carnarvon, but there was no need for Broad to divulge that to the *Dominee* if the man didn't already know it.

"Now Bruce y'all sure you wanna run on foot t' town?" Broad asked of his pilot.

Bruce Matterson had been Broad's pilot of the private Gulfstream jet for the past three years. He was a keen runner and had announced to Broad that rather than accept a lift into town he'd jog the distance to loosen up from too many days cooped in the cockpit and hotels. They'd take his bags in the vehicles and he'd follow directions to the guesthouse.

"It's a straightforward road I scoped it from the sky, it's not real far," Bruce replied, "so I may do an extra lap somewhere. Don't you worry about me, I enjoy getting lost, if that's possible here. Oh… no wild animals to worry about in these parts I read?" He added as an afterthought.
"No four legged animals," Jan had scoffed implying that two legged predators might abound.
The men all shook their heads at the notion of running, it seemed madness to them.
"I'm personally not one for a-running," Broad proclaimed, polishing his belly again. "Sometimes I think 'bout exercise but if I sit myself down awhile the feeling passes."
There was consensus from the hosts.

The reason for the run was motivated by more than Bruce declared—he simply did not relish spending more time than he had to cooped up as he'd been for days on end with Broad and Bud.
With two preachers and an understudy meeting for the first time, he had a pretty good idea from past experiences that they'd drone on for an age; a pissing match to see who had more Faith.

In his association with Broad, Bruce had endured countless of these engagements and they wore on him. He simply did not care for, or about, religion. Whenever he could he avoided the company of those 'afflicted', as he termed it. But Broad paid well enough for him to shut both his mouth and his mind when it was unavoidable.

The preachers climbed into Gert's freshly washed aging Toyota sedan while Willem rode separately with Jan who had privately confirmed his disquiet; "I dislike them both just like I thought I would. The young one won't look you in the eye… I don't trust him. And the fat one talks too much, thinks he's better than us… condescending bastard. I never question, but I think the *Dominee* is making a grave mistake with this."

"I'm sorry for your tragedy," Broad was saying to Gert as they pulled away. "I understand y'all lost a good man."

"One of the best," Gert inclined his head a moment. "It's a big loss to the community."

"Amen to that," Broad said and maintained a few moments of respectful silence.

"These are difficult times," Gert picked up the conversation, "A lot of change… We don't like change here."

"Change is opportunity, boy," Broad suggested. "Y'all gotta take the right attitude to it. Look, it's brought us here; you and me. With me… *together*… you can be stronger than you gonna be alone."

Gert nodded agreement but he suddenly didn't feel it. He certainly didn't like being called *boy* even if it was cultural. He'd seen Jan also recoil when it was said to him.

"Together…" Broad's words kept echoing through Gert's mind.

This is what it was coming down to; this was real, these men were here, in his car and overbearing; and Gert didn't like how he was beginning to feel.

His character was to go it alone and apart. His culture had a legacy of being apart from all others for so many generations that the inclination was ingrained in him. He reveled at being a pastor out on the fringes of civilization where he could avoid the politics of the cities and other *Dominees* in the more densely populated areas. Out in the forgotten areas he could be king of his own domain and answer only loosely to the *Synod*—the governing body of his church.

For a lifetime he'd dutifully followed the core of their prescription, but he'd been left to run his territory like a private fiefdom. They knew it and they let him be, trusting his judgment.

As he drove onward, his mind worked it over and he found himself second-guessing his decisions; this affiliation with the Americans might be a bridge too far. He was, he admitted to himself as the low-slung town came into view, on dangerous turf—holding talks and committing to paths without sanction or even informing his superiors.

And if Gert was honest to himself, Broad had cunningly sold this course to him over the months since their conversations had begun. It was not easy to admit it to himself and the realization of being sold-to made him uneasy; it emasculated his self-esteem.

But it was there... the nagging voice that now wouldn't let up; Broad had convinced him to keep the plans to himself and he now deeply regretted being mute so long and not sharing the details and magnitude of his plans with even Andre—his most trusted advisor.

The more he thought about it the more uncomfortable he became, grudgingly admitting to himself how Gabriel Broad had smuggled his mind, had made him dance to an unaccustomed tune.

In this instant of self-honesty and sudden doubt he felt overwhelmingly lonely... isolated.

Thinking about all of this made him uncomfortable, made him feel like a weak man; and weak men were despicable to him, so he tried to put it aside.

"I hear your congregation is now less than three hundred?"

"Some days," Gert parried.

"And y'r tithe?"

"We don't tithe," he blocked.

"We gotta teach you 'bout church business. What y'all doing to increase the flock?"

"God takes care of that."

"What 'bout your Negroes? You thought to bringing them in?"

"Our church is open."

"Y'all can run separate services to keep from trouble a-making with your folks."

"Our people are accepting."

"What's a Sunday collection bringing... in your money?"

Broad's barrage of questions as they drove onward were unrelenting... too probing, moving too quickly for Gert's liking... too focused on cash; constantly seeking with devious triangulation to uncover the details of matters far beyond the brash man's right to know. Gert felt his hackles beginning to rise again; his mood descending into a defensive laager.

"Y'all seem reticent, friend. Don't mean t' offend; just trying to get to know one another... And... man—is this place *beeeeudif'l* hey Bud? Just heavenly. Y'all sure got a peach of paradise here preacher!"

"We are very proud of it," the compliments brightened his gloom.

He knew he was being prejudicial and he tried to reverse the emotions. The first minutes since they'd first shaken hands out on the runway were not enough to judge these men and build *rapport*, he reminded himself. He was grasping little of what was being asked of him; his mind a flurry of contradiction; These guests were being outrageously rude, immediately quizzing and demanding so much of him so early and so vigorously—did they not realize...? He was not *their* man.

"Perhaps..." he thought, *"I must put my foot down now... sooner than later."* But to come straight out with a challenge like that would go against everything the hospitality of his culture stood for.

It was a sea of endless conundrums; the small town preacher far out of his depth with no hint of experience to navigate his way out of the territory, so he went silent; the brooding inclination of his people.

Then a better plan struck him—he'd go on the offensive. He'd choose the topics and drive the questions.

"I understand you have significant oil interests?" Gert inquired of Broad.

"Fam'ly business," Broad confirmed.

Gert was pleased to see that the man shifted easily to responding. Perhaps, he thought, he could take the reins back and keep control after all.

"…It pays the jet 'n ministry," Broad was still rambling. "But I do enjoy it too. It takes me to interesting places. Just ahead of Uganda we were in Saudi, met with some towel head, *Faizel El-something-or-other*. Gonna sink some wells and take an interest there, but I don't trust 'em. Don't trust those sand-niggers at all."

Bruce; back at the airfield; saw the meetings in Saudi, the trip to Kenya, and now this detour down South, quite differently to the account his employer was describing to the *Dominee* in the car.

He habitually kept opinions to himself, though doing so was an exhausting yet necessary task. The meetings in Saudi had been vastly taxing on his will to remain silent. All of the cultural ceremony and personal posturing of the wealthy man he served, and the wealthier men his employer had met with, tedious; each man pretending to compliment the other while trying to get a leg up on him.

Had the Sheik known what Broad thought of him and his religion, the meeting would have been off before it started… the plane would never have been allowed to land. Indeed, Bruce was more than a little concerned for his own head remaining attached to the rest of him amidst the gross insults and opinions Broad regularly made only just out of earshot, in uncomfortably close proximity to itchy-fingered Islamic zealots.

"Bunch of misguided goat herders," Broad repeatedly called them, "but somehow their Satanic *Gaaawd* has fixed it for them t' be camped on a whole lake o' black gold. The sooner we smoke the lot of them the safer the world'll be."

He'd said much worse of the Kenyans whose backs he'd recently slapped and hands he'd warmly shaken and lined with cash; ugly and bigoted utterances Bruce would prefer to forget.

"They're tools for spreading the Grace 'a *Gaaaaawd*, son," Broad had kept telling him. "The only value these jungle-bunnies' bring, is to incite the cultural war at home. That's what *Gaaawd* has told me he wants, son… Outlaw the faggots here in Africa and God's people back home will sit up 'n take notice."

Now it was South Africa and using the *White Tribe*, as Broad referred to the Afrikaners, to achieve yet other objectives.

Here he found himself, Bruce, talking to an imposing and handsome representative of the White Tribe who'd introduced himself as "JJ."

"She's sure a beauty," JJ whistled with approval at the Gulfstream Jet. "She's the G650 if I'm not mistaken?"

"That's the one," Bruce agreed with vast pride.

"First I've seen in the flesh," JJ's face beamed. "Mind if I take a closer look?"

Bruce gladly agreed. Anyone who complimented his bird was automatically up and past the first rung of friendship.

JJ had come to the airfield to check over his charted plane in which he'd flown his mom and sister up from Cape Town, making sure it was fueled and ready to go if the unscheduled meeting that had suddenly come up in Johannesburg materialized.

On his way into the field, he'd been surprised to pass *Dominee* Gert who was leaving the airfield with an obese looking stranger wearing a Stetson hat inside the car, and then the realization struck him that it could only be the American delegation in from Kenya. They evidently hadn't recognized him in a borrowed car.

"Not just from Kenya," Bruce went on to elaborate the Saudi trip.

They'd been scrutinizing the plane for the past few minutes and had settled in the lavishly appointed lounge to share a cup of premium Arabic coffee that the Sheik had included in his parcel of ritual gifts he'd handed over when they'd touched down.

During the past few minutes, into the flow of conversation Bruce had injected searching questions and established to himself that JJ was entirely without a religious affiliation. In his experience, the keenly religious always advertised their viewpoint in the first moments after meeting. In the past several weeks, he'd been cooped up with nothing but dogmatists, and he was keen and relieved to at last get a break and be in the company of someone likeminded.

"Jeez, no," JJ confirmed. "I grew out of that nonsense when I left this place ten years ago."

Bruce nodded knowingly.

"What's Saudi really like? Like we imagine?" JJ quizzed.

"It's as unpleasant as you'd imagine," he confirmed. "Hot, sticky... dusty. Feel like you want a shower every few minutes. The women... what can I say about the women...? Nothing to look at for sure—then again, wearing bin bags over your head is just never gonna be flattering."

JJ was starting to like the man.

"You gotta feel for the average person there, though. They're like us, just trying to get by but their system is screwed up. It's like the dark ages. The ones on top are deranged." Bruce hesitated, "But I must tell you... what goes on, what I see... it's bewildering... I don't get these types."

"I can only imagine—I can't deal with them anymore. The willful ignorance is what gets me."

"Ignorance? Try full-on *cognitive dissonance*, complete inconsistent thoughts... I mean, complete and utter disconnects between their fictions and realities. We met with this Sheik," he pointed at the coffee, "and he had a whole entourage of geology advisors. For the first half of the meeting Broad and the Sheik preened and congratulated one another on the other's Faith, and how misunderstood they each were of one another... how similar they each reckon the two opposing Faiths are... just a big circle-jerk... It's complete bullshit of course, they hate one another."

"Seen it myself," JJ agreed.

"Oh… it was spectacular… They went on and on, pretending to fawn. Then they edged closer to the business of oil and spent another age talking about how, a few thousand years ago, their invisible sky-daddy had put all this oil in the ground as a present and gift to them… I mean personally, for them… you can't understand the egos."

"Oh… I have a pretty good idea."

"Well… this got them into the carbon emissions debate and their take on it…. Evidently it would be terribly *rude* if they did not accept their Heavenly Father's gift and thank him by burning all the oil they can lay their hands on."

"Nothing self-serving in that at all of course…"

"Nothing at all… And then, *poof*… they both seamlessly switched tack; it was down to the real business of yields and ratios and the quality of the oil in the ground. Suddenly they were conversing in eloquent detail about the deposits. I mean, *intricate* details about the strata; the *Permian, Jurassic, Carboniferous, Devonian*… staggering. Without a hint of shame or irony they shift from fairytales to profits achieved through the stark realities of the very science that they reject."

JJ topped his coffee mug but Bruce refused more as he kept explaining.

"One minute they were talking thousands of years and some sky-magic and the next they were bandying about *hundreds of millions of years*…. the intricacies of geologic processes… and I just sit asking myself 'how?'… *How* do you keep both of those contradictory ideas in your head and believe both of them?"

"Have you never asked? In private, I mean?"

"No point. My job is to fly, so I fly. I just endure the meetings when I'm invited and hold my tongue."

"I couldn't do it," JJ said. "I just couldn't do it. Does your man know how you feel?"

"He might suspect but I keep it low key. I bow my head at the frequent prayers before meetings and meals and use the time to think about important things."

"And if he finds out?"

"As long as I shut up and do my job, probably nothing…" Bruce said, and then added. "Now I think about it, if the plane's ever in a crisis… gonna crash… I think he'd rather I'm not distracted with praying; he'd want me getting on with the mechanics of all of it—so there's the hypocrisy again."

"He's a big oil man? Gabriel Broad... I don't really follow the oil game... I know he's a preacher."

"Well, then his PR is working a treat," Bruce suggested. "If you speak to him, he'll tell you that the oil is only there to fund his 'missions'... But, not true, not true at all. Oil's a very traded market and he's on the periphery with it. Selling religion gets him through back doors... and its cash cow in it own right. As it stands oil is lubricant for his empire, but what he takes out of his mega-churches would make that Sheik blush with shame. He's into all sorts of things I'd be wise to forget about... hence this leg of the trip."

The statement puzzled JJ, but he let Bruce talk and determined silently to return to the odd statement, *"...things I'd be wise to forget about... hence this leg..."*

"In my opinion... for what it's worth... I think Broad's a bad businessman—that's why he's nowhere in the formal markets; all his deals fall out of bed. He's too aggressive in the deal... leaves nothing on the table for the other guy. It's in backwaters that he can dominate; it's where he outmaneuvers everyone... he gets the politicians in his pocket."

"Interesting..." JJ said. "And this leg? In Africa?"

"The Kenya trip was with select parliamentarians, *gee-ing* them up against homosexuals. You know—he was the catalyst getting the death penalty pushed through into their law..."

"They reversed that," JJ reminded him.

"Sure... but he'll still got mileage out of it."

"What's his game?"

"We wing in... he slaps some backs, greases some palms... gets them riled up. I sat through some of the meetings and it blew my mind. Broad had some outrageous videos on his tablet... where he gets the stuff, I can't even imagine... Evidently homosexuals *'eat poopoo'* and rub it all over themselves. He had videos of it, and these guys just took it all onboard, got themselves into a lather over it."

"Astounding."

"Well, now you know the Red-White-&-Blue source and inspiration for it."

"I never doubted it. But what these clowns don't get is that over here, in Africa, that kind of evangelizing turns *real-serious, real-quick*. Our locals don't picket, they go on the rampage... they kill anyone they suspect."

"You're wrong... Broad understands perfectly well, he just doesn't care."

"Disgusting," JJ agreed. "And here? Carnarvon...?"

"Oh, Carnarvon's just one part of our South Africa leg. We have meetings with your Parliamentarians. I probably shouldn't mention this, but you don't seem likely to hijack us... there's a big suitcase of dollars in the safe on the plane, to... you know...."

"Persuade?"

"Yes, *suggest* to those in authority to see things Broad's way."

"Hard dollars?"

"That's the tip of the iceberg—these days he's mainly using Bitcoin—cyber currency... totally untraceable... safer. But in Africa dollars still speak loudest."

"Shew! So what's the flight plan?"

"Cape Town, Pretoria and back through here. Then Nigeria—interests there too—mega-churches... Then back to the States via Germany." Bruce caught himself, "But... my mouth's running away with me. I've been cooped up too long," he cautioned himself aloud.

"Talking's a risk," JJ agreed openly. "I'm no threat to you, I'll lay my cards on the table with yours."

"Your cards won't save my job or neck. You're a very likeable guy," Bruce admitted, "...had my mouth running itself."

"I'm intrigued. Your information's fascinating... It's timely... there's a madness here in this town right now that I'm trying to figure out, and what you've just told me hints at what I've been missing... details I couldn't know."

Bruce fidgeted with a loose thread on the hem of his shirt sleeve, his forehead creased, weighing thoughts;

"I don't know why I trust you," he declared. "I don't know why I *should* trust you, but I do. Maybe I've been locked into this bullshit world for too long, but I feel like I've got to get this burden off my shoulders to a stranger not in it." Bruce was studying JJ, trying to figure himself out, "I must be nuts..."

"I don't want to compromise you. Tell me what you're comfortable with, I won't pry... Tell you what... I'll tell you what I think is going on and you can just ignore it if it puts you in a position.

"Reckon you have a theory?" Bruce challenged.

"One's forming. I'm interested in all kinds of things—this new global evangelism intrigues me... The tie-up with the local church... what's broad getting out of it? A publicity stunt?" JJ didn't want to blunder in this delicate dance; he was working carefully to avoid spooking the man.

Bruce raised an eyebrow and a barely perceptible nod to the question—it indicated limited agreement; its lack of enthusiasm suggesting that there was much more to it;

"The *Answers in Genesis* crowd... Broad is affiliated to them?" JJ took it further.

"In bed with them... and others. Like... really in bed. They're his front."

"Ahhh... This spear head in South Africa and Carnarvon is to broaden the fight they're putting up over evolution and science in general, States side?"

He nodded, "And...?" Bruce encouraged.

"And they'll make the news?"

"Why? Why's making the news important?"

"Attention... a spotlight on them?"

"Look... Outwardly, Africa's the newest and most lucrative growth market for evangelism; South Africa's a gateway, a strong base. Announcing a mission here... the press that comes with it... legitimizes frequent return visits... no-questions delegations, easy visas, unchecked movements."

"I'm sure... and it grows their base... sort of an economies of scale"

"Also... influence. They've got a lot of traction now in your government—pushing to pass laws that religion influence in the legislature, slowly closing the rights to talk against it."

"Have you heard of Andy Selbourne," JJ was connecting dots very quickly.

"We were supposed to collect him in Cape Town to bring him up here, but he's busy buying up a church not far from here, so he'll drive in later."

"Buying a church?" JJ was surprised at that.

"Yes—expanding his little piece of Broad's empire. Traditional churches that are in decline of membership, they're under financial pressure; the youth turning away from old-fashioned religions. They want something more with more pizzazz... something... *sexier*. This is fertile ground for evangelism with its flash and upbeat razzmatazz... You have a little town down here called *Swellendam*? And another called *Oudtshoorn*."

JJ agreed, "Yes, up on our east coast—the Garden Route, why?"

"The main NG Churches there are gone, did you know that? Swallowed up by the Evangelists... and, all financed by...?"

"By Broad? You're kidding?" The pieces falling into place.

"That's what Bud-Junior is here to do, oversee the terms of surrender."

"What?" JJ was bewildered.

"Sorry—you probably missed the man, he was in the back of the car, he's the other party with us. Looks much younger than he is. His name is Bud-Junior, travels as the understudy to the preacher, but he's a lawyer, you'll never hear him preaching. Broad constantly reminds him, *'listen and learn'*—it sounds like they're talking preacher speak, but it's business; code for when Broad has seen something he really wants Bud to take note of. Very cloak 'n dagger."

"Jesus..." JJ exclaimed, "quite a tangle."

"More tangled than you imagine.... Do you have vested interest here? In the town?"

"Not anymore," JJ declared, and admitting it hit him in the gut. "I grew up here, but have grown far apart from it. I just lost my dad last week and my mom and sister moved to the city with me. I was just up for the funeral and extended my trip to sort out the estate."

"I'm sorry to hear that," Bruce said. "But you'll be relieved to be out of here with what's going to go down."

"Have you any idea how Broad and Gert, our preacher here, became acquainted?"

"I know exactly how. Broad wouldn't have given your preacher or this little town the time of day, but with the SKA coming… well… the potential for PR in the long run… As the town becomes a center for science, he wants a hand on the lever… but there's more to it…"

Shadows moved behind Bruce's eyes—he was calculating something; JJ could see there was something he wanted to share—something that begged to be shared, and he was assessing if JJ could be trusted.

JJ picked his moment and prompted him.

"Sounds like more than evangelism going on…?"

"…Broad says he just wants a stake in the ground here… but… Well… anyway… stuff I'm, uhhmm… not supposed to know… much less *talk* about."

Those phantoms were eating at the man and JJ was certain that, with patience, Bruce would crack and reveal them… JJ could see him fumbling for a new tack, trying desperately to divert from the secret he was straining to hold back.

"If you're from here," he was saying, "you'll know the church attendance is dwindling… losing money."

JJ knew it and agreed.

"It's a drain on the parent church. Like any business, they'll only carry it for so long. Broad knows it's ripe for acquisition, just like those other two towns. Just like the deal Selbourne is cutting right now. They targeted your preacher here, baited up a hook for him, stroked his ego a bit… spoke a lot of bullshit of common goal… told him to keep it to himself and not elevate it to his superiors or share it with anyone. They got him believing that he could be a hero if he was seen to take the fight against this internationally recognized scientific initiative, this great Satan, single handedly."

"And he swallowed the hook and sinker?"

"As we speak, they're probably sinking the gaff in. These guys are laughing at him. It's small potatoes for Broad."

"So he is being used? The *Dominee*… the preacher… the folks here being… used?"

"Sure… Used."

"And Selbourne?"

"A loyal dog. He's helping build the empire and thinks he's a partner in it." Bruce contended.

"So he isn't in the inner circle? He talks like he is. I've seen some video—on about his *'meetings with partners abroad'*. Claims he's having all manner of *'high-level'* talks."

"They always do, don't they…? Elevate their own self-importance and imagine they're in the inner circle. No… Selbourne is oblivious. He's a stooge. He'll run himself ragged to bring any dusty corner for his master. Him, you… *they*… you've no clue of the extent of all of this."

As Gert had swung off the highway he'd seen the first of the placards up on streetlight poles. He caught a glimpse just too late to read it, but every second pole repeated and heralded the forthcoming debate he had only just announced at the tail end of Andre's funeral; and he read more and more of the detail as he passed each pole.

It spelled out the venue—his own NG Church—and the participants; Broad himself and internationally famous *evolutionary anthropologist* Alok Singh—Al—Andy Selbourne and Marsha Martin, the famed astrophysicist.

Gert had been urged by Broad on an earlier phone call to announce the debate but assumed that he would be the main participant and hand-pick an opponent, preferably holding the debate in his native Afrikaans. He'd confirmed to Broad that he had made the announcement when they'd last spoken two days earlier.

Broad saw the shock written on Gert's face so he took the initiative, pointing to the posters; "Our PR folks been good and busy," preemptive strikes always-beat defensive responses.

"You arranged this?" Gert was outraged and it showed.

"We talked 'bout it, m' boy." Broad ignored Gert's look of outrage and stormed directly onward, "I get jobs done, don't have time t' waste with chicken-shit jibber-jabber—so it's arranged for this Saturday night, the media invites are out, we've some mighty impressive coverage lined up and the other side's opponents are in agreement already. I must fly t' Cape Town for meetings, but I'll be back for the event."

"You did not tell me about this," Gert's mind was reeling from the blow, his voice betraying that.

"What was there to tell y'all, son...? Y'all said we could use the church and Y'all agreed to announce it. I didn't intend to burden y'all with arrangements at a time of sorrow as y'all have been through. Y'all did your job inviting the good folk o' the town and I'd like t' thank y'all by having y'all chair the 'vent."

"This is not how we'd planned it!" Gert blurted.

"There w's no '*we*' to do the planning, son," Broad pointed out. "I planned it. Y'all are just to provide the venue. I mean y'all no disrespect, but this is a tad over the head of a small-town preacher like *yerself*. These character's we debating are internationally accredited and I doubt y'all would survive the first round. I'm a pro… do it *aaaall* the time. You'll see, it's the better option. You'll be relieved to not participate."

The impertinence of the man slammed Gert down a slope, into a dungeon of surging wrath. His mind shut down on him and he did not know what to think, much less what to say.

He drove the rest of the route to the guesthouse in a mute world of voices inside his head, while Broad pointed with oblivious indifference to inanities of topography and architecture around the town.

Gert dropped his guests without more than grunts and monosyllables escaping the shroud of his icy rage.

Broad seemed unmoved by the frosty mood. He slapped Gert heartily on the shoulder and assured him that there was "nothing to be emotional about," it was, "all just business".

"All just business!!" Gert repeated bitterly to himself as he drove away. "This is not business, there is only God's business, and this doesn't sound like God's business to me," and his mood grew yet more bleak and despondent.

He began to dread the forthcoming hours when he would have to fetch the men after they had freshened up; he'd have to pretend to be a good host—to discuss plans in earnest that he now grudgingly admitted to himself, were not his plans—plans he was not even part of.

To extinguish the voices and seek guidance, he withdrew to his church to pray and to ponder what calamity he had unwittingly inspired.

Chapter 33

"You never take them at their word, Marsha," Al cautioned his wife. "When you shake hands with these guys, you count your rings when you get your hand back."

"Oh Al, that's rather melodramatic?" She accused.

"I've been dealing with them for a decade. It's not at all dramatic. They justify any contravention of ethics or morals with an out-group bias."

"Out-group bias?" She frowned.

"If you're not in their group, you're out of it, and therefore beyond any moral or ethical code they need to uphold. You're either in lockstep with their specific worldview, or they consider you an enemy. They project that you're trying to bring them down, and that's how they justify bringing you down with any dirty trick they can."

"Come on Al… you've been doing this too long. They're not as bad as you make out."

"I'm not saying they're intrinsically bad people…. I'm saying that their outlook allows them to justify unscrupulous behavior."

"Hmmmm," she bit her lower lip and rolled it between her teeth. She always did that when she was thinking. "And how does this manifest?"

"Well… There's something that just doesn't feel right here. Three weeks ago, after a debate put on by the *Revelations Institute* that this Broad character is tied in with, I got into discussions about your work here, and one of those hicks said some very strange stuff…. That I'd *'be surpriiised at how the territory's gonna change'*. I didn't think much of it then, because that type are always making wild predictions. I don't want to create a false memory for myself here, but there was something in the way he said it that had a *knowing* to it."

"Now you're psychic," she challenged with irony.

"No… it's just loose ends falling into place. I shouldn't even be here—only because of Dara I am—it's suspiciously convenient that we get a call out of the blue challenging us to debate the Evangelists, just after the local preacher has announced a debate."

She cocked her head. "What's going on then? What am I missing?"

"Maybe I'm imagining it, but everything seems to be falling into place too neatly."

"You seem to think it's sinister?" She asked. "You suggesting they knew Dara would… would be attacked to get you here? It seems far fetched."

"No—that's ridiculous, obviously. The coincidences are just… odd…"

"You met Broad before?"

"No—not personally, but I know *about* him; I've debated his colleagues; I know the type. I know he's got fingers in more pies than you can imagine, Marsh. Extreme right-wing, *uber*-Republican… pro-oil, pro-coal—anti-renewable, anti-conservation, anti-anything that he can't exploit."

"If he's such a man of God, why's he like that?"

"Why, ever…? It comes from his and their philosophy."

"Mom, I've been telling you this for an age," Dara had come into the kitchen with Sonja and caught the tail end, "… she's so gullible, dad. So innocent. Just refuses to believe anything can be sinister."

Marsha did not admonish or challenge her son, she knew he was right. She was innocent, she actively *wanted* to remain innocent and un-jaded; she wanted to always give the benefit of doubt.

"Everything in their philosophy is about death—*'things will be better when we're dead, we'll go to a better place. We'll sit at the side of our Father, we'll judge the wicked'*… that's why."

"Earth is Satan's place, it is flawed." Dara jumped in. "Heaven is perfect, mum, so the sooner this all ends the better."

"You two a tag team?" Marsha challenged.

"He's right, Marsh, those are their mantras. Dangerous, sick, anti-life obsessions," Al paraphrased them, rolling off the list of standard fundamentalist dogmas.

"Think about it, mum; every time a natural disaster strikes, they celebrate because it confirms their perception of negativity. They speak in grandiose terms about love, fellowship and charity, but their obsession with humans bringing natural disasters on themselves through their behavior just erodes their humanity and numbs them to real suffering."

"It's a death cult," Al amplified it. "It's all about celebrating death."

"I told you, mum."

"You're just repeating what your father keeps teaching you," Marsha challenged.

"No, Marsha. Listen to him. He's got his own mind," Al pointed out. "Fault him on the merit of his argument if you can. Why can he see it and you can't?"

"I don't want to," Marsha admitted. "It's bleak to think that way. I don't want to believe that there are still people like that."

"But it's reality, Marsha. They're barking mad... worse than that, they're in charge because democracy hands the power to politicians who appeal to the lowest common denominator. If you don't recognize it, you don't take action to oppose it. You become complacent," he paused, "...as you are."

"Oh, *I-am-not*... you should've seen me on the podium... my Kardashev talk... But I don't dwell on it. I want to see the best in people."

"Oh... *Phahhhh*, Marsha... Don't give me that. That's a cop-out. You're too smart to claim that defense."

She didn't argue, he was right.

"And, as to your moral integrity—they'll attack it from every angle. I can almost guarantee that in the debate they'll try to spin on it that you're... satanic."

"Oh, Al, you're such a cynic."

"I'm telling you because that is the flavor and tone they'll try to set."

"How can I be satanic? Satanism's a superstition... an aspect of religion. I reject superstition, it's illogical to even suggest it."

"But they will. Their world is dominated by the superstition you reject."

"There's only black-and-white in their minds, mum. If you're not sailing under the flag of their version of God, they'll insist that you're duped by some sinister force."

"You can't argue *logic* to persuade someone out of a dogmatic position; if they applied logic they wouldn't hold the opinions in the first place."

"You both sound jaded... Why accept this challenge if it's all such a lost cause, Al?" She came directly to the point as she always did.

"You're right... I've been at this too long..." he paced. "We can't back out... the media's already invited... there's a PR machine in overdrive, very coordinated. If we're not in the debate, they win by default." Al could see that Marsha was very uncomfortable, "I know you're not keen on the podium, but you're a natural talker. Look, after the presentation at the school, how long did it take us to leave. People practically wanted your autograph."

"Long enough to have our tires slashed," Marsha said bitterly.

They'd gone out to the parking lot to find her car standing on its four-rims. She'd had to borrow a car for four days while new special-order tires were brought up from Cape Town.

Frustratingly the CCTV footage was mysteriously not available. It took more effort than she had time available to pursue a follow up.

Fortunately, the owners of the other two cars who'd engaged them in discussion after the event, people who were openly supportive of their opinions, were fighting vigorously to uncover the perpetrators of the violation to their own vehicles; and the police were being cooperative but hitting headwind.

"What else have they got left?" Al asserted. "They lost the argument and bombastic attitudes and intimidation is their last bastion. It's how they got to dominate in the first place, through fear, threat, torture... Those old habits die-hard. Ostracization doesn't work anymore."

"Oh, before I forget," Marsha suddenly changed tack, "JJ called and is coming directly over with some *'very surprising'* updates. Says he may have to fly out on short notice. Whatever it is, he says, it can't wait."

Sonja briefly smiled at the mention of her brother. She'd been predictably glum under the circumstances—the shock and the funeral.

JJ and Sonja had stayed over with Marsha at the compound for several nights since flying in. Neither of them felt comfortable to stay in the family house where their father had so recently died. The compound was bright and new, and held more distraction with the cosmopolitan mix of foreigners and families, than all the reminders of their sudden and shocking loss that staying with friends in the region would trigger. They'd opted against staying at a guesthouse, which, in the small town, amounted to the same thing as staying with friends.

This decision to live with the outsiders had set tongues to wagging across the village and beyond. And, some of what was being whispered was true, Sonja and Dara had formed a warm bond; it was fuel to *skandaal*.

Johanna, their mother, was staying with Andre's mother, helping the devastated old lady cope with the loss of her son. Much as she wished to be with her mother in this trying period, the aged grandmother's cottage was too dark, cluttered and depressing for Sonja to contemplate.

JJ arrived a few minutes later and filled them all in on what he had just learned from Bruce, the pilot.

"Is this confidential?" Marsha wanted to know.

"He really didn't want to tell me… agonized over it. I could see him trying to hold back, but eventually, well… I guess its' been eating at him… said he had to tell someone," JJ grimaced. "It's a bit of a burden now though. I don't want to compromise him, betray his confidence, but this is a crossroads. Let me start with my personal feelings; What I don't want are the real lunatics getting a hold here in this country or my town. Their goofy ideas are very infectious, particularly to the youth. But I think the shakeup of what Broad and that Andy Selbourne are up to will be good for the old guard, they've had their way so long they think they're invincible."

"I knew there was more to it than met the eye," Al crowed gleefully. "Marsha... I told you! I've just been telling her," he turned to JJ, "I foresaw this."

"He's been having a lot of psychic insights today," Marsha teased.

"It's not psychic, my darling. This conservative old Calvinist church is a little like the Church of England—it's fat and happy and doesn't go looking for a fight. From the moment I heard there was trouble here I could smell the whiff of the evangelic big-business churches. It's their style."

"You two can squabble about that later... I've got more pressing news, and it turns everything we're thinking on its head; it's the real interesting part of what I learned with the pilot... let's call it a *speculation* at this stage," JJ said. "The German withdrawal of funds and support for the SKA project.... Bruce tells me it's his man, Broad, and his people behind it."

"Reeeally...?" Al's voice sang with intrigue and triumph at the claim.

"Now, come on... that's nonsense!" Marsha retorted.

Al gave her a smug *'I told you so,'* expression of victory.

"No... There's just no-way... Impossible..." Marsha said categorically, "Their withdrawal's for financial circumstances. Al's going to argue it's all some hidden hand."

"Officially?" Al quizzed, "financial issues are the official stance, Marsh?"

"Yes," Marsha replied. "Now I know you're going to immediately discredit official statements, but I mean... how...? How and why would an American evangelist have influence to get Germany out? That makes no sense."

"It does if you know how deeply he is entrenched in oil..." JJ left the unmentioned accusation hang there, and it even caught Al by surprise, but Marsha beat him to the question.

"Oil? What's that got to do with the SKA? It's a bit of a leap..." she challenged.

"Okay... not literally oil, but fracking...?" JJ posed it as a thesis in a single word; in a question. In truth it was a statement. "You do know that the big oil companies are circling like sharks, wanting to get into production in the Karoo."

"Uh-Huh...!" There was a hint of triumph in Al's exclamation.

"They're building the SKA here, also in the Karoo, and…?" JJ begged somebody to finish the sentence.

"And you're saying that powerful interests wanting to frack for natural gas don't want the SKA getting in the way of their operations?" Al volunteered.

"You… you're saying that fracking will put a spoke in the wheel of the SKA?" skepticism fleeing from her face ahead of real concern.

"Fracking requires construction, infrastructure, communications and disruptions that are fundamentally at odds with the SKA's needs," JJ posed, "…you can't put them side-by-side—one must go, that's what's at stake. They could still pull the plug here and curtail the project."

"They'll *never* allow that," Marsha asserted.

"Germany just backed out… America never came in," JJ challenged. "And… I'm curious why key figures in government are buying up huge tracts of otherwise worthless land?"

"It makes sense, Marsha," Al added. "Science will always come second to profit."

"So spell out what you're claiming," Marsha came to the point.

"I'm not claiming… I'm not claiming anything… yet. I'm repeating what was suggested to me, and I'm guessing we should be circumspect in repeating it, but it is something to keep track of. This Broad character evidently whispered in the right ears in Germany that the politicians down here are probably on the make and will push legislation to allow fracking to happen, no matter what. That in turn is going to put the SKA in some jeopardy. With a flea in their ear, the Germans are stepping back. They're not saying they're out, they've just cut funding and everyone has put a brave face on saying it doesn't really matter. But with them gone, who is left?"

"Australia, Canada, China, India, Italy, New Zealand, South Africa, Sweden, the Netherlands, and of course the United Kingdom," Marsha listed them.

"And the USA?" JJ challenged, "You'd expect them in that list, right? Maybe France, maybe Russia or Japan? All the big ones, but they're absent."

"Your Bruce says that this Broad and his merry men got to them?" Al asked.

"He only mentioned the US consortium. I think we can take it as read that he had the kind of influence there to sow doubt and keep them from ever getting fully involved."

"It just sounds so fantastically conspiratorial," Marsha didn't want to believe it.

"It does, I agree. But I mean, all of the wealthiest countries are citing lack of funds to participate…? In this, the greatest scientific cosmological implementation in history? Come on… Does it make sense to you? I battle to make sense of it. The US spends more on sweets for a single Halloween night than the whole SKA will cost over ten years to build and run…. I know that's a simplification, but it does give some perspective to think about… over the decade you build this machine, with its untold spin-off benefits into commerce and wellbeing, the investment into ten nights of chocolate binges and tooth decay… in one single country… could pay for ten of these initiatives. It's just ludicrous."

"Okay, fine, I just don't see that happening."

"Marsha," Al stepped in. "You're approaching it from the point of view that the SKA *'has to happen'*—in your mind it's too fantastic not to. But business and politics come at it from the other direction—they want immediacy. If there is profit under the ground, then whatever you want to build on top of it will have to wait until it can be exploited."

"Have you not followed the media on this? There are laws to stop the two coming into contact," Marsha played her ace.

"And, of course, big oil always fastidiously obeys the laws," Al retorted.

"There are going to be *buffer zones* around the astronomy facilities. And, wise guy, the *2007 Astronomy Geographic Advantage Act for protection*… Go look it up."

"I'm sure *aaaaall* the assurances are there as they always are… but oilmen have delivered countries into war for less. Just wait till they find a mother lode where you want your radio silence," Al was relentless, "we'll see an amendment to your 2007 Act pretty quick."

On impulse, cornered, Marsha stuck her tongue out at him.

"You know what happens to naughty girls who do that," Al rubbed his hands gleefully.

"You two can get a room... and there are kids here... Seriously, this is pretty heavy," JJ pointed out.

"He's just so irritating sometimes," Marsha admitted. "And I don't really have the coping skills to deal with this. I studied astrophysics for God's sake; precisely because I didn't want to deal with all the bull of humans and their political maneuvering."

"And... yes, I've read media reports on this issue... all the assurances, and one thing strikes me—it's always the SKA spokesman saying things like, *'we're always mindful that there might be instances where we will collide'* and *'we will seek to co-exist peacefully with the frackers'*... all very hat-in-hand. I'm yet to hear a statement from the other side, not that I'd have faith in it if I did."

"So, you're telling me that at this late stage these guys are still hopeful of stopping the project in order to get at the natural gas in this region?" She asked.

"I'm telling you that politicians play to their bank balance first and only... to get support they simply tell the public that if they don't immediately allow the natural resources to be tapped, fuel will double in cost and the currency will halve in value." Al stated. "You and I *get* it that this is a short-sighted view... we understand that, to permanently get away from fossil fuels we need a breakthrough... like figuring out anti-gravity technologies, and that we'll only achieve this by digging into the fundamentals of cosmology and particle physics through the SKA and CERN.... But the general public aren't sophisticated enough to make that leap... and the average voter in the street, battling on with their mundane and difficult lives carry the votes."

They were silent a moment, absorbing the thought.

"So Bruce is claiming that by getting Germany—and before that the States—out of the project, the project stumbles and the headwind disappears for him and his cronies to get their hands on the gas reserves," JJ summarized it.

"That's what it sounds like."

"If you're a cynic," Marsha added.

"As a businessman, it's actually a master stroke," JJ changed the spin on the matter. "What he's done is use a smoke screen to get his way. He got the old pastor to do his bidding, to keep it secret from his superiors and set himself up for failure when the news breaks and the church fathers come down on him. When they do, his man with the new Evangelic church sweeps in and cleans up so that he has a beachhead in the region. He can easily launder money through his own church to keep opposition to the SKA going, while he secretly cozies up to politicians and they survey the ground together for oil explorations. Brilliant…!"

"It's also speculation," Marsha added.

"That it is," JJ admitted. "I'm not telling you this is even what I believe yet, I'm still brainstorming to test if it's feasible. That the local church is getting shafted is now clear and obvious to me; and that the oil-man posing as a religious leader is up to his neck in it—and probably instigated it—also seems pretty clear." He hesitated a moment, weighing the ethic of disclosing more. "…I've been going through that video recording of the meeting with the inner circle of the local church. They're trying to mount a land claim using the Bushmen as a front."

"Oh, come on…?!" Marsha was aghast, "That is ridiculous."

"It seems like it, I have the video and their plans are advanced. I've been out to see the old clan leader and he confirms that they're in discussions,"

"Dawie's grandfather?" Dara ventured. The two youngsters had been silent and almost forgotten by the adults. "Dawie told me the lawyers were out there two days ago."

"Why didn't you mention it?" Al challenged.

"I didn't know what it was about. Dawie got out of there when they arrived, he thought that it may be to do with him…"

"Poor bloody kid," Marsha said. "I think he could do with some help… some post traumatic therapy. He's been forgotten with all that's gone on."

"I'll see to it," JJ assured, "I'm in contact with him and helping where I can. I think he'd do better out of this town… his grandfather agrees."

"And his parents?"

"They're… well… they're not really parents to him. Alcohol."

"Shame… I had no idea."

"It's a plague."

"And his friends?"

"I'm his friend," Dara volunteered and the adults smiled at him.

"It's complicated, Dara," Marsha pointed out. "Even if it's not ideal… impoverished, he's got a community here."

"He says he wants to go," Dara made it sound so simple.

"He does," JJ confirmed. "I've talked with him... chatted with Karel... the grandfather. Even Fiske at the school says he's not a fit here; has too much potential... could lose a year and still be better off."

"Well?" Alok posed in the long pause as they each contemplated it.

"Well, it's something to explore," JJ suggested.

"We've veered a bit off track with so many topics on the table," Marsha tamed the conversation. "The Land Claim... what's that about?"

"I also heard them talking about it," Sonja ventured—the first meaningful participation in open conversation she'd offered since the shock of her father's death, and glances about the room told the story of relief that she was emerging from her dungeon of grief.

Not wanting to make too much of this sign of recovery, JJ went smoothly on as if there had been no concern for his sister's wellbeing all along;

"I'm using Land Claim too loosely—technically, it's a *Cultural Heritage Claim*. The townsfolk... the *Dominee* and his cronies are trying to find a way to keep the land ownership but have the indigenous Bushmen get it declared out of bounds for any development that might interfere with their traditions and ancestor grounds."

"Could that fly?" First the speculation about fossil fuel prospecting and now this prospect of Heritage rights slammed Marsha from the opposite direction. She was seeing the hopes of her life's work circling the drain in a game she was ill equipped to play.

"If they get money behind it for a legal battle, they could probably put a moratorium on construction for a while; maybe stir up trouble through the unions of workers who'll build it. It depends on how big the claim is and how deep pockets go," JJ speculated. "It would not be as catastrophic to the project in its entirety as Doominee imagines it might be. Then again, their concerns are only for the local territory anyway. They just got riled up about it being in their back yard."

"But such a land-claim does fly in the face of the fracking theory you've proposed," Marsha challenged.

"It does… it absolutely does." JJ agreed. "And I'll wager that the local guys who don't understand the game here are doing it renegade—without the Americans knowing about it. They think they've hit on a foolproof way to come out winning. What happens next will tell us how close our speculations today are to the truth."

"And why would the *Heritage Claim* stop the SKA but not stop the fracking?" Sonja took another step toward proving her recovery was happening before their eyes.

"Unfortunately," Al stepped in, "I've seen this kind of thing happen the world over, it's called *realpolitik*…. The reality, even in a democracy like this, is that money talks louder than any rights or sentiments. If your brother is right, you won't hear another word about this Heritage Claim if it is going to get in the way of big oil and politicians. It will all just go silent."

"So, do we tell them?" Marsha asked, "The preacher… Gert?" she pronounced it badly. "Do you take it to him? Suggest he's being a puppet?"

"Yes, Gert," JJ amended the pronunciation. "I don't know. I think we must, but I'm not really on talking terms with him. You saw how he looked right through me at the funeral. I went afterward to thank him and he wouldn't shake my hand."

Chapter 34

"These fuckin' local yok'ls," Broad spat. "…tryin' t' go it alone."

He was livid.

Earlier, he'd struck up a conversation with the guesthouse owner who was a devoted NG Churchgoer. Her husband was close enough to the inner circle to hear what was going on behind the scenes.

Gabriel Broad had poured on the Southern-Charm and warmed the plump old lady to give him all the dirt on the town. He'd successfully convinced her that the two branches of Christianity that they respectively sat on were mostly adjacent with only small cosmetic differences. With that notion and thickly laid charisma, he'd won the lady's confidence.

With great pride she'd let Broad in on a secret—that the Church Elders were well advanced with their cunning and devious plan to lock the SKA development up in Land Claims Court for long enough to send it somewhere less offensive—like Australia.

He'd smiled and thanked her warmly, congratulating her that she'd secured a husband who associated himself with people so wile and devious, and then he'd stalked off to find Bud.

But, before he got back to the room, his mobile had rung with interesting news from Neels' hosts in Kentucky. Indeed, the news was spectacular; with the mood of stubbornness he could see brewing within his host, the *Dominee*, the news in from States-side could not have been better; it gave Broad a brilliant idea to swing the shifting balance of power back into his own favor, so he issued his strategic instructions on what ought to happen next and then he'd headed once more in search of Bud.

"If these clowns lock that land up und'r a Land Claim… worse yet… some kinda indigenous *Sacred Site*," Broad had ranted, "that'll lock the natural gas industry outa here for the rest'a time."

He'd barely finished venting his anger and had begun to reveal the details to Bud of an unexpected new ace that the call from Kentucky had suddenly slipped up his sleeve, when there'd been a knock at the door.

It was Andy Selbourne.

The men had first met years earlier and become associated. Two months ago, Selbourne had visited Kentucky. They'd assembled at the *Genesis Museum* with Bacon and others of the inner circle, and Selbourne had reported on his progress in Southern Africa, setting up a *'Religious Freedom SA'*—RFSA— with powerful government ties that would push through favorable legislation to benefit them.

Andy had been instrumental in making first contact on Gabriel Broad and his associate's behalf. He'd acted as intermediary and now felt rather smug knowing that pretty soon his influences would extend into this region too, as they ousted the local church in favor of his Evangelist Faith; so much more loyal as he knew they were to *The Word* than the incumbent.

"Now I heard me a strange *rum'r*," Broad was smiling at Andy, but his eyes weren't, "…that there's some kinda Land Claim y'all got going on in these here parts? A Sacred Heritage Claim?"

"Yes," Andy confirmed with some surprise at the man's knowledge of an initiative he personally had conceived and sold to the *Dominee*.

But it shocked him to now see the death in Broad's eyes, so he quickly covered his surprise, feigning matter-of-fact neutrality in his reply; giving him the stance to leap in any direction that the flow of conversation might require.

"You certainly keep your ear to the ground!" he complimented Broad, "...I think the *Dominee* intended to disclose and discuss it at the meeting later. The local preacher thought it a good idea to stall the SKA process by bringing in a *Heritage* claim that wi..."

"Y'all don't think it's something we should've discussed beforehand?" Broad's voice was brittle.

"I... we... never thought it an issue. You know, the situation is local, the best solution will be local. We're well placed—the local church is well placed—to have influence over the claimants. It's a pretty solid plan."

"That's presuming y'all know what the plan is...," Broad bit back, and Bud shot him a look that said, *shut up—don't pique his curiosity.*

"The plan seemed pretty clear to me," Andy stammered, but tried to sound authoritative. "We want to bring the *Word* to the people, we need to save the youngsters here who have lost their Faith in a church that history is leaving behind. Particularly here where there is now so much distraction from the scientific community who are pouring money in and winning hearts with it. We talked about this when..."

"That's the plan *y'all* working on, yes," Broad cut him off disdainfully, then reigned himself in from betraying any more than that. He admonished himself internally for being so emotionally rocked by what amounted to a business management error in communication. "That's the plan y'all working for us toward, yes, boy. That's the goal we'll be wanting. But there's gotta be cohesion in our implementation of the plan. Y'all understand?"

Broad's mind was racing to weigh up the angles, so he culled the conversation to buy himself more time to think;

"...But y'all put it aside for now. It jus' caught me unawares. Just stay 'way from that there topic today with y're pastor, I'll give y'all instructions when I've considered it by its merits."

"How do you like him... the Pastor?" Andy was keen to leap far from the morass and minefield he'd suddenly found himself in. The look on the two American's faces had shocked him, the devil was in them and he welcomed the backdoor that Broad had opened for him to avoid what looked like an ugly and evidently ego-driven power play. *He didn't come up with the Heritage Claim—*

which is inspired, he was thinking to himself, *…so it's a bad plan? Typical… egotist!*

"How did you like the *Dominee?*" he repeated.

"Not a bad sort, but I don't get that he likes me a whole great deal," Broad volunteered. "He didn't appreciate the advertising of the debate."

"He said so?" Andy asked.

"He said nothing… that said it all."

Gert had been on his knees in the pew for longer than he had ever knelt in his life. At his age it would normally have seized his ailing back, but he felt nothing.

He'd prayed earnestly for direction. In his mind he'd mulled what was at stake and how much he'd exposed himself to sanction from the synod. The more he'd thought about it, the more he'd convinced himself he was free and clear. All he'd done was interpret the scriptures literally—that the earth, heavens and man were made when the bible said they were; and from this perspective he had preached against the newcomer scientists seeking to entrench an alternative claim.

Indeed, he'd convinced himself, the synod might well thank him for taking the stand afterall.

He'd also been in dialogue with Selbourne and his *Religious Freedom* group—but that was not a violation of any kind? He had not committed the church or its members to any official course—or, not yet officially committed it at any rate.

"Indeed," he thought, "when the troublesome female scientist, the mother of the black devil child, had brought the matter up with the Minister for Science and Technology at a recent engagement, he'd brushed it aside." The *Dominee* was very pleased to have such a network of informers feeding him vital information like this.

The more he thought about it, the more he diminished in his own mind the negative impact to the church. Indeed, the more he thought about it, the more he began to feel that this whole sojourn was going to pay off in positive outcomes for him. He gained strength from it, prayer had worked for him as it always did.

At last he had his answers... he would face the Americans down and send them packing; but then the issue of Neels popped into his mind.

Neels was in the Americans' hands, at their whim. It wasn't exactly a hostage situation, but it did make it awkward. Neels was emotionally brittle right now and Gert didn't want to create any situation to aggravate that. It was a delicate situation, he realized; it just might cause an issue if his emotions ran from him and he became confrontational with the boy's benefactor today... *What to do about that...?*

Neels coming back at this time was out of the question; Beatrice, the legal secretary of that turncoat Pieter de Villiers, was keeping Gert well informed of the meetings and correspondence being produced against the lad, and it was ugly; it seemed half the girls in the area were coming forward now that Sonja had gone against him and alleged his sexual predations. It made him wonder if the stories she was making up were the result of grief at her father's loss and bitterness toward the boy who had such a strong bond with him. But it seemed inconceivable that she could have turned the whole community against a boy whose reputation had always been impeccable; and, not just the girls, many of the boys too, especially the coloured and black ones had jumped on the bandwagon claiming Neels was a racist and filled with hate.

The hate was theirs, Gert decided; venom they were producing to bring down a boy who represented an older, purer, better era.

So—Neels could not come home and Gert was loath to make waves for him.

Just then the three men arrived through the church door.

"*Whad'a* place, huh?" Broad bellowed. "Like something from th' Ark, not that it'd be a bad thing if all y'all want is creaking and aging bones on the pews."

A worshipper who had quietly and privately kneeling in silent prayer startled at the brashness of the man's loud voice. She gathered her belongings and hastily made to leave.

The church was austere—it was in keeping with every other NG Church one would enter and it was precisely the way Gert liked it. He didn't appreciate the bombastic insult.

"We keep our voices down out of *re-spect*," Gert hissed 'respect' in two syllables.

"Oh, gotcha... I'm used t' a more lively house-a-prayer; y'all gotta know the lord's a lively fella and it comes kinda naturally to me."

"The Evangelist churches are much more flamboyant," Andy tried to quell the obvious tensions already entrenched between the two men.

"And us evangelicals also go in for a bit more colour and glamour. Somthing we all can help out with if y'all want the good advice."

"We are quite fine without any help, thank you," Gert said curtly. "Let us go to my office."

Gert did not want them defiling the sanctity of his church another minute, so he led them back out through the doors and up the side to his office at the back.

He crowded them around the table and did not offer them refreshments—what he had in mind would have them off the grounds and preferably out of town in quick order.

"There seems t' be a problem?" Broad went directly to the issue.

"I am afraid that I may have overstepped my jurisdiction," Gert responded plainly.

"This was something we were planning to take up with y'all. Y'all mean this Land Claiming business?" Broad made a snap decision to broach the topic himself.

"That... and the challenge to the SKA project. I did it without authorization from the synod."

"Y'all did what I told y'all to do... that'd be the best strategy. Take them head-on, they're a-violating your jurisdiction."

"Well that's not how we work in *our* church and I made a serious error of judgment which I must now correct. It is also not policy that I pursue this discussion with other denominations without direction from my superiors," Gert was angling to bring the entire discussion and matter to a hasty close.

"So y'all gonna run? They got y'all licked? All the fight outa y'all gone? I'm mighty disappointed. Thought y'all made of sterner stuff?"

Broad had done his homework on the mindset of the Afrikaner—there is no more certain way to strum his ego and drive him in a direction you want him to go than to effectively call him a coward who is not up for a fight.

Gert was up for a fight, and he still firmly believed the SKA's objectives threatened to violate his deepest held Faith, but he did not want this foreigner as his fight manager. It took all of his self control not to lash out at this brash and arrogant man trying to toy with him, here, on his own turf. He would fight, but he would now only do so under the direction of his own church. He would convince them that this was a fight they needed to allow him to take up.

"I think we have taken this as far as I can take it," he was being genial, not wanting a total confrontation. "I am sorry for the disappointment, but I'm certain that if I can convince my superiors as to the urgency of this, they will give me the authority to proceed again to work closely with you."

Andy saw his opportunity to gain a foothold in this region starting to slip.

Since he'd gone in league with the Americans, he had only seen success; moving in and taking over every suburb or town they'd targeted.

But the last few moments were unsettling and he was about to venture an opinion to smooth the path and bring the old *Dominee* back into the fold when Broad beat him to it.

"Well I'm real sorry that y'all *gotta* create such a difficulty at this time. I'm particularly sorry to give y'all the bad news I only just received myself minutes before we left t' come on over… It's about your boy back in Kentucky."

"Neels?!" Gert had detected the severity in Broad's voice and his face was a mask of horror, "Bad news?"

"Afraid so… that boy's gotten himself into some *seeeerious* troubles. *Seeeerious-seeeerious* troubles…" Broad had sunk the hook deep and was letting the old man stew and work for the details.

"Is he all right? I've heard nothing like that. His parent's would have called me," Gert insisted, suspicious of the American's maneuvering.

"Oh, they'd not be a-knowing yet," Broad pointed out. "The boy's awake but not discharged yet from the hospital. I have to tell y'all that there's a-high probability there'll be *chaaarges* pressed... *chaaarges* for rape."

"For rape!?" Gert stood from his chair and started to pace. "Rape...? Impossible!"

"I'm afraid it's not. Seems your boy pushed one of the little coloured girls a bit further than she wanted to go."

"A coloured girl?" Rape was one thing, but Neels having sexual liaisons with a coloured girl was entirely out of the question.

"It's 'a *seeeerious* matter. My people can take most of the sting outta it. But I understand he's in a little spot of bother this side o' th' water too?"

Broad ground away at his advantage. Now the preacher needed him and would have to kowtow and toe the line.

"I, I... I really don't know what to think. I need more information and to talk to his parents immediately."

"My people are a-calling his folks *riiight* now. I'm pretty sure y'all can have a discussion to see how y'all *wanna* work it out. Under the circumstances, we can reconvene later to discuss the upcoming debate."

Gert agreed; he could see no other option. In agreeing, he'd agreed to the debate too.

Chapter 35

"A most peculiar situation…" JJ disclosed to Marsha and Al, hastily called to a meeting with him at Meerkat restaurant in the town; conveniently close to de Villiers attorneys. Pieter the attorney was already drawing documents to affirm the matters under discussion;

"I just got a call from the Vermaaks, from Neels' parents. It seems their son's landed himself in very hot water in Kentucky and needs to be extracted in a hurry. I already have wheels in motion… my wife's visiting family one state over and she's already taking care of things over there for us. I'm hoping to get your agreement on this, he's returning."

The Vermaaks had, after agonized discussions with *Dominee* Gert, concluded that their son needed to be extracted in a hurry from the serious repercussions he faced in the United States. It was clear that the only person with the resources to do this in an emergency was JJ Kruger.

Angling to pre-empt what was generally considered JJ's traitorous shift of allegiance to outsiders, they'd pitched their plea to appeal to his deep cultural roots and family history in the community.

Long before they'd come to their point, JJ had seen through their convoluted *Afrikaner-against-the-oppressors* appeal, and their desperation lent him the levers he sought to secure favorable terms in return for his help.

"What's the scoop?" Al was bursting with curiosity.

"That proverbial old leopard hasn't change his spots," JJ bopped his head in a nod of victory. "Neels has been involved in exactly the kind of thing in the States that we've uncovered about him here. Happily this time, he seems to have come off worst."

A waitress arrived and set down coffees, fussing with minor arrangements, clearly trying to pick up threads of gossip. JJ paused till she left.

"The details I have are that he went to a house party, got out of hand… drunk… was dancing with a girl, and… *same-old, same-old*… The pair went out to the back garden… Next thing she shouts for help and a bunch of home-boys jump in and beat the tar out of him. He put two of them in hospital, but they knocked him out cold, and he's been brought down a good few notches."

"This lunatic's a real loose cannon," Al observed.

"…It gets better; we know there's a connection to Broad's crowd. Latest in from the gossip mill, things aren't going swimmingly here for Broad with the *Dominee*, so, all of a sudden there's muttering from Kentucky that she has the option to claim attempted rape… you know, if Broad's hosts don't warm to him over here."

"Good… let him rot," Marsha folded her arms.

"It's an option," JJ shrugged in agreement, "He's discharged from hospital, and of course claiming it's a setup. So… yeah… we could let it be… let him sit… but will sitting fix him or this situation here? It's retribution, but is it rehabilitation?" JJ posed.

"What's a better option?" Marsha kept her arms folded.

"I think there's a win to be had… Whatever he's done there he already got swift justice… *physical* justice, the kind he's used to dishing out… I've talked to him and he's really shaken; rightly terrified and sheered off his foundation… So… we could leave him there, sure. Even if what they're muttering about is trumped up, he certainly deserves justice for what he's done on this side of the pond, yes. That's the one option, but maybe it's the option that pushes him the wrong way… and nothing actually gets learned?"

Marsha unfolded her arms and joined Al with her forearms on the table, listening intently.

The waitress was in conference with her colleague, glimpsing their way, clearly plotting a new strategy to get a toe-hold on the tantalizing conversation at table seven.

"I think that while he's rocked we get him on *our* turf."

"Hmmm…" Marsha was grappling with the notion, "…and? To what ends?"

"Well, the objective… your objective… is, what? To get an apology? To see him rehabilitated…?" JJ countered. "To have him pay… and I mean money and more… for what he's done? I think we can get it all."

"I don't care about money," Marsha insisted.

"Well, I think the money does matter. They have to pay… his folks… for all the medical at the least. And this is our moment to turn the screws. He's on the run, scared as hell… way out of his depth. There's no friendly *'Andre'* the policeman to make it go away…"

Al saw as JJ uttered his father's name that he did not flinch; this was about business and not emotion.

"…he's a typical bully;" JJ continued, "…a dog behind a fence. His family's wealth and influence has let him throw his weight around."

"What exactly are you proposing?" Al chimed in.

"Between my US partners in my business and some strings my wife, Morgan, has, we can make things happen quickly. As I speak he's being bundled off to the airport. I have agreement from his parents already that if he returns here the civil and *Equality Court* cases against him will be suspended but only with their and his agreement to undergo anger management and other psych evaluations."

Both listeners were nodding and the waitress was hovering.

"…His parents will pay full medical… plus a very handsome grant to a charity… a charity that makes sense to this cause."

"You have that agreement? In writing?" Al asked.

"Not in writing… yet. That's what Pieter is doing now."

"Anger management and psychological assessment, in a town like this?" Marsha huffed her doubt.

"Definitely not. No. There's no way he can be rehabilitated here. No, no, and no. The terms are that he is extracted from this environment for at least two years. I watched him grow up, I know how to handle this boy. He's pretty much *me* fifteen years ago."

"Really?" Al seemed aghast. "Surely not literally?

"As close as *dammit*, yes." JJ assured. "I was... well, very unpleasant.... a bully, headstrong, and I'm ashamed to say I... well... I'm ashamed, let's leave it at that."

"That makes it sounds like we've got bigger problems than one renegade," Marsha observed.

"We do... yes. Absolutely we do. It's a culture of this nonsense, and this is an opportunity to break it. It's guys like me who are to blame; when I left and got enlightened, I never came back to face down others like me. *That's* the mistake, and that's why the Neels' of this world keep cropping up in little forgotten villages all over the place. The few who recover from bigotry want nothing to do with it."

JJ covered his mouth, looking away, feeling ashamed to admit who he had been.

The restaurant owner came over to ask if they had everything they needed and they assured him they were happy. When he went to the kitchen, the two waitresses followed.

"Now's the time for change," JJ went on. "Let me pick it apart for you; my dad, whom I loved dearly, represented that ongoing thread of infection into the youngsters. He was assisted by it in this Calvinist tradition of stern old men who are a sort of cabal— they're the Church Elders. They've celebrated in it for decades, they have the whole system down to a fine art; the school principal handpicks the *alpha* personalities in the next generation, they groom them through sport and captaincy, and refine it in the Youth Group of the church. With my dad gone and not replaced, they lose their grip on smoothing over any abuses that crop up."

Al could see emotions written across JJ's face as he disclosed his culture's deepest secrets to outsiders; "I'm sorry you have to admit all of this."

"Yeah... admitting it's not fun. They got it so deep in me that even now it feels like I'm betraying something sacred... makes me feel treasonous, and that gets me angry..."

He paused a moment, his head shaking minutely with internal dialog.

"...It really starts with the *Dominee*; he plays the pivotal role... everything that's done round here is because God wants it thus.

You heard it from Dara when he laughed about it from the staff… *'When the Dominee's angry, we must all be angry…'* It's a crazy mantra. It's the source of years of tension between my dad and I. When I think about it, he was actually the victim… a puppet always dancing to that tune. And of course, I'm from a line of cops—they're the henchmen who perpetuated it. And it's just like this across every town and back through time. I suppose, like the sheriff in the old West always running interference for *'his people'* to have things go their way. It's convenient when the law looks the other way, and the preacher justifies bad behavior with Old Testament assertions of the right bigotry has to impose itself."

"Wow… That's a hell of an assessment," Marsha said just as the waitress's ears arrived to straighten the already impeccable tablecloth on the adjacent table, so conversation dried till she left.

"It's necessary, Marsha," JJ looked her in the eye. "And, the *Dominee* is now reeling because he's been caught in a trap of his own ego… and this has given me a plan. I'd prefer him as an ally."

"Will he get behind it?" Al asked.

"Hard to know. He's a stubborn old bastard… On the other hand, I'll say this for him; he's a very moral man—it's sometimes very odd morals, but if he decides Broad's dishonest…" he left the thought without conclusion.

"Since your disclosure I dug around about Broad and he does seem rather checkered," Al said.

"*Checkered* would be quite a euphemism," JJ suggested. "This is my game, digging into facts and looking for legal loopholes, and this guy is buried in a tangle of them and I mean a really ugly birds-nest of fraud, and corruption and outright hijacking of decency."

"Why's it not come to light before?" Marsha posed.

"It's there if you scratch enough, Marsha," JJ began, "…but the press won't touch it when the big fish are involved. With Broad, too much rides on his *philanthropy* and connections to make waves. The trail isn't easy to follow…"

JJ was cut short; the waitress had come back yet again to see if anyone needed anything; she was clearly consumed by curiosity by the juicy tidbits her earlier foray had yielded.

"Do you want to pull up a seat?" JJ offered her and she scuttled away.

They all had a mild chuckle around the table as the other waitress and owner simultaneously evaporated to the kitchen to hear what she'd discovered.

"Believe me, I'm even shocked; Broad is knee deep in it all; in coup plots to install puppet leaders of tin-pot dictatorships in Middle America and Africa—anywhere there is a whiff of oil or diamonds... and God-knows what else. I've traced him to financing completely bogus climate change denial organizations running fraudulent petitions by scientists who are dead or never existed. As you know, he's up and down Africa agitating against homosexuals in countries like Uganda and Nigeria... And of course here through front companies, trying to get his hands on a piece of the fracking action they're angling for."

"Wow... but how will we use this? Your information? This Neels situation?" Al was not a strategist and didn't pretend at it, and he'd sensed that JJ had a plan formulating.

"Several ways. I'll handle the *Dominee* and put an end to this undercover nonsense they're up to with the Bushmen. We can expose the pressure groups fronting with *faith* to cover their tracks. The implications of why countries stayed out of the SKA funding could be far reaching; maybe it shoots dirty politicians in the foot... I've found that there's insider trading going on here too, snapping up cheap land... everyone knows it's earmarked for radio silence, so the value's tanking, but if they bulldoze their objectives through and overturn the moratoriums on radio silence in place, the land explodes in value. If we throw a spanner in those works, we leave crooks holding worthless land and we even put a spoke in the fundamentalist juggernaut. And then there's finding other Neelses in other regions."

"Quite a list," Marsha rolled her eyes.

"Quite a list..." JJ paused. "...And Neels...? I have another plan... it's going to sound a bit crazy at first... Remember I told you I was '*a*' Neels? I know how a bully thinks and I know how a bully reacts when he's put in an environment that's tougher than him? I'm going to propose that we have a six-month trial of something—an experiment. The school Dara is going to is just around the corner from a house I own..."

"He's going to school in the Southern Suburbs," Marsha pointed out. "Don't you live on the Atlantic Seaboard?"

"That's my beach cottage," JJ corrected her, "...An investment we enjoy on weekends and summer; but our main family home's in the Southern Suburbs, I run my office from it.... Well, I think I told you before, that Morgan has a psychology degree? She's not in active practice anymore, so she's very excited to get back to it... I've been talking to her about this plan as it formed. Let me first say that she's tough as hell; takes no nonsense, so she's keen to make what I'm going to tell you a project..."

Marsha sucked air and emitted a light groan of concern, guessing at what might come next.

"I want to put all three boys under the same roof for a time; Dara and Neels... and Dawie if he wishes. Morgan's behind it... feels she can take it on full time."

Marsha's mouth began to hang agape, "You're not serious?"

"Well... I sort of was... Morgan said the same thing at first."

"Before you did a sales job on her?" Marsha challenged.

Al's brow was furrowed, calculating the possibilities, "Let's hear him out, Marsh."

"I'm really not *selling* it... just putting it on the table. It's up to you...."

"Maybe Dara should be part of this discussion... and Dawie," Al suggested.

"Dara always thinks he can cope," Marsha added with concern.

"Please... I'm just offering and suggesting," he held up his hands, surrender style. "These aren't snap decisions, they're possible courses."

"The outcome?" Al tilted his head.

"Constructive engagement, you can't change anything when it remains in isolation."

"Hmmm..." Marsha's hand muzzled her mouth, her eyes betraying cogs clicking over.

"Dawie...? Could he really cope... with the city, under these circumstances.... Should he *have* to cope in his second last year of school?"

"I've chatted again with Fiske... the science teacher. He's adamant that boy is gifted and incredibly stable—*'wasted here'* is what he repeated... those were his exact words. So.... sure, you can leave him here, as he is—he can battle forward... I'm sure he'll be fine. Or... you can open the cage and see if he wants to fly. There are no guarantees and it's a compromise whichever way it goes. We can't prescribe... let's leave it up to him."

"And you're not selling this?" the first twinkle of smile returned to Marsh's eye, JJ returned it;

"I'm going to start selling now," JJ assured. "...He's the right age for his grade, so that even if he loses a year... if he re-does this year in a new environment... he really loses nothing."

"And culturally? We talked about this... you take him away from it, and...?"

"I've spoken again to Dawie, he's keen. His grandfather's his only positive influence and, uhm.... Well, that's not looking good... the old man's health. If he goes...?" He let the statement hang. "...Anyway..." He gathered his keys off the table, "It's food for thought; we have a few weeks before we need decisions. Right now I've got to go across to the clinic to see the situation with *Oom* Karel, I just heard that they've booked him in as an inpatient, which is about the worst thing they could have done..."

"Hmmm...?" the same sound came from Marsha, but now it was quizzical with a question mark that lifted both her eyebrows.

"Let's think it over," Al spoke for them both.

JJ looked at his phone and nodded at what he saw there; "So if we have agreement...? Pieter said he'll explain the documents he's been drawing for Neels... It needs your signature, can you stop on by there?"

Marsha looked at Al and they both nodded, "The Neels bit..." Al already nodded agreement to what she was going to say, "...I think we can go with it, I... we... we trust your insight."

Al checked his watch. "Oooh... for a lawyer's meeting you have to count me out, it's too tight now, I'm flying later and haven't packed yet."

JJ sucked air through his teeth and they both read that it meant urgency.

"I could do it," Marsha volunteered to Al, "...if you drop me and collect me later?"

"I could play taxi if it helps...?" JJ suggested, "Pieter says he'll only need you for twenty minutes. By then I'll be done with my first errand and can pick you up on my way back, then drop you at home after I've popped by the clinic, if you don't mind waiting."

Chapter 36

"Do you have no respect for my Faith? For the Faith of your father?"

"Oom, I respect you as a man as I respected my father," JJ countered. "I respect your... and his... intelligence. I respect this intelligence so much that the way I honor it... the way I show it respect, is to say that I think you are more intelligent than the ideas you hold," and he braced for the backlash.

JJ was not disappointed; the *Dominee* grew red in the face and growled about the insult the younger man had served to him, proceeding to admonish him for degrading his Belief and Faith as mere ideas;

"How *dare* you?...!"

"It is not about 'daring' or my arrogance, *Oom*. What I said I really mean. I felt the same emotion of Faith as you do... you and my father crafted that in me but I have since then exposed myself to the medical realities of how the brain works and through that knowledge I came to understand that..."

"I've heard enough of this modern rubbish to last me a lifetime," Gert cut him off. "And this is why I am against Neels going to Cape Town and living under your guidance,"

"I'm afraid there is no option to that, *Oom*," JJ did not take offense, and he tried to deliver his message without unduly giving any. "With all respect, that *Dominee* is against it, is academic. Neels is guilty of offences here and in America too that will send him to a far worse place than living under my rule. May I ask what offends you about my influence?"

"Since you went to the city and married *that* woman, you changed. You left here as a good young man strong in your Faith. You have become influenced by *her* and the modern world and I don't like the modern world and its teachings. I don't like what you became… All the nonsense from the city and that foreigner changed you; that's the evil they're trying to force on our children here…"

"Really?" JJ kept his voice neutral and resisted the urge to add a provocative response. "What of the modern world offends you? We have better communications, easier travel, safer food, better medicine… the list goes on."

"I'm in favor of these things," Gert declared.

"You say you are, and then you actively try to suppress them at the school," JJ charged.

"Suppress? What do you accuse me of?" Gert's affront was real. He was unaware of suppressing any of these matters.

"In the science class. I met with the new teacher, Mr. Fiske. As just one example he says you are pressuring him and the other teachers to leave evolutionary studies out of the biology syllabus. Pressuring the children to boycott it."

"Yes… evolution… I don't like lies and evolution is a lie. Another of these modern lies to confuse and mislead the children. It has no benefit to them," the *Dominee* insisted.

"It's a hundred and sixty years old, I wouldn't call that modern; But it does underlie all modern medicine… antibiotics… cancer treatments, anaesthetics, yes *Oom*; in that regard it is perhaps *modern*. You've said you were for medicine but you want to ensure that the children in your care can never understand it? That makes no sense to me."

"Well, I don't believe in evolution and I can't support children learning what I don't believe in."

"And I don't believe in evolution either," JJ let the statement hit the *Dominee* and gave it a pause to let it sink in.

"You don't? I thought you did? I thought you were arguing for it?"

"I am arguing in its favor, yes; but, of course I don't *believe* in evolution… Then again I also don't *believe* in arithmetic—I *understand* arithmetic, *Oom* … understand and apply it. That is the proper way with science we don't ever *believe* in any of the sciences. We only aspire to grasp them so that we can apply them and master our world, master engineering and master biology."

"You have developed an answer for everything," the doominee accused.

"Thank you," JJ took the insult out of it, "that's because I think deeply about everything *Oom*, and I'm not ashamed of that. I expose myself to others far more intelligent than me who are experts in understanding and studying about things...." He paused, "I did not come here to argue about these things. The matter with Neels is settled. His parents have signed the *Memorandum of Understanding* already, the document I need as a surety to help them get him back here and to have the charges here suspended against him. I only wanted to inform you of it as a courtesy."

The *Dominee* shook his head, turned, and walked slowly away down the aisle toward the altar. His head was bowed and JJ could see from behind that he had his right hand up to his mouth—his finger would be crooked like a question mark tapping his pursed lips; the pose meant he was deep in thought digesting the angles to see if there was an escape out of the trap.

"What I really came to do, is talk about your problems," as he said it the *Dominee* whirled and looked at him.

"My problems?"

"Yes *Oom*, with the Americans,"

"What..." Gert was going to ask *"What Americans?"* but he caught himself—JJ was too smart and connected to be unaware of their presence in town, "What *problems*?" Gert tested him to see how deep his knowledge of the details and his folly ran.

"Oom, I don't want to waste our time so I will come directly to it. There are two Americans in town and they have with them Andy Selbourne; a man who has been dazzling you with his salesmanship. I know about him, I know about their arrangements with him. I know about their interference outside of South Africa… about their angles and arrangements with government, I know what their agenda is and that part of it is to swallow up churches that are in trouble…."

Gert was trying to keep the surprise at the succinct summary and reference to additional information that even *he* did not know about off his face.

"…When I was youth leader here," JJ went on, "…people queued out the door on Sunday—only white people, the blacks and coloureds went elsewhere. Now everyone comes here, and yet there's still plenty of room…"

"There is nothing wrong with our attendance," Gert bridled at the truth.

"Maybe… maybe not. We're in tough financial times, and even a parent church has a budget…"

"They would *never* allow that to happen," Gert blurted his deepest fears and wiped the expression of worry from his face a moment too late.

But for all his emphasis on *never*, his voice and eyes did not have conviction, and JJ saw it, "Perhaps in *Oudtshoorn* and *Swellendam*—and now in *Kimberley*… there is an ex-pastor who said the same thing?"

The truth stung Gert and his mouth set to a thin and hard line. He brought his fist down on the back of a pew, "Never!"

"I am not the executioner here, *Oom*," JJ reminded him. "I am just an observer. You believe I have moved so far from my Faith that I have no regard left for my culture and my people, but that is unfair and untrue; the two are not indivisible. I can still love my people and yearn for my memories of how it felt, and want to protect this simple way of life without agreeing with its every detail."

Gert was stationary, paused with his fist still down on the back of the pew.

"Religion *is* our culture, *Dominee*. Without religion, we don't really have a culture—and I've recognized that."

The two statements staggered Gert. The prodigal had turned, he was facing his home for the first time in a decade; the boy had called him by his religious title; he had not done this in years, always pointedly preferring the neutral 'oom' since he'd lost his Faith; this instantly softened the old man's heart and Gert saw that the Lord was at work here so he let the boy talk.

"Much as I'll not deny how I'd like to see our culture evolve toward reason, I recognize that it is a slow process. Accepting that things take time to change," JJ was explaining his mind carefully, "the bigger threat to us all and to progress in general is *not* the old church that you represent; for all its follies of the past and faults of the present. Much as I've come to disagree with it; you and what you represent is sincere. The threat is the moneymaking churches—they are conniving. They appeal to the youth, they are positioned like the business that they are, to draw the new generation away from our culture. They don't have the welfare of the individual or the community at heart; what they want, are mind-slaves contributing into their fund. That is the threat and that is our common enemy."

Gert turned and faced the man who he had once known, the man who was like the young lion his father once was.

"What are you proposing," he looked JJ in the eye.

"I propose that you were duped, *Dominee*. I'm not going to sugar coat it and pay you the hollow respect of pretending that it didn't happen—you were *had*. I don't doubt that your heart was in the right place, but somebody with an agenda—a businessman—did a sales job and convinced you to pick a fight you shouldn't have picked, a fight with progress."

Gert was about to argue against it, but JJ held up his hand.

"I am not insulting you, *Dominee*, I am telling it as it is. There is no argument the NG Church has with science… perhaps there is one they should have, because science does corrode faith; I don't want to argue that… In this debacle you were convinced by someone else to take the lead role without elevating the proposal up the chain of leadership to the synod; am I wrong?"

Gert couldn't deny it and he was surprised at the man's insight to how it had in all fact happened.

"I get a sense that you know this already… the signs on every street pole out there…"

The look on Gert's face confirmed to JJ all he needed to know.

"…they're taking control already? Acting like they own this *gemeente*—our *parish*. They think they already own *you*."

Gert was nodding on the outside, seething within; seething that the whole true state of affairs was so obvious to a man who he'd rejected, one whom he'd come to despise and now found himself grudgingly having to respect.

"We fix it by recognizing that it is true. We reconcile it by making apologies—you to your superiors, to the *gemeentelede*—to the *parishioners* who you have wound up on this issue. And you let them think they are winning, you let the outsiders have this media event, you let it go ahead and you watch them fail in front of the *volk*."

"You propose that I give them my church and my altar? That I expose my flock… to people with an agenda?" Gert asked, squinting with deep skepticism. "Tonight you have spoken more sense than I knew you had, but this… this idea…"

"You think it's too much of a risk? You have that much faith in their ability to swing our people?"

Gert heard the conviction in him as he said *"our people"* and he knew instantly that JJ was in the fold of the community again.

"The world we are entering is not like the one we are leaving, *Dominee*. When you did your ministry the world was closed, there was our church and few others out here, very little other influence. Out *there* has come *here*. Whether we or you like it or not, it is an open market of ideas and only those ideas that can compete on their own merit will survive. If you try to keep the lid on and pretend there are no other ideas for the next generation to choose from, those ideas will come right in past you and take them away. No… you give them your stage and let them compete—then you rely on real strength of character to come through in the people you have served for so long. These newcomers will make no inroads here if you allow them to be defeated in open battle… If you deny them an open battle, they'll do it with stealth, that's precisely what they're masters at doing… and that's an infinitely tougher fight for us to win."

"Allow them to be defeated?" Gert was cynical.

"Yes, with no shadow of doubt they'll be defeated. I'm so sure of it I would also like to make a donation… a donation I would like to see them match. A big donation for all that I learned from you as a young man."

"I can't be bought!" Gert snapped.

"I'm not suggesting you can be, *Dominee*. But it is in my capacity to help this community… and I believe you help this community, so I will help you to help. I would like to see these people do more than talk. I'd like them to show their commitment."

"You surprise me," Gert admitted. "But I do have serious reservations."

"It is your choice… cancel the event here in the church and they'll take it elsewhere to another hall. If you hold it here, our people coming in will already be on *their* own familiar turf aligned to you and less open to persuasion as they'll be if they're on more neutral ground in another hall."

"I don't know..." Gert shook his head.

"This is what I do, *Dominee*... I strategize. I know what I'm talking about .... Why not think on it? Pray on it," JJ suggested.

"I will do that," Gert agreed.

They began to make their way to the exit door, walking slowly, contemplatively, each in thought about the world they'd shared, their paths that had diverged; now, a glimmer of finding commonality seemed possible.

As they reached the daylight, still under the shade of the tall spire, the *Dominee* put his hand on JJ's shoulder as he would when the boy was youth leader. Back then he'd have reached down to do so, now he had to look up as he put an earnest question;

"For many years I have feared and prayed for you. I have feared that you left the path and will only inherit hell. Do you not fear this? Do you have no dread for the hell that your path has surely put you on?" Gert implored.

"Yes I fear hell, *Dominee*," JJ responded.

He allowed the old man a moment to think he had a triumph, and then he went on;

"But I want to first tell you about heaven. My heaven is the knowledge that this is the only life I'm going to get. It is that thought that makes me fall in love with reality every day. To savor that reality... Even when I sat saying my private goodbyes to my father in this church just days ago I was at peace that I will never again see him or anyone else that dies. This makes me value those who are alive. This makes me deeply grateful for the curious experience I am able to have of being alive and with people I love. In the tragedy of my father's loss... in all the other tragedies and challenges I face, I keep in mind that just being alive and experiencing life... and family, and community, is the greatest privilege. And it is this heaven of truly living that makes me want to make the world a better place and treat others more kindly."

"Then death becomes your hell?" Gert challenged him.

"No, *Dominee*. Hell is far worse than that.... Hell is for the living... for those who believe it exists. It is their hell to torture themselves with that idea every day that they live. It is their hell to reach the end of their finite time of being a living and thinking person and realize they have wasted it on hope."

Chapter 37

"They want to kill me *Baasie!*" *Oom* Karel had visibly aged in the past weeks since JJ had last seen him. When he'd come in for his checkup the X-Ray had revealed the lethal progress of the growths in his lungs, and the young doctor had insisted he remain as an inpatient.

As he lay there now, he was drawn, his complexion sallow, his eyes sunken with the opacity that comes near death but he still mustered plenty of energy to deliver a good argument and a smile that imploded his toothless face.

When he needed it, like now when he was angling toward an objective, he could also somehow manufacture the old twinkle of health in his eyes;

"They say I must have clean air so they take my tobacco," he grumbled, "and then they put me in this place that smells so bad. I would be better if I could have my tobacco… and be home."

"It's antiseptics," JJ assured him, trying to justify what had been done to the old man, taking his will to live with it, "it kills disease."

But Karel would have none of it; "It makes a man sick…" he insisted.

The old bushman's sense of smell was, in spite of a long career devoted to smoking everything that came to hand, refined far beyond the olfactory reach of even a virile young city dweller.

JJ appreciated how the old man must be suffering from the astringent chemical odors and the cultural deprivations away from his people, "I'll fix it," he promised.

"And the light is terrible. So bright, everything so white," Karel wanted to leave no room for misunderstanding.

"It's how we keep the hospital as clean as possible; but I'll get you home today, *Oom*. In the meantime I'll have them turn the lights down," and he sent for the administrator to see that it got done immediately.

"Ja... but my poor old eyes..." Karel groused, sounding instantly weak to the point of expiring.

While he had the young *Baas JJ* ready to argue his case and get him concessions, Karel was determined to negotiate all he could;

"These blankets are too much. They want to keep me covered, but it's smothering me. And... I don't know..." he shook his head with a great tragedy and weakly lifted his arm, festooned as it was with drips and monitors, "How can an old man survive with so many pipes and wires... And the food..."

Just then the nurse came in to check readings on the monitor and Karel managed to devise the kind of appearance and manufacture a cough that would ensure him extra special attention. JJ took the opportunity to step into the corridor where Marsha, catching a ride back from Pieter the lawyer, was waiting. She'd heard the exchange and had sneaked a peak past the door.

"Is it a good idea to have him discharged?" Marsha asked quietly, "He looks like he's at death's doorstep."

"Don't let him fool you, he's stronger than he looks," JJ assured her, his voice warm with affection and assurance; but he couldn't cover the real pang of concern he felt, and she knew she was right. "They're the best actors in the business. I'll bet he bounces right back as soon as we get him home. Right now he's angling for his tobacco before anything..."

"You don't think it's as serious as it seems?" she quizzed, trying to tease the facts out of JJ.

"Oh... it's very serious but it comes down to his will now. I wish they hadn't kept him. These people are extraordinary... unless you work with them you'll never believe it; tough beyond imagining. I'd wager that even in this condition he could still keep going for years—it comes down to his will to fight, and they took it away by trying to nurse him better. They took away his reason to keep going."

"You think?"

"Without a doubt, Marsha; he doesn't think of himself as an individual like you and I do. Nothing in his background has given him that perception—he was probably conceived in an open room full of other families, born into it, grown up in it, and conceived his own kids that way. To him, his community matters much more than himself. He thinks of himself as just another actor in the unfolding drama of his clan."

Just then the administrator arrived and JJ followed him into the ward. To much protestation from the man, JJ instructed that they were to turn down the lights and begin discharge procedures to get the old man home.

Earlier, Karel had confirmed that nobody had come to discuss the Heritage Claim with him as the *Dominee* had said they would. He'd of course heard about the death of Andre and was remarkably sad given that his own grandson had suffered so terribly at the man's hands.

"I wanted to apologize in person," JJ had told him, "for the terrible things my father did. They were inexcusable."

Karel had nodded solemnly and then had countered, "He was a policeman, that was his job."

"No it wasn't *Oom*, not like that. The time is over when police could act that way. He was wrong." JJ had insisted.

"Dawie is a strong boy, it did him no harm," it was a long custom for his people to justify the injustices, and though he may well have thought differently about it he would never stand up to authority, certainly not to the man whose father had wielded it over him and his people so thoroughly for decades.

"Any harm that's been done I want to help fix it, *Oom*. And that is why we are here… and making sure you get home today." JJ had gone on to lay forth the option for Dawie to come with him to Cape Town and the new opportunities it would bring the boy—and through his success, success to his community too.

"It will break this old man's heart," Karel had confirmed, "but it is my death wish that you take him…"

"You are far from dying *Oom* ... but if you allow this, I will bring him back here every holiday—four times a year," JJ assured.

"He has been my reason to live, and I am only holding him back by staying..." no amount of arguing against this dire prognosis would sway him from his decision that it was time to go.

And, it was true—in spite of JJ's hopeful claims that the old man could beat his condition if only he could be back home, the doctors had confirmed to JJ that the old man's time was running short, the lung cancer was advanced; the weeping puncture wound made to drain fluid from his lungs was uncovered to let it dry out. It looked like a small mouth between ribs that stood in stark relief of the baggy old skin.

JJ asked if it was painful and the old man insisted he could not feel it at all.

"I think I have an idea," JJ told him with a wry smile, and in a conspiratorial voice he suggested something cunning; "we get one of the nurses in here and ask her to make wounds in each hand and maybe a few prick-marks around your scalp."

"And then?" The old man squinted, puzzling the suggestion.

"Well—when you get to the pearly gates, St. Peter there may confuse you for the Son of the Big Man in the sky."

Karel began to laugh, the little mouth in his side chortling along with each compression as laughter morphed into a life-threatening death rattle. He thought it a fantastic idea that, in his own words, a little *"Lelike ou Boesman"*—ugly old Bushman—might be mistaken for the handsome son of God he'd seen in the statues and stained glass when the farmer Bauer had once taken him to the big church.

Karel told them that Dawie had got his phone back, but the screen was cracked and the battery missing.

"That's nothing," JJ told him, "I will get him a better phone. I will also get you a phone too... I'll go buy it right now and get it to your house before you get there."

The old man heartily laughed again at the thought of it. He had no need for a phone, not now or before, or ever.

"I am serious," JJ had insisted. "Your community needs at least a phone between you. I will talk with *Baas* Bauer and ensure that this is done."

Karel conceded that it might be a good idea—he had a good eye for trade and he'd seen how cleverly Dawie had used the device to make some money and begun to arrange improvements in their lot, so Karel agreed to identify the next best individual to whom JJ could entrust the valuable asset.

"I only ask for one thing," the nurse had finished her fussing and gone; Karel looked drained from acting so deathly sick, "that I can lie on the sand again." Afraid that, in his weakened condition, JJ might deny this extreme wish to him, he quickly played out a trump card, "I want to see the sun one more time, because I don't have much time *Baasie*. I have already seen my people here at my bed, come to fetch me."

The way he said it, JJ instantly knew what he meant—he'd already established that the old man had received only scant few visitors who'd managed the trek in from the farm; "You have seen people?"

"Ja, coming into the room to look at me," the old man confirmed.

"Do you recognize them? Are they ancestors," he asked gently.

"I think so, *baasie*… I know you will say they're not really here, but they do look friendly and I'm not afraid. They want me home."

"I'm arranging it already, *Oom*. As soon as our new ambulance is back from the emergency it is on, they'll get you straight home," he assured Karel.

Another small interruption and he stepped to the door, admitting to Marsha that her the worst were true, "I think he's slipping faster than I thought, I hope we can beat the clock. His brain's shutting down, I've seen it before."

"I know, I can hear," she said, "and it's heart breaking. I've never met him, yet it feels like losing an old friend."

"He is an old friend, an old friend in an instant, because he's a piece of us deep within that we can all recall."

She wiped at the tear that welled and fell from her eye.

JJ stepped back inside, "The visiting time is almost up, everything is in place… I must go buy your phone now," JJ assured him.

"That would make me very pleased, *baasie*." Karel wasn't laughing, it was the first time JJ had seen him so earnest.

JJ went out to ask the doctors to make all haste with preparations, then returned to say that it would all happen within the hour.

They said their goodbyes and as JJ went out through the door he heard the old man say something so he stepped back inside.

"I am very proud to know you," Karel told him.

JJ's throat locked up and his mind clamped fast, he could only repeat the same sentiment to Karel, "I am proud to have known you too, my old *Oom*."

He quickly left before the old man could see him cry.

Before JJ could reach the phone shop, his own mobile rang; it was the hospital.

"He is going fast *Meneer*, and I'm afraid we didn't manage to let him see he was unplugged from the machines as you'd asked before he slipped…"

By the time they'd doubled back and hurried into the ward, *Oom* Karel looked peaceful. The drips and monitors were gone and serenity had returned to his shell, lying neatly covered by the light sheet he'd earlier kept pushing aside.

The look he wore on his face said he had seen the sun after all and that he had returned with it to the wild *bushland* of Africa.

Chapter 38

Months had passed since the funeral of the old man and the subsequent fiery debate in the NG Church between the warring parties. Broad had flown away and people had gone back to their small lives in a big place.

Oom Karel had been interred into a simple grave, the way he had wanted to go; not in a cemetery with a marble headstone and bouquets, but out in the deep bush with living shrubs and wildlife for company.

Even *Dominee* Gert had evolved; his sermons now trumpeted how *God Himself* had privately disclosed that this technology, revealing as it would the magnificence of His Creation in their very town; marked them out as his favorite flock in all the world.

And it was then, in the settled dust of a town once more at peace with itself, that the need to lodge a Heritage Claim had found its belated way into Bennie Pieterson's cluttered office. In the weeks since it was whispered to him that *Oom* Karel had this important matter on his mind just before he died, Bennie began to weigh the situation. The more he thought about it, the better the idea became; it was just the kind of social victory he needed in order to win his way back into active politics.

By the time the idea had reached him, the broken telephone of rumour had already shed all connections between the initiative and the *Dominee*, its architect. It had also become much more ambitious; taking aim way beyond Heritage and, seeking a full Land Claim.

Armed with this ignorance, he'd begun his inquiries that very day.

And a few days later the threatening call had come; a Texan drawl startling him awake just after midnight, the caller suggesting that he drop all ideas relating to Claims of any kind. The voice was laced with threat and cancerous in its details— intricate and deadly details of both his private life and, more corrosively, the situation that had hoofed him off into the political wilderness that could never be allowed to reach the media.

Pieterson had tossed through the long night, eventually giving up on sleep and trudging under the burden of peril and decisions to be made, out along his favorite pre-dawn beat. The meander through deserted streets took him down to the grove of willow on the banks of the town's dry reservoir. There he stood under that timeless pale rash of the Milky Way overhead, weighing the odds and the threat. The wind was up and the tendrils of the trees lashed in the pale of a streetlight, tinted to yellow by a decade and more of dead insects that lined its glass bowl.

The longer he stood, the more the gusts of the wind became a mournful dirge through the branches. Its sound slid deep within him, probing… seeking… ferreting out the ancestral parts of him; the ingrained KhoiSan that coursed his veins—the legacy of the Bushmen that were in his Coloured heritage, their eons of shuffling and chanting around fires, begging the ancestors. It was like this windsong under these stars and in this place, rising over a billion nights that had gone before, now echoing back through the wind.

He listened to the song, trying to discern its voice and meaning, straining for its advice, but the tangle of too many saying too much drowned itself out.

Then, plaited into the wind's haunting lament, came a long low rumble of discontent in the tinder dry reeds where the water had receded, and Bennie's skin crawled—it said nothing, but it had the cavernous drone and throaty rumble of the long dead Constable interred in the graveyard not far away. It was a trick of his mind, Bennie knew it, but it was enough to snap him out of the hypnotic stupor of exhaustion and worry, and he turned his back on it and trudged home again.

Later that day, the haunting intone so like Andre's voice had nagged and rolled relentlessly onward in his mind, repeating itself until he reached for his phone and out to the son of the departed man.

"Bennie…?" JJ's voice betrayed the puzzlement he'd felt when he'd seen the name appear on his ringing mobile phone. He'd had limited dealings with Pieterson early on during the planning phase of the clinic and had forgotten that he had the number still saved.

They spoke some pleasantries before Bennie came to his point; "…this Broad character, my *broer*… I heard you keep tabs on him. He's a Texan, hey?"

JJ answered all that Bennie asked, and added; "I know he's in the country at the moment," a tone of deep concern in his voice. "Don't screw with this guy, Bennie… he's really bad news."

Bennie made his inquiries and learned that Broad's jet was due at Carnarvon's airstrip the next morning. Further inquiries revealed that a helicopter was already standing by to take the jet's occupants on a sightseeing adventure over the dull and nondescript desert scrub.

The next day, Bennie sat in his car out on the national road and watched the chopper with a square contraption and radar-style dish slung below its belly as it clattered it's way out and off into the distance.

He watched till the machine was a dot and then nothing in the sky. The wind was still up, singing a pennywhistle note in the key of the ancestors on the barbed wire fence that divided the newly re-surfaced road from the ancient land.

Tall thunderheads, like the phalanx of foreign invaders in centuries past, began to march once more abreast, steadily forward, and salvos of thunder began to reverberate off the surrounding mountains.

Bennie turned the engine over and drove slowly back to town, pondering who the occupants had been, what the heavy load of technology slung below the beast might be, and what their persistent business was.

The next morning's front page news report only hinted at the possibilities: "FATAL KAROO CRASH: Chopper Struck by Lightening—Oil Tycoon Dies..."

> THE END <

The Debate? See Epilogue…

Epilogue

Thank you for taking the time to share this journey.

In draft copies of this novel there were two additional chapters inserted after Chapter 38; these dealt with the debate on ethics as challenged by Dominee Gert at the funeral of Constable Andre Kruger.

In editing, it was decided to remove this debate as it interfered with the literary flow of the story.

However—if you have interest in reviewing the debate, you are encouraged and most welcome to visit the home page at: www.SKA-at-Carnarvon.com and navigate to the very bottom of the page—click the very last item in the list entitled "Removed Chapters"

If you enjoyed what you read, please share your thoughts at:
- facebook.com/SKACarnarvonBook

Of course—reviews at Amazon.com and GoodReads.com will help bring this story to the attention of others—please visit:

Please do stay in touch:
- I use: #skaNOVEL
- facebook.com/MichaelSmorenburg
- www.ska-at-carnarvon.com
- www.MichaelSmorenburg/TrojanAffair
- MichaelStheWriter@gmail.com

About the Author

Michael Smorenburg

Born in 1964, I grew up in a fabulously stable family with the best siblings one could ask for and an embracing community. I also landed with my *derrière* firmly in the proverbial butter in another way; home was a piece of paradise; the beach community of Clifton, Cape Town, South Africa.

Today, Clifton is world renowned as a playground of the super-rich, but back then it was all a boy could want; a wild and bounteous southern ocean on the doorstep flanked by towering mountains on all sides, and precious few rules in between.

It was there that I fell in love with adventure and nature, and these in tern prompted in my endless questions about what made everything tick. Religion, back then, provided the stock standard answer, but as time went by, science increasingly won my inquisitive vote.

In my mid 20's, the travel bug bit, and when my head cleared, it was the millennium and I found myself living in San Diego, California, founding an online marketing company—but Africa has a heavy gravity, and I was drawn back home, where I have happily remained.

Humans are, of course, the universe finding out about itself. We are of nature; we are matter… the stuff of stars, all too briefly made conscious and self-aware. Each of us is privileged to add our small voice to the symphony of life.

SKA@Carnarvon (and my other books) is my small contribution into that great chorus.

Wherever you may be in time and place, it's been a very great privilege to entertain and now chat to you.

Please do keep the conversation moving.

Glossary of Terms

Almagtige	Almighty
Apartheid	a policy of forced separation of races
Astrophysicist	the branch of astronomy concerned with the properties of stars
baasskap	boss-ship or domination; where the white man must automatically be in charge
Baster	literally, a bastard—a 'half-breed'—of mixed race
bakkie	a pickup truck
bedonered	crazed with anger
belaglik	laughable
bekommer	worry or troubles oneself over
Burgemeester	Mayor
besete	infected
bliksemse	(derogatory) bloody
bobbejaan	baboon
boere	farmer—(derogatory) Afrikaner whites
boesman / bushmen	see san and khoisan
boetie	brother or friend
bokkie	a fawn, term of endearment for a female, a plaything
braai	barbeque
Broederbond	brotherhood, an officially abandoned secret society devoted to furthering white Afrikaner influence
CERN	European organization for fundamental nuclear research
coolie	an unskilled native laborer from India's south
dagga	marijuana
dankie	thank you

diaken	deacon
dief	thief
Dominee	a clergyman, a preacher, in the NGK or Dutch Reformed Church
donner	to beat up / also, 'rascal'
donnerse ding	damned or bloody thing
Doppers	a member of the most conservative Afrikaner Church, which practises a strict version of Calvinism
dorp	small village
duiwel	devil
duiwelaanbidder	devil-worshipper
eie	own (people)
ek	I
evolutionary anthropology	the study of the evolution of human physiology and human behaviour
fantasties	fantastic
fok / fokken	fuck / fucking
gedoente	contraption
gee	give
gekry	acquired
gemeente	parish
gemeentelede	parishoners
geraas	noise
groot geraas	big noise
haasbek	toothless
Hadron Collider	World's largest and most powerful particle accelerator (at CERN)
hemel	heaven
hominid	a primate of a family (Hominidae) that includes humans and fossil ancestors.
Homo Naledi	A hominid sub-species found in 2013 in the Rising Star cave system of Maropeng, South Africa.
Hotnot	(derogatory) coloured person, derived from Hottentot; used to refer to *Khoi* peoples.
Israel-Visie	a collective term for a variety of conservative religious groups who aim to

	prove that they are direct descendants of Israel's chosen people
iron maiden	medieval torture device—a coffin-like apparatus festooned with inward pointing spears to skewer a victim
ja	yes
Jislaaik	an exclamation similar to "Jeepers"
jou	you or your
Kaffer	(extremely derogatory) a black person
Kaffir-boetie	(derogatory) a white person who speaks on behalf of blacks
kak	shit or nonsense
kakpraathout	a variety of wood used for bonfires but not for cooking meat due to noxious fumes that taint food.
Kardashev Scale	Named after Russian physicist, Nikolai Kardashev, a method of measuring a civilization's level of technological advancement, based on the amount of energy a civilization is able to utilize
khoisan	a collective term for the *Khoikhoi* (*Hottentot*) and *San* (Bushmen) peoples (not black African see *nguni*) of southern Africa: see also Coloured, *boesman/bushman, hotnot*
klap	hit or smack
klein	small
kleinbaas	small boss
klim	climb
klomp	lot of
kom	come on
kont	cunt
landdros	magistrate.
larney	posh
lelike	ugly
lekker	great and enjoyable
luister	listen
ma	mother
mal	mad or insane
manne	men

masjien	machine
meme	cultural analogues to genes; infectious ideas that self-replicate, mutate and respond to selective social pressures
mense	people or culture
meneer or Mnr.	mister or Mr.
moffie	(derogatory) queer, homosexual
momparas	idiots or fools
Mother City	Nickname for Cape Town
Munchausen Syndrome	Munchausen syndrome by proxy is a mental illness and a form of child abuse. The caretaker of a child either makes up fake symptoms or causes real symptoms to make it look like the child is sick.
Nguni	the black-African group of closely related Bantu language speakers, including Ndebele, Swazi, Xhosa, and Zulu
niks	nothing
non sequitur	a situation where the conclusion one is drawing does not logically follow from what is at issue
nooit weer	never again
onbeskof	immensely rude
Oom	uncle
opskud	get a move on
oens	guys, fellows, boys or men
oupa	grandfather
pa	father
pro bono	a free service
putch	a secretly plotted and suddenly executed attempt to overthrow a system
realpolitik	a perception of politics or principles based on practical rather than moral or ideological considerations
rooinek	a foreigner, particularly an English speaking person
seun	son or boy
SKA	Square Kilometre Array (Radio Telescope)

skandaal	scandal or scandalous
skelms	crooks
sommer	just
staan	stand
stilte	quiet
swart	black
staan	stand up
synod	the governing body of the church
tannie	aunt
tik	methamphetamine
uitlanders	outsiders or newcomers
vang	catch
vark	pig
veld	bush or scrub, uncultivated land
verraaier	turncoat
verdomde	damned
voetsek	get-lost, go, get away
volk	peoples, culture
voortrekker	Dutch-speaking people who migrated away from the Cape Colony from 1836 in order to live beyond British rule.
weer	again
weg	away
xenophobia	fear of foreigners
Young Earth Creationist	(also *YEC*) Christian sects who believe in a literal interpretation of the bible and a 6,000 year old earth